Reading Kenneth Frampton

Reading Kenneth Frampton

A Commentary on *Modern Architecture*, 1980

Gevork Hartoonian

ANTHEM PRESS

Anthem Press
An imprint of Wimbledon Publishing Company
www.anthempress.com

This edition first published in UK and USA 2024
by ANTHEM PRESS
75–76 Blackfriars Road, London SE1 8HA, UK
or PO Box 9779, London SW19 7ZG, UK
and
244 Madison Ave #116, New York, NY 10016, USA

First published in the UK and USA by Anthem Press in 2022

Copyright © Gevork Hartoonian 2024

The author asserts the moral right to be identified as the author of this work.

All rights reserved. Without limiting the rights under copyright reserved above, no part of this publication may be reproduced, stored or introduced into a retrieval system, or transmitted, in any form or by any means (electronic, mechanical, photocopying, recording or otherwise), without the prior written permission of both the copyright owner and the above publisher of this book.

British Library Cataloguing-in-Publication Data
A catalogue record for this book is available from the British Library.

Library of Congress Control Number: 2023948339

ISBN-13: 978-1-83998-637-6 (Pbk)
ISBN-10: 1-83998-637-9 (Pbk)

Cover image: By Simon Menges

This title is also available as an e-book.

CONTENTS

Acknowledgments vii

Introduction 1

1. The Violence of Quotation 13
2. A Trilogy 33
3. The Vicissitudes of a Critical History 59
4. In Defense of Architecture 81
5. The Agency of the Critical 105
6. Aalto Contra Mies: A Conundrum? 139
7. From the Critical to Resistance 163

Postscript 199

Index 207

ACKNOWLEDGMENTS

At the outset, I would like to thank Megan Greiving, senior acquisition editor, and her team at Anthem Press. My special thanks go to Andrew Metcalf for commenting on an early draft of this project. I am indebted to Mary McLeod for her enthusiastic support of this project and her valuable suggestions for the book's title. I also want to thank David Chipperfield Architects for providing images of the refurbished Neue Nationalgalerie in Berlin from which the cover-page image was chosen. Finally, I want to thank the anonymous readers of the final text for their constructive feedback.

INTRODUCTION

> In many works, searching from this viewpoint for this or that trace, for something that can give you information about an author, you practice an essentially biographical investigation of the author himself, you don't analyse the meaning and significance of the work as such.
> —Jacques Lacan[1]

This book is neither a biographical investigation of Kenneth Frampton, a renowned historian, architect and architecture critic, nor a study of his oeuvre in its entirety, a huge task that would take into consideration many volumes, including the fifth editions of his *Modern Architecture: A Critical History*, in addition to the numerous published books, essays and forewords that he has written for scholarly books to date. Instead, it is a modest yet timely project: focusing on the first edition of *A Critical History* (as it will be referred to throughout this volume), published in 1980, it is a search for clues and positions that will provide the reader with a partial view of the significance of Frampton's historiography of modern architecture—"partial" because, in this volume, each chapter of the first edition of his book has not been examined. Although particular attention has been accorded to Frampton's work, the scope of this book is comprehensively narrow. Rather than reading the first edition of *A Critical History* through the lens of contemporary fashionable ideas and transient themes, the approach here is somewhat archeological: zooming into his book and simultaneously building out, an attempt has been made to historicize Frampton's positions, with a critical eye on the contemporary state of architectural praxis. The following reading of Frampton also offers a "prism" for comprehending architecture in global capitalism. Critically significant to this retrospective reading of Frampton's book is the fact that in the course of its subsequent editions, the first two parts of the first edition have remained almost unchanged, and also that its content comprises the core of the Modern Architecture movement, which still influences the course of future actions. For instance, among the many themes discussed in the second part of Frampton's book, his interpretation of events from 1930 to 1945—a watershed in the developmental process of modern movement architecture—is highlighted.

On the other hand, the thematic continuity and crisis of postwar architecture is demonstrated by a focus on selected themes from the other two main parts of *A Critical History*. This book explores the historical constellation in which Frampton held onto his anteroom view of history, even amid the flow of *time* and the flood of temporality. In this mediated interest in historiography, our contemporary involvement in the subject foreshadows the appeal to retrieve the historian's intentions.

Following on from continued scholarly interest in teaching and writing on modern and contemporary historiographies of architecture was this author's *The Mental Life of the Architectural Historian* (2013), a volume that examines tropes central to the work of selected architectural historians, including Frampton. In particular is the question of how each historian approached the historicity of modern architecture. The present book is different: it neither looks exhaustively at every subject and building densely elucidated in the first edition of Frampton's book nor pursues what might be considered a textual reading of his book. The reader will note the diachronic temporalities that weave my reading of Frampton's project with the historicity of his *ecrire*. Obviously, "Kenneth Frampton" means many things, not only to this author but also to the many architects, critics, historians and academics who have been reading, reviewing and critiquing his work since he attained *visibility* in the architectural circles of London after graduating from the Architecture Association in 1956, and more so after he decided to settle in New York City and teach at Princeton University in 1972. In addition to his affiliation with the critical theory of the Frankfurt School, and with Martin Heidegger's writings on subjects such as "the work of art," technology and "dwelling," what is intriguing about Frampton is his analytical approach to, and criticism of, the architecture of the past and the present—an approach that, even during the high days of post-structuralism, was neither formalistic nor textual. Although exposed to the significant theoretical discourses disseminated during the late 1970s, this author's central intellectual inclination was coloured by Marxian readings and criticisms of art and architecture in general and Manfredo Tafuri's in particular. On the other hand, Frampton's take on critical theory and his engaged criticism of architects' work were appealing to an architect and educator who was a latecomer to the primal scene of the postwar crisis of architecture—America!

As for the book itself, *A Critical History*, each chapter begins with an appropriate quotation from the text of another architect and/or thinker. This became a motivation to write an essay on "quotation" that was presented at the annual conference of the SAHANZ (2017)[2]—a revised and extended version is compiled in this volume (see Chapter 1). Equally important was the fact that, in the first edition of Frampton's book, an image preceded the text of each of the three main parts. These three cover-page images are considered here as "postcards," pregnant with clues to the problem suggested by the title of each part, which Frampton critically unpacks in the relevant compiled chapters. Each of these postcards is also read as a visual emblem communicating between the author's text and the reader, who would be expected to encounter the book in different geographic temporalities, especially as the book has been translated into several languages. Here, the reader is reminded of two things: first, that these postcards and the idea of starting each chapter with a quotation are considered as an attribute of artifact, an analogue to Frampton's book; and, second, that the image preceding the introduction to the first edition of the book was removed in the second (1984) and subsequent editions.[3] Though Frampton never stated as much, this excision was perhaps part of the "minor corrections, to enlarge the existing final chapter substantially, and add a completely new chapter at the end," he outlines in the preface to the second edition. Toward the end of the same preface, we realize that this "new chapter" will introduce the concept of Critical Regionalism, Frampton's major contribution to the criticism of contemporary architecture, which he revised and expanded upon on several subsequent occasions. This is one reason why the last chapter of this volume is dedicated to Critical Regionalism. And yet, the omission of the cover image from the book's introduction says something about Frampton's skilled sensitivity concerning the images he selected to accompany his text, a vital hallmark of his career since he took on the job of technical editor of *Architectural Design* (*AD*) in 1962, a position he held for three years. Frampton's reserved admiration for photographic techniques is evident in most of his published manuscripts to date. This is an extremely important attitude in the context of the current commercialized nature of everyday life when the photographic reproduction of a building is often abused, its potentialities narrowed to *image-making*, a snapshot substitute for the experience of architecture as such. This development confirms today the distinction Walter Benjamin made between watching architecture with a pair of touristic glasses and experiencing a building in a moment of distraction.[4] This is a critical-materialist understanding of "experience," the anthropological dimension of which Frampton shares, though in his work this is toned down by a phenomenological concern for "essences," rather than for the Benjaminian notion of "bodily sphere" associated with the developments taking place in *technique*.[5] In the same text, Benjamin wrote in parentheses that "Heidegger seeks in vain to rescue history for phenomenology abstractly through 'historicity.'" Frampton would agree with Benjamin's disappointment at witnessing the demise of traditional experience (past historical life) due to the distance technology inserts between the past and the present and the subject and the object.[6] In the following chapters, the reader will also notice Marxian traces in both

Heidegger and Hannah Arendt.[7] Even though Arendt is not mentioned in the first edition of Frampton's book, these two thinkers' discourse problematized his affiliation with Benjamin to the point where Benjamin would remain in their shadow. Frampton's post-1980 writings demonstrate that he did not keep Benjamin and Heidegger at an equal distance, even though, as we will see in the following chapter, a Benjaminian vision of history casts a long shadow on Frampton's historiography of modern architecture.

The third significance of Frampton's book relates to the following statement extracted from the introduction to the first edition, which, interestingly enough, remains the historico-theoretical regime of *A Critical History* today:

> Of the courses of action which are still open to contemporary architecture—courses which in one way or another have already been entered upon—only two seem to offer the possibility of a significant outcome.

This statement discloses the dialectical coexistence of the "operative" and the critical in Frampton's historiography. What seemingly interested Frampton were the moments in the formation of modern architecture when a work either tried to exacerbate "meaning" to the point of inexpressibility or recoded the culture of building toward a poetics of placemaking. Thus, Mies van der Rohe's "ideal" of *beinahe nichts* (almost nothing) is tacitly introduced as a source of future action. According to Frampton, Mies's lack of interest in engaging with the urban enclave is "patently visible and often takes the form of masonry enclosure," without associating the implied *character* of architecture with any particular architect. In retrospect, the reader of Frampton's oeuvre will not fail to associate this suggested "visibility" with a specific group of modernist architects, among whom Alvar Aalto stands tall. Pursuing Adolf Loos's strategic approach to modernity, Aalto attempted to emulate the "cracks" existing between the past historical life and technologically motivated experience, aiming to create an architecture that would avoid the avant-garde's transgressive agendas.[8] Yet, call it *misreading*! In the present volume, Frampton's two suggested opposing sources of future action have been read allegorically. It is hoped that the reader will extrapolate its potentialities from "Mies Contra Aalto: A Conundrum," discussed in Chapter 6 of this book. Still, having come across Fredric Jameson's reading of the Heideggerian rift between "world" and "earth,"[9] this alleged misreading sheds critical light on Frampton's reserved position on Mies, whose work complements Aalto's while keeping the Finnish architect's "biomorphism" at arm's length. This implied ontological separateness can be read in analogy to the "bridge" Heidegger discusses in his famous 1954 essay on "dwelling." Reflecting on Frampton's reading of

Heidegger's essay, as suggested elsewhere, amalgamating material with technique, the Heideggerian bridge can evoke a sense of nearness by keeping the banks of the river apart.[10] As such, dialectics structures the proposed "Mies contra Aalto" paradigm.

A fourth interest in Frampton's vision of history concerns themes that led him to choose *A Critical History* for the book's subtitle. These themes are differentiated from those of another prominent historian who also took a Marxian approach to architectural history, Manfredo Tafuri. While this has been extensively discussed elsewhere,[11] the difference between the two historians can be briefly articulated thus: both remain critical of the avant-garde aspiration to reconcile formal autonomy with the prevailing zeitgeist; and each approaches architectural praxis differently. Drawing from the historicity of the nihilism of the project of Modernity, Tafuri's critical discourse remains focused on how *architecture* at its best anticipated an eventual failure, despite or because of its attempt at decoding the capitalist production system. Frampton, by contrast, tends to highlight the marginal victories of singular works that have been able to preserve aspects of "placemaking," as instrumental reason tightens its grip on architecture. While both historians share the idea that architecture should address a historiographical problem, Frampton's commitment to semiautonomous architecture has uniquely positioned him to interpret the architect's continuous encounter with the contemporaneity integral to a broader crisis of architecture. Whereas Frampton plots the ongoing development of the concept of crisis throughout the short history of modernity, Tafuri traces the genealogies of the crisis back to the springboard of Western Humanism. The important dimensions of Frampton's critical regime are discussed throughout this book, particularly in Chapter 7, and in connection with the author's Critical Regionalism.

Having plotted these four cardinal points, we need to remember two additional considerations: given the three postcards mentioned above, the scope of this book remains "confined" to discussing themes coterminous with the historicity implied in the division of *A Critical History* into three main parts, as listed in the contents of the first edition. Following Walter Benjamin's distrust of historicism, the narrative form that ends with the totalization of history in one way or another has been avoided. This is important given not only my sympathy with the German thinker's messianic Marxism[12] but also the fact that Frampton's "Introduction" to *A Critical History* begins with a famous quotation from Benjamin's "Theses on the Philosophy of History" (1940). Apropos, the present book should be considered a collage of separate plots,[13] short sketches on topics relevant to Frampton's discourse on the historiography of modern architecture that have been sewn together into seven chapters with an absent central theme: to reflect and expand on the theme of the *critical* that peppers the first edition of *A Critical History*.

The present book thus approximates Benjamin's concept of "constellation." He wrote, "It's not that what is past casts its light on what is present, or what is present its light on the past; rather, image is that wherein what has been coming together in a flash with the now to form a constellation."[14] As such, the past/present dialectic sets the agenda for this interpretative reading of Frampton's text, which means that, although I had read *A Critical History* several times before, whenever teaching courses on the history of modern architecture, reading Frampton's book anew, and writing this volume, involved more than "understanding" the author's intentions. Instead, I read the first edition of Frampton's book in the image of the constellation wherein the past, the temporality of Frampton's writing of *A Critical History*, and that of my writing of the following pages, could not but lead me to choose an interventionist strategy, which is evident in between the lines of my discussion of Frampton's positions on the themes elaborated in each chapter of this volume. Accordingly, this project neither attempts to "discover" what Frampton thought when he wrote *A Critical History*, especially during the ten long years that ended with the publication of the book's first edition, nor intends to contextualize his book historically, though "contextualization" remains integral to the critical rewriting of history. Moreover, the formation of Frampton's book has not been "reported" in a chronicle-like fashion, as is the case with semi-documentary work. However, this is a fashion in recent writing on past events, a follow-up to the mass media production of documentaries on diverse subjects! And yet, particles of these methodologies might have unconsciously slipped into the chapters, and the reader is sure to detect them here and there.

To reiterate, *A Critical History* has been approached as an artifact stripped of temporality. The book's major tropes have been unlocked toward two ends: first, to elucidate how Frampton's critical presentation of the history of modern architecture, and the book's classificatory mode (periodization?), have contributed to our understanding of the contemporaneity of architecture. Second and related to the first, it concerns the particular theoretical strategy for mapping Frampton's historiography over time, from the modernism of the 1920s to the crisis of the project of Modernity (starting roughly from the mid-1930s) to the postmodern condition. The themes Frampton attended to, the formation of which has shaped his singular approach to the problems of modernism in architecture, which is integral to the historical progression in this book, have been emphasized. Frampton had the privilege of seeing the 1930s retrospectively, from the viewpoint of the Cold War era, when capitalism in America had shifted gears to not only consolidate its presence in known industries, including the building industry, but also, more importantly, for the first time, expedite the formation of the "culture industry," as formulated by Theodor Adorno and Max Horkheimer in 1947. While these developments' socioeconomic and cultural impacts in so-called Third-World countries have not been explored,[15] Frampton's recently published work is proof that he sees architectural history from an Archimedean point on the fringes of the western hemisphere.[16]

Along with these developments, ample attention has also been focused on Frampton's exposure to several critical texts and concepts, including Hannah Arendt's *The Human Condition* (1958), Heidegger's notion of "dwelling" and Walter Benjamin's "Philosophy of History," mentioned earlier. The impact of these texts on Frampton's oeuvre—the shift from his earlier reviews of buildings, which could be labeled journalistic, to his later, more distinctively critical work—is studied here. Imbued with a phenomenological reading of Marxian concepts such as labor, materiality and technology, Frampton's later work tries to move away from his earlier style of criticism, which was primarily focused on "design" and the architect's *intention* in handling issues internal to architectural design—even though the various dimensions of design should be the concern of every historian even today. Since the first formulation of "Critical Regionalism," however, Frampton has consistently contributed to identifying the scope of the ongoing architectural crisis in late capitalism, while at the same time highlighting strategies of resistance intended to postpone the total takeover of architecture by the regime of technological instrumentalization. This historical phenomenon has attained global visibility through the expansive strategies of late capitalism. Not only Frampton's various reworkings of the text of "Critical Regionalism" but all the revisions of his book should be considered a strategy to resist the reduction of the *project* to an object, the repetition of which undermines its capacity to face the present, the now-time. The many editions of the book do not speak to any strong desire to keep himself on the stage of contemporary architectural debates on Frampton's part. Rather, they speak to a desire to see the continuation of modernity, though with advanced awareness of its problematics, while at the same time searching for effective critical channels to postpone the moment when architecture disappears within the multitudes of effects emanating from the floating images that structure the future propagated by the global networks of capitalism. This dimension of his work places him squarely in opposition to Tafuri. Whereas Tafuri consolidated himself as a *classical* historian working within historical totalization, Frampton's insistence on revising and expanding the book during the past four decades demonstrates the possibility of a critical assessment of the ongoing conflict between architecture and capitalism, even as the latter's master-code constantly reimagines modernity anew. This is the negative dialectics that has unconsciously sneaked into Frampton's project, and it is a positive change.

As mentioned earlier, the text of Chapter 1 emerged from the idea of the role quotation plays in historiographies in general and in Frampton's narrative in particular. Each chapter of *A Critical History* begins with a carefully chosen quotation. However, the choice turns out to be particularly significant when Frampton opens his short introductory remarks with a famous quotation from Walter Benjamin's essay "Philosophy of History." In this chapter, extensive attention is given to Benjamin's "Angel of History," mapping its critical importance for Frampton's historiography of modern architecture. Chapter 2, "A Trilogy," focuses on three dates, 1939, 1967 and 1978, claiming that each of these years saw particular historical events destined to limit the scope of architecture's drive for autonomy. These dates also designate the periodization that underpins the three-part organization of Frampton's book. The three cardinal transformations that thematically structure Frampton's position on the history of modern architecture have been highlighted: these are the cultural, the technical and the territorial, which are discussed in the first three chapters of Part I of *A Critical History* and encapsulated in Part I's cover image, an interior view of Germain Soufflot, Ste-Genevieve, Paris, 1750–1939. Inspired by the cover-page image of Part II of the book, a photomontage of Giuseppe Terragni's Casa del Fascio, Como, 1932–36, Chapter 3 in this volume argues for the criticality of the events of the 1930s, particularly the rise of Fascism in Europe, a pivotal moment in Frampton's retrospective account of the period spanning 1836–1967. Comprised of twenty-seven chapters, Part II of *A Critical History* comprehensively covers Frampton's story of modern architecture. The study of the major players of this rather long period was guided by the insight that, between 1914 and 1918, Benjamin had already sensed the crisis haunting Europe. While Frampton might not share Benjamin's position that technique is more than a tool—that, rather, "it is a condition of the invention of the human itself"[17]—he would be unlikely to disagree that the decade of the 1930s transformed the "structure of experience," which in its many manifestations, including architecture, was until then directly or indirectly influenced by the metaphysics of Humanism.[18] No wonder then that in Chapter 3, and throughout this volume, Frampton's obsessive focus on Hannah Arendt's call for "the space of public appearance" and the Heideggerian notion of "placemaking" is important. These two concepts have been taken up in Chapter 6 to demonstrate their centrality to Frampton's appraisals of Aalto's architecture on several occasions since the first edition of the book. What makes the uncharacteristic juxtaposition of Aalto and Mies significant is the type/tectonics manifested in these two architects' best work. Another difference relates to the geographic temporalities that each of these two architects had to work through as part of the project of Modernity. Herein lies the essentiality of regional difference— Finland for Aalto, Berlin and Chicago for Mies—even within Europe and from the bedrock of the formation and transformation of modernity. The significance of *distance* is discussed in Chapter 7, which primarily focuses on Frampton's Critical Regionalism. The historico-theoretical trajectory of his discourse on the "critical" since the book's first edition in 1980 is also demonstrated. Chapter 5, by contrast, presents an in-depth reading of four analytical essays on selected works of postwar British architecture that were written before Frampton's total appropriation of Arendt and Heidegger. Despite this, his later writings show the persistence of particular concerns about the culture of building that were formative for his earlier work. In this regard, the culture of building is for Frampton the site where the *image* of the past turns out to be the nucleus of resistance; he has launched against the colonization of architecture by commodity form.

This book deliberates on matters related to the history of modern architecture and contemporary historiographies of architecture. Besides this, it stresses the relevance of modernity and modern architecture for contemporary architectural criticism and praxis. In the present state of digital reproducibility and global capitalism, it is convincing that, at best, both architecture academics and students have lost sight of architectural history. At worst, they presumptuously proclaim the irrelevance of history for contemporary architectural praxis. Perhaps a different architecture could emerge from the prevailing depthless intertextuality, when all that is solid, including the subjectivities nurturing class conflicts, melts away! It is not the task of architecture to expedite this process in any form; it should, however, be theorized to offer a clear demonstration of ideologies of architecture across history. The following pages aim to establish Frampton's historiography and his ongoing endeavor to promote a critical understanding of the historicity of architectural crisis.

Notes

1 The final draft of this manuscript was prepared by mid-2020; thus, the fifth edition of Kenneth Frampton, *Modern Architecture: A Critical History* (September 2020), and K. C. Britton and R. McCarter, *Modern Architecture and the LifeWord* (January 2021) were not consulted.

 Jacques Lacan explaining his methodology, quoted in Fredric Jameson, *Allegory and Ideology* (London: Verso, 2019), 97. For Lacan, the problem was the articulation of "desire." The ambition in the present volume is rather modest!

2   Gevork Hartoonian, "The Violence of Quotation," in *Quotation: The 34th Annual Conference of the Society of Architectural Historians*, ed. Gevork Hartoonian and John Tying, Australia/New Zealand (SAHANZ), 2017, Canberra, Australia.
3   Another curiosity is the photo of Alberto Santori's project for Notre-Dame du Phare (1931), used for the book's cover since its first publication. Neither the project nor its architect is mentioned or discussed in any of the chapters of the book's first edition!
4   Walter Benjamin, "The Work of Art in the Age of Mechanical Reproducibility," in *Illuminations* (New York: Schocken, 1969), 217–52.
5   In "Convolute N" of his *Arcades Project*, Walter Benjamin distinguishes his concept of historical materialism from a phenomenological emphasis on "essences." See Benjamin, *The Arcades Project* (Cambridge: Harvard University Press, 1999), 462. For Benjamin's affiliation with "anthropological materialism," see John McCole, *Walter Benjamin and the Antinomies of Tradition* (Ithaca, NY: Cornell University Press, 1993), 172. The chapter "Benjamin and the Weimar" is recommended.
6   Recalling the mutilated bodies returning from the scene of World War I, Walter Benjamin writes, "With this tremendous development of technology, completely new poverty descended on mankind." He continues, "Indeed (let's admit it), our poverty of experience is not merely poverty on the personal level, but the poverty of human experience in general. Hence, a new kind of barbarism." See Benjamin, "Experience and Poverty," in *Walter Benjamin: Selected Writings, Vol 2, 1927–34* (Cambridge: Harvard University Press, 1999), 731–40. The essay was originally published in 1933.
7   In his autobiography, Robert Maxwell recalls that Thomas Stevenson, known as "Sam" in the architectural circles of the University of Liverpool, United Kingdom, recommended Hanna Arendt to Kenneth Frampton. Robert Maxwell, *The Time of My Life in Architecture* (London: Artifice, 2016), 27.
8   The idea of "crack" has been borrowed from Hal Foster. See https://news.artnet.com/art-world/hal-foster-1251083 (accessed August 13, 2019).
9   Fredric Jameson, *Raymond Chandler: The Detections of Totality* (London: Verso, 2016), 76–81.
10 Gevork Hartoonian, *The Mental Life of the Architectural Historian* (Newcastle: Cambridge Scholars, 2013), 169.
11 Ibid., "Coda," in Hartoonian, *The Mental Life*, 160–77.
12 For work on Walter Benjamin, see Gevork Hartoonian (ed.), *Walter Benjamin and Architecture* (London: Routledge, 2010); and Gevork Hartoonian, "What Is the Matter with Architectural History?" in *Walter Benjamin and History*, ed. Andrew Benjamin (London: Continuum, 2005), 171–81.
13 A shorter version of the first chapter of this volume was presented at the Society of Architectural Historians Australia/New Zealand, 2017. On two separate occasions, the concept of Critical Regionalism discussed in Chapter 7 in this volume has been addressed.
14 Walter Benjamin, "Awakening," in Benjamin, *The Arcades Project*, 462.
15 Lukasz Stanek's book sheds fresh light on the center-periphery debates. See Stanek, *Architecture in Global Socialism* (Princeton, NJ: Princeton University Press, 2020).
16 The speculation here was recently confirmed in Kenneth Frampton's email to the author dated Monday, January 11, 2021. He wrote, "I assume that you have obtained a copy of the 5th edition of my so-called Critical History! You seem to be referring to it in your current critical take on operative occidental histories?" The author had

not yet received the fifth edition of the book when adding this footnote (Saturday, January 24, 2021)!
17 David Cunningham and Jon Goodbun, "Marx, Architecture and Modernity," *Journal of Architecture* (April 2006): 173.
18 See John McCole, *Walter Benjamin and the Antinomies of Tradition* (Ithaca, NY: Cornell University Press, 1993).

Chapter 1

THE VIOLENCE OF QUOTATION

> The quotations in my works are like robbers lying in ambush on the highway to attack the passerby with weapons drawn and rob him of his conviction.
>
> —Walter Benjamin[1]

Kenneth Frampton is one of the few historians who have used an epigraph at the start of each chapter of their work, in his case the famous volume *Modern Architecture: A Critical History*, first published in 1980. Throughout the book, each epigraph either sets the basic theoretical tone of the chapter or plots the premise of Frampton's take on a subject, which is further elaborated on in other relevant chapters. Following Walter Benjamin, we could say that Frampton's appropriation of quotation intends to rob from the traditions of the historiography of modern architecture: an interventionist strategy and one in lieu of dismantling a linear vision of time central to the preceding historiographies of modern architecture. If we do not reduce historiography to the factual presentation of data, dates and building types, then historiography proper involves a philosophy of history by which the historian maps a constellation of architects' work abreast of available textual interpretations, critical or otherwise. This definition of "historiography" was not popular a century ago, and the absence of such a perspective along various discursive formations necessitated the emergence of different approaches to the formation of modern architecture during the 1960s. Frampton's book, among a few others, is a case in point: it was written with an eye on the suggested theoretical vacuity. However, it would be premature at this point to reflect on the word "critical," which has particular sociopolitical connotations for most of what Frampton has written to date, not to mention its implications for the history of modern architecture discussed throughout *A Critical History*. Considering the epigraph Frampton chose for the introductory chapter, it is appropriate to recall Benjamin's dream project: to write a book compiled from quotations! A brief discussion of a few writings that also influenced Frampton's positions on architectural history and criticism will shed light on his appropriation of the discursive differences between Benjamin and Martin Heidegger, especially the issue of technology. In reflecting on the work of these figures, this book hopes to provide the reader with a retrospective view of Frampton's book, casting light on his short introductory text to the first edition of the book.

I

To quote an author in confirmation or refutation of an argument is one thing, to write a book of quotations is quite another. Whatever Benjamin's intention, a book peppered with quotations page after page would elucidate two theoretical strategies that he pursued in his philosophical reflection on history, montage and constellation. Montage is a conceptual and technical device to make a *thing* (text) out of various fragments, a technique exemplified by both carpentry, one of the oldest crafts, and cinematography, the most modern technical artwork today.[2] Constellation, by contrast, connotes "a group of stars forming a recognizable pattern [totality] that is traditionally named after its apparent form or identified with a mythological figure."[3] The implications of this definition of "constellation" for the historiography of architecture, in general, and for Frampton's take on the subject, in particular, will be discussed in this book. There are two interrelated types of *violence* involved in using a quotation: the first concerns the extraction of a sentence or two from its original context, while the second involves the insertion of a quotation into the text of an author. Whereas the first case is justified based on the content of a text—the direct or indirect need to confirm an argument with the help of another author's words—the second is considered part of a writer's judicious right to violate his/her own text using another author's statement(s), as long as it is properly referenced in footnotes or the bibliography. In both cases, however, "the authority invoked by quotation is founded precisely on the destruction of the authority" sealed by the history of culture.[4] Thus, provisionally we should say that the totality a narrative evokes is nothing but *fabrication*, a montage of statements and quotations that, similar to a constellation, tries to disclose a myth (ideology)—perhaps a historical fact, if not a lucid historical observation, or a detailed representation of events, as is the case with the nineteenth-century novel.

These preliminary remarks are important not only in reference to Frampton's use of quotation at the beginning of each chapter of his book but more so in consideration of the image accompanying the book's "Introduction," the text of which is introduced by Benjamin's statement borrowed from *Theses on the Philosophy of History*, discussed below. This cover-page image (Figure 1.1), though removed in subsequent editions of the book, is remarkable. It depicts the demolition of C. N. Ledoux's *Barrieres de l' Etoile*, engraved by Henry Duff

Figure 1.1 Demolition of C. N. Ledoux's *Barrieres de l' Etoile*, engraved by Henry Duff Linton in 1860. Image courtesy of Chronicle/Alamy Stock Photo.

Linton in 1860. Allegorically, it represents the singularity of modernity as the messenger of "ideological and political changes," compared with previous periods of Western civilization. Both here and in the remaining caption of the frontispiece, Frampton tries to encapsulate modernity as a destructive, but at the same time inevitable, historical force, the wind of which, as we will see shortly, propels Benjamin's Angel of History forward.

In Linton's engraving, the two buildings standing unharmed say something about the two sides of the coin of what we might consider the humanistic impetus of the Enlightenment: that "ideas created buildings and ideas destroyed them." In the same engraving, one of the buildings that stands tall is The Arc de Triomphe, conceived by Chalgrin in 1811 and completed in 1836. By contrast, at the forefront of the engraving we see workmen demolishing the Barriere, an emblem of the Ancient Regime that was "stormed and damaged during the Revolution as symbol of oppression," Frampton added to the caption printed at the foot of the frontispiece. The engraving's compositional message is convincing: the Arc de Triomphe is positioned away from the picture plane occupied by the workmen and closer to the spectator than the Barriere. As such, the composition, particularly the proximity of the Arc de Triomphe to the spectator, confirms Frampton's emphasis on "ideas" as a transformative force throughout modernity, itself loaded with utopic visions (constructive or destructive) that were most often expected to take place sometime in the future. In a nutshell, the image reiterates the temporal and ideological dimensions of the famous French literary debate between the ancients and the moderns, the modus operandi of the project of Modernity even after it was usurped by capitalism in the late 1930s. Baron George Haussmann, the ideologue behind the genesis of this engraving, is discussed in the next chapter. What should be noted in passing is the importance of Walter Benjamin's philosophy of history, which also covers Haussmann's surgical operation,[5] mapping the ideological regime of the territorial and technological transformations unfolding throughout modernization, as hinted in Frampton's caption, mentioned above, and discussed convincingly in Chapter 2 of *A Critical History*.

In what follows, Frampton's short introduction to *A Critical History* in the purview of Benjamin's concept of history, a lengthy quotation that provides a window into the mental life of the historian, is analyzed. Thereafter, Benjamin's notion of the constellation as it concerns the two realms of the cultural and technical transformations that structure Frampton's historiography of modern architecture is discussed.

II

The quotation Frampton included in the introductory text of *A Critical History* is a well-known passage from Walter Benjamin's "Thesis on the Philosophy of History" (1940),[6] which is frequently discussed and widely quoted. Numbered IX, the passage starts with a poem written by Gerhard Scholem, a close friend and confidante of Benjamin.[7] Scholem's poem, "Gruss vom Angelus," was written in reference to a 1920 Paul Klee painting, *Angelus Novus*, a print of which Benjamin had purchased in 1921. Both the painting and Benjamin's interpretation of it have become allegorical for Left-oriented scholars, and thus the main points of his take on the painting are worth summarizing here. Essential to an understanding of the quoted passage is the physiognomy of the angel, which is depicted against a storm "blowing from paradise," as Benjamin reminds us. The force of the storm propels the angel forward, and yet in a gesture of *resistance*, the angel's head is turned back, with its mouth open and wings widespread. What makes this image associable with history is the figure of the angel even though we do not know why the angel's mouth is left open, for example. It might be that the angel is screaming in reaction to "the catastrophe which keeps piling wreckage upon wreckage and hurls it in front of his feet," as Benjamin wrote. It might also be that the angel's mouth is open in analogical reference to the shock effect of the storm of progress depicted in Edvard Munch's *The Scream*, first painted in 1893. In Munch's painting, the central figure is painted in a ghostly form, with its mouth hanging open in anguish at the stakes involved in reconciling "the individual with the metropolis," according to Manfredo Tafuri, another historian sympathetic to Benjamin's philosophy of history.[8] Whereas Tafuri's interest is channeled toward the historical avant-garde's responses to the schism capitalism introduced into the traditional fabric of cities, Frampton instead seeks the architectonic responses that avoid internalizing technological nihilism into the work, as has been the case with most avant-gardes. Still, while Tafuri closely investigates the work of the avant-garde to sharpen his own criticism of architecture in modernity, Frampton sees "salvation" in the work of architects who would sidestep the modernist reduction of architecture to the exigencies of technology, the driving engine of capitalism as we know it. Thus, Frampton's notion of resistance attains both conceptual and pragmatic complexity, not only because a more sophisticated capitalism has prevailed since the Second World War but also because of his own juggling of the most relevant critical discourses focused on architecture, particularly those formulated by Walter Benjamin and Martin Heidegger outlined below.

Head turned back, the forward-moving figure of the Angel of History can be considered a proper analogue for the ontological posture of the historian. So too can the angel's desire "to stay, awaken the dead, and make whole what has been smashed," an impossible task since the storm has already lifted the angel off the ground, "propelling him into the future to which his back is turned." Benjamin ends the passage with a reminder that "this storm is what we call progress." Thus, eyes turned to the past, armed with the will (desire?) to reconstruct the past out of *memory* and factual and textual evidence, Benjamin outlines the task of the historian as such. Central to this task is the messianic dimension of Benjamin's project, which, interestingly enough, has the least passion for utopic visions. Its main commitment, rather, is rescuing the progressive aspects of the past that are essential for the formation of an image of the bygone *totality* that progress has smashed to pieces. For those who have followed Frampton's oeuvre closely, the above reading of the *Angelus Novus* should convincingly justify his appropriation of a long quotation from Benjamin in support of his historiography of modern architecture and the criticism he has launched against the mainstream architecture produced during the second half of the century.

Read in conjunction with other passages, Benjamin's text discloses both a vision and a strategy for historiography that, in addition to defying the linear vision of history, also plots a discourse of temporality that is not homogeneous. He highlights the anachronism involved in most cultural production activities and puts forward a concept of time, now-time (*Jetztzeit*), that is pregnant with the revolutionary ethos of the past that is most often suppressed by the victor's vision of history. Since the publication of Benjamin's text, historians sympathetic to Marxism and scholars affiliated with the critical theory of the Frankfurt School (Frampton included) have appropriated Benjamin's vision of history.[9] Frampton writes,

> My affinity for the critical theory of the Frankfurt School has no doubt coloured my view of the whole period and made me acutely aware of the dark side of the Enlightenment which, in the name of an unreasonable reason, has brought man to a situation where he begins to be as alienated from his own production as from the natural world.[10]

Having established this, Frampton quickly reminds us that, in spite of the fact that he has been influenced by a Marxian understanding of history, his book does not follow "any established methods of Marxist" analysis.

III

In addition to Benjamin's text, which supports the general outline of his book, Frampton also uses quotations from other prominent architects, writers and thinkers in the remaining chapters. He writes, "I have endeavoured to use these 'voices' to illustrate the way in which modern architecture has evolved as a continuous cultural effort and to demonstrate how certain issues might lose their relevance at one moment in history only to return at a later date with increased vigour."[11] The statement echoes a general Marxian understanding of modernity articulated by Harry Harootunian, among others. Harootunian writes, "All production immediately falls into ruin, thereafter to be set in stone without revealing what it had once signified, since the inscriptions are illegible or written in the dead language." He concludes that "beneath the historical present, however, lie the spectres, the phantoms, waiting to reappear and upset it."[12] Nothing short of this statement confirms the devastation caused by the wind of progress, which paradoxically secures the return of certain aspects of the past in the form of either kitsch, which works against the transmissibility of tradition in now-time,[13] or fragments of a bygone project to be enlivened once more when the time is ripe. This much is also evident in Fredric Jameson's observation that, as an external factor, *history* cut short the ideology of modernism developed in Russia and Germany in the 1920s,[14] an unfolding that nurtured the theoretical seeds of what we might call the state of unequal development of modernism. These observations solidify both Jürgen Habermas's theorization of modernity as an incomplete project[15] and Jameson's particular theorization of postmodernism.[16] Having established these Marxian dialectics between past and present, it is not far-fetched to claim that, against postmodern abuses of the past, Frampton turns his attention to the culture of building pregnant with the dialectics of inspiration and resistance accumulated throughout the history of various geographies. In a nutshell, this is a strategy of resistance against the drive for formal autonomy and other ideological manifestations of architecture's drift into the production and consumption systems engineered by postwar capitalism, the theoretical gist of which would culminate in Frampton's formulation of critical regionalism, discussed in Chapter 7 of this volume.

Having mapped these observations, interpretative methods and influences, it can be posited that central to Frampton's historiography are dichotomies such as tradition and innovation, métier and technology and also site and materiality. Frampton reads these dichotomies through Benjamin's discussion of the loss of aura and Heidegger's *Building, Dwelling, Thinking* (1954). Six years before the publication of his book (1980), Frampton wrote an editorial in *Oppositions* plotting the implications of Heidegger's essay for the state of architecture thwarted by postmodernist simulation of historical forms.[17] Starting with the differences between architecture and building, and the effectiveness of generating a built environment that society is receptive to, Frampton's short editorial presented a criticism of late liberal capitalism and the postmodernist exaltation of the mainstream commercialization of the urban fabric under the spell of "illusory vernacular," and the dissemination of abstraction as part of the enforcement of commodity form in everyday life and architecture. Frampton visits these developments and their consequential tendency to overstate the importance of *space* at the expense of the dialectics of *production* and *place*. His convictions regarding the state of architecture and the city under the auspices of late capitalism, and the architects and theoreticians who embraced the postmodern condition with the least reservation, were enough for him to curtail his collaboration with the editorial group of *Oppositions*, although he was one of the three founding editors at the time of the publication of his editorial text on Heidegger in *Oppositions* 4 (October 1974).[18]

One of the implications of the aforementioned editorial relates to the critical implications of Frampton's juxtaposition of quotations from Walter Benjamin and Heidegger for the opening and closing chapters of his book, an issue which will be taken up on another occasion in this volume. What should be mentioned here is that his appropriation of Benjamin and Heidegger hinges on a third figure, Hannah Arendt, and her famous manuscript, *The Human Condition* (1958), which has influenced Frampton's oeuvre more than any other contemporary thinker today. As early as 1969, and in a collection of essays that today can be considered an opening into the state of uncertainties permeating postmodernism in architecture, Frampton made a case for the stakes involved in Arendt's differentiation between labor, work and action.[19] His didactic text expands the etymological dimensions of Arendt's triad, relating each to *architecture* and to his own discussion of the city and how the classical and holistic meaningfulness of what Arendt coined "the space of human appearance" has not been attainable since the advent of industrialization, to the point where the railway station would be taken for the *res publica* in Tony Garnier's Cité Industrielle of 1904. At these two levels of consideration, Frampton's text seems written in anticipation of the three first chapters of "Part I," where he maps the historico-theoretical premises of *A Critical History* under the rubric of cultural, territorial and technological transformations, respectively. Following Arendt's association of *labor* with the biological and ephemeral attributes of the individual (domestic cell), and *work* with the world of lasting things distinct from nature, the reader will not dismiss the permanence of dwelling in the form of *edifice*, an idea essential for the meaningfulness of what Frampton considers the "cultural context." Be that as it may, Frampton traces the loss of a constructive dialectic between the domestic cell and the city in projects that most often are overshadowed by the emergence of a contemporary Megalopolis, where various infrastructural elements substitute for the role *edifice* used to play in the built environment. The following dire conclusions speak for themselves: that "an arbitrary individual vocabulary wilfully used is relatively in-effective,"[20] and that things do not last long enough to be part of humanity's needs for permanence and stability. It can be speculated that Frampton's formulation of "critical regionalism" and "Megaform" was in response to the ongoing crisis of architecture, and the expectation that the culture could charge "meaning to architecture," to recall the central theme of the book edited by Charles Jencks and George Baird (1971), which was titled accordingly. Furthermore, as we will see shortly, their book announces a new turn in architecture, with most chapters, including Frampton's, trying to rethink postwar architecture based on the direct or indirect conviction that the core principles of modernism are not sustainable in the built environment and that architecture should be retooled using theories such as semiotics (Jencks), humanism (R. Wittkower, 1949), phenomenology (N. Schultz, 1962) and a nostalgic view of vernacular (B. Rudofsky, 1964).

The two main tropes Frampton draws from the discourses of Benjamin and Heidegger are *technique* and *place*, one born out of the spine of modernization and the other rooted in ancient times and congenial to most existential aspects of the lifeworld. He pursues the impact of these two themes' uneven rapport with architecture in light of the ever-acceleration of temporality experienced in modern times. Frampton discusses the concept of place-making in reference to Heidegger's and Benjamin's proto-anthropological understanding of history. Disregarding their philosophical differences, what makes the juxtaposition of these two figures plausible is their critical reflection on technology and time. Both Heidegger and Benjamin "opposed the progressive view of history which regarded the present as the untroubled heir of the past." Peter Osborne continues that, for both these thinkers, "the act of 'handing over' destroys the object it surrenders," and "tradition is not only that which is handed over within a given time, but also the giving of that time itself in the distinction of past and present."[21] Interestingly enough, time and technology, the engines of the so-to-speak progressive view of the Enlightenment, constituted the two major vectors of the historiographies of modernism written by Reyner Banham and Sigfried Giedion. Unlike these two historians, Frampton neither bets on technological determinism (Banham) nor presumes the totalized experience of time and space exemplified in modernist abstract painting, the architectonic implications of which are paramount in many historiographies of early modern architecture, and Giedion's in particular. And yet, what differentiates both Banham and Frampton from Giedion relates to the strategy of periodization and a complex approach to technology.

While acknowledging Giedion's contribution, Frampton tries to put behind him the zeal for capturing and projecting a coherent concept of the Zeitgeist of modernism exemplified in the Swiss historian's pathbreaking book *Building in France, Building in Iron, Building in Ferro-concrete* (1928), which, interestingly enough, was also noted by Walter Benjamin.[22] Frampton instead recognizes Banham's persistent sympathy with the main ethos of modern architecture, disregarding Banham's inclination toward high-tech architecture and his tendency "to structure his arguments around persistent antinomies—tradition versus technology, aesthetics versus ethics, style versus performance—that he saw as key features of modern architecture and central to his discussion of High Tech."[23] These dichotomies have been important for Frampton as he takes note of Banham's strategy of breaking down modern movement architecture into various thematic segments, each championed in the work of one or two architects. Frampton seems also sympathetic to Banham's later writings, which, according to Todd Gannon, "assumed a staunchly critical stance to postmodern architecture and laboured to make a case for the continued validity of modern architecture."[24] Mention should also be made of Frampton's attempt to recode the aforementioned dichotomies without giving lip service to the aesthetic of high-tech and its implications for the postwar consumer culture. In retrospect, Frampton's discourse on tectonics[25] was a response to the dichotomy between the engineer and the *bricoleur* implied in Banham's criticism of Charles Jencks's turn to the communication theories of the 1960s and the subsequent theorizations of the architecture of postmodernism.[26] For Jencks, the debate between the master and his pupil was the tip of the iceberg of crisis, a crisis he plotted at the two levels of "revolution and change" and "architecture and meaning."²⁷ By contrast, in *Studies in Tectonic Culture* Frampton underlines the significance of "public architecture," in place of Banham's proposition for the responsiveness of architecture to the individual. Their differences attained a new visibility in Frampton's *A Critical History*: while radicalizing Banham's strategy of periodization, Frampton subdivides his own book into three main parts, each a constellation wherein every chapter covers the work of a particular architect, to the point where each chapter can be read independently of what has gone before and what follows after.

The first two major parts of Frampton's book explore dichotomies that were essential to the schism between the cultural and the technical as architecture entered (1750–1939) and exited (1925–78) the vicissitudes of the project of Modernity, respectively. The taxonomy Frampton follows in the middle section of the book works like a historical construct in its own right (1836–1967). For one, he rips objects out of their context and places them in reference to an architect's interpretation of the suggested dichotomies. The anachronism informing the dates of the two major parts of the constellation defies historicism: it departs from the vision of history that would try to establish totalities based on one or two major principles, that is, the organic (Bruno Zevi), or space and time (Giedion), let alone the totality constructed in analogy to a Marxian interpretation of capitalism (Manfredo Tafuri). Frampton's periodization of modern architecture instead conjugates the dynamics of time and technology with the geopolitics of placemaking as architecture puts behind itself the historicity of modernism. This strategy of periodization is implied in the work of many theorists, including Habermas, a thinker Frampton has been sympathetic toward. It also draws from ontologies inherent in Heidegger's critique of technology. What makes Frampton's take on periodization interesting is the concept of placemaking, which meets technology halfway.

This much is clear from the last chapter of the first edition of Frampton's book, titled "Place, Production and Architecture: Towards a Critical Theory of Building," where he discusses postwar architecture in the light of technological optimization, on the one hand, and the urge to recognize the existential demands of *dwelling*, on the other. Starting with a quotation from Heidegger, Frampton departs from Benjamin to follow Heidegger's distinction between space and placemaking.²⁸ The distinction, however, does not fault Benjamin's thesis as discussed in the "Work of Art" essay.²⁹ It rather allows for "crossing-over [...] between the categories of Marxist materialist explanation and those of Heideggerian ontology, which ascribes the age of modernity to the unfurling of the essence of technology."³⁰ This understanding of technology turns out to be central to Frampton's theorization of a semiautonomous architecture, the thematic of which, paradoxically, is defined and redefined by the unpredictable path capitalism travels to smooth its internal contradictions.

THE VIOLENCE OF QUOTATION   23

Even though the outdated distinction between "the base" and the "superstructure" is itself a by-product of capitalism, in its evolutionary process the system has shaped and reshaped itself to the point where culture has become a production system in its own right. This development has led historians and critics to rethink the production of subjectivity anew and beyond the mechanics of the base and superstructure paradigm. However, as far as Frampton's project is concerned, we ought to ask: what is involved in discussing architecture in relation to the human condition, especially the idea of placemaking, at a time when capitalism has taken over the project of Modernity? In Chapter 7 of this volume, Frampton's critical regionalism is discussed in depth. For now, suffice to say that Frampton was aware of the total disintegration of the craft-based tradition of architecture, the loss of aura as the art of building encountered the instrumental logic of technology and the impossibility of sustaining the old homologies between the body, language and landscape. If the implied homology fits with our understanding of vernacular, Frampton is pretty consistent in underscoring the uniqueness of critical regionalism compared to the vernacular. Gone also is what Arendt termed the *excess* of labor, when the latter was not yet fully absorbed into the production and consumption cycles of capitalism.[31] Even though the consequences of these so-to-speak "negatives" for the art and architecture of early modernism were reapproached by both revolutionary and conservative politics,[32] Frampton has not yet given up the angel's mission of rescuing those aspects of the culture of building, type/tectonic in particular,[33] that could resist the current flood of commodification.

IV

How then do the symptomatic readings charted so far structure Frampton's introductory text? Similar to the Angel of History, Frampton's attention is focused on the past, especially the culture of building, without dismissing the *natural* flow of progress that has been at work since the Enlightenment, and this in conjunction with an experience of temporality that is measured not in terms of nature but history. Frampton reminds his reader of the fact that construction of the lifeworld demands both formal and spatial solutions, which are essential for architecture's rapport with the city and urban design as history moves from the pre- to the post-Enlightenment appropriation of reason. This historical trajectory, which Frampton sees as the dark side of the Enlightenment, is enforced by a production system that differs from the pre-mechanical process of reproducibility when most construction materials were extracted from nature and skills and techniques of surface embellishment were rooted in the traditions of handcrafts. Even though architectural production and reproduction have always used construction methods internal to the building's historical development, this limitation, if you wish, did not stop the art of building from sharing motifs developed in other areas of cultural production. The vicissitudes of this Semperian position (*Stoffwechsel*) were drastically transformed as architecture entered into the production and consumption cycles of capitalism, wherein industrial technology overdetermined the *natural* transmission of those aspects of the culture of building that were not profitable in terms of the de- and reskilling of labor. One consequence of this was the urge to use industrial materials and techniques. The implications of this process of reskilling for the work of art and architecture, as discussed in Benjamin's "The Work of Art in the Age of Mechanical Reproduction" (1934), is another topic informing Frampton's introductory text. In the tradition of critical theory, Frampton suggests that, in addition to performing its purpose, technique sets up a particular movement and rhythm, the temporality of which, interestingly enough, coordinates the body's action and its relation to place. Recalling Heidegger, Frampton's criticism seems to be focused on architecture's one-dimensional appropriation of technique, and this is in spite of Benjamin's belief that the exhibition value of the artwork, itself one of the consequences of the infusion of the aesthetic of commodity fetishism into the cultural realm, will one day be integrated into the general ways in which architecture is appropriated and apprehended. No wonder then that the first edition of Frampton's historiography does not fully cover the aesthetic and formal consequences of what he would later frame as the "product-form."[34]

Frampton's introductory text also touches on the daunting issue of the date and period when the modern movement in architecture began. He sees the diffusion of industrialization and prefabrication into the production process of architecture as the agent not only of the transformation of the culture of building but also of the dissolution, slowly but surely, of the Humanist precept of unity between architecture and the city. Frampton correctly argues that, with the proliferation of positivistic and technocratic approaches to planning and built-environment, the split between "architecture and urban development has led to the situation in which the possibility of the former contributing to the latter and vice versa, over a long period of time, has become extremely limited." No wonder then that the two opening chapters of the book are dedicated to the theme of territorial and technological transformations, which, interestingly enough, happens to be the core subject of his critical interpretation of modernism in architecture at least until the arrival of the postmodern moment. This interpretative regime not only structures the entirety of the first edition of the book but also opens a particular vista into what was and was not included in the second part, a major section of the book. However, the introduction fails to provide detailed criteria for the inclusion and exclusion of architects explored in the second and main part of the book.³⁵ It is left to the reader to speculate on how the work of the discussed architects relates to the specificity of the "subject under consideration" in each chapter of the book; how a particular design is "inflected by the given socio-economic or ideological circumstances;" and/or in what conditions the author has restricted his analysis to formal issues. What we do know is that these exclusions concern projects that were motivated, in the first place, by the architect's subjectivity—expressionism as one example among other omitted themes—instead of disclosing the ways *external* factors (the dichotomies mentioned earlier) influence design and its execution. Similar to Benjamin's characterization of "expressionism" and the *Neue Sachlichkeit* architecture of the 1920s as a "delusional belief in the efficacy of intellectuals and of moral appeals for progressive causes,"³⁶ the exclusions noticed by Tafuri and others disclose another side of Frampton's critical discourse, wherein the individual quest for *freedom* (liberalism?) is seen as inadequate to stand against the totality enforced by capitalism. The implied "collective" is a major clue to the labyrinth of Frampton's Marxian approach to the historiography of modern architecture.

V

At this point it is important to reflect on the differences between Heidegger's and Benjamin's take on technology one more time. As mentioned earlier, in Benjamin's account, the angel's physiognomy is positioned between the two moments of the past and the present. The temporal passage between the now-time and the past is inflected by Benjamin's take on the historical loss of the aura. However, he does not specify the timing of this historical unfolding; instead, he associates its occurrence with techniques internal to the age of mechanical reproducibility. This entails a concept of periodization that separates the Classical age from the Modern, the two major and long-lasting periods of Western humanity that were still in progress during Benjamin's lifetime (1892–1940). The posture of the Angel of History also suggests that the now-time stands for modernity, a longue durée *event* driven by the repressed dynamics of the past, and a perception of temporality that is in tune with technological innovations. Unlike Heidegger, Benjamin does not lament the loss of the classical comradeship between the body, place and the act of making, a constellation shaken by the rise of the instrumental appropriation of science and technology,³⁷ another theme dear to Frampton's critical discourse. Unlike the concept of the body foregrounded in phenomenology, the "anthropological materialism" attributed to Benjamin draws its conclusions, first, from the conviction that "the idealist tradition of humanism, and the classical ideal of humanity itself, were thoroughly compromised. Not the preservation of these traditions but only a purifying liquidation could hope to save what had once animated them." Second, Benjamin's position benefits from an experience of "bodily collectivity" that is traceable in the realm of images, on the one hand, and in the bodily self-consciousness that is touched by technological development, on the other.[38] These brief reflections on the body, place and making are important because, among other things, technique also sets a particular movement and rhythm, the temporality of which coordinates the body's action and its relation to *place*. According to Wolfgang Schivelbusch, who is occasionally referenced in Frampton's lectures,

> Pre-industrial traffic is mimetic of natural phenomena [...] Only during a transitional period did the travellers who transferred from the stagecoach to the railway carriage experience a sense of loss due to the mechanization of travel: it did not take long for the industrialization of the means of transport to alter the consciousness of the passengers: they developed a new set of perceptions.[39]

In reading Heidegger through the pen of Arendt, Frampton foregrounds an understanding of the culture of building that is not yet reduced to its "lowest common denominator, in order to make production cheaper and to optimize use." He goes further, suggesting that "in its well-intended but sometimes misguided concern to assimilate the technical and processal realities of the 20th century, architecture has adopted a language in which expression resides almost entirely in processal, secondary components" of buildings.

The aforementioned two poles of periodization, the Classical and the Modern, underpin Frampton's *A Critical History* and disclose the paradox of his historiography. This means that in order to exert its disciplinary autonomy, architecture in modernity has to stand against its context—that is, against the hegemonic aspects of the functionalist reduction of all expressive dimensions to the exigencies of instrumental reason, and the simulacra of the postmodern historicism of the 1970s. It seems that, at the time of the publication of the first edition of *A Critical History*, and in reference to Frampton's later publications, Alvar Aalto was the architect whose work came closest to Frampton's hope of reconciling the Miesian "obsession" with technology and the notion of "almost nothing" with the traditions of the culture of building.[40] Such a work, according to Frampton, is "patently 'visible' and often takes the form of a masonry enclosure that establishes within its limited 'monastic' domain a reasonably open but concrete set of relationships linking man to man and man to nature."[41] Here, Frampton tries to unpack the paradox permeating Benjamin's and Heidegger's positions on technology, which, interestingly enough, demonstrates the subject's importance for historiography of modern architecture. Benjamin's tacit acceptance of technology as the force propelling the Angel of History forward does not overshadow the critical task of the angel in saving the radical potentialities of the past. It was clear to Benjamin that technology had already tossed the earthly bound culture into the orbit of relentless technological innovations and into the mutation of a landscape that is charged with the desire for nothing less than mere consumption. This suggested negativity is balanced dialectically in Benjamin's formulation of the "loss of aura," meaning, among other things, the impossibility of critical praxis without technological progression as it has taken place. Heidegger's project, by contrast, was centered on the recollection of work that might turn his hypothetical spectator's attention from the bridge (a technological spectacle) to the apartness of the two banks of the river.[42] It is the distinction between Benjamin's and Heidegger's interpretations of the loss of aura, on the one hand, and Frampton's empathy with Heidegger's notion of *Raum* and the loss of "nearness," on the other, that led Frampton to compile his book as a *constellation* of various architects' responses to the nihilism of technology, and the way each had tried to recode the culture of building, major aspects of which are particles of premodern times in the first place. Setting aside philosophical differences, what made Frampton sympathetic to Heidegger, as discussed in Chapter 7, was the historicity of the 1960s, when a different understanding of the nation-state prevailed in countries then viewed as "underdeveloping," whereas Benjamin's overarching position on modernity and modernization remained focused on Western geographies. In Heidegger's notion of placemaking Frampton saw the seeds of a resistance that might be workable in the context of developing nations (peripheries), turning it to strategic criticism of architecture produced in Western centers. What we can expect from the concept of "resistance" is a general stance with no strategic future goal.[43]

VI

Walter Benjamin wrote the "Thesis on the Philosophy of History" in 1940, when the war had already shown the atrocities that un-reasoned reasoning could commit under the guise of populist political slogans. The sleep of reason followed by the destructive war had political, economic and humanitarian consequences that touched both architecture and the built environment. It was a wake-up call to witness how architectural ideology could operate within a system with a preprogrammed intellectual game, a unique unfolding as far as the genesis of critical thinking is concerned.[44] The historicity of the 1930s set an alarming precedent for the contemporary enthusiastic embrace of mass dissemination of information that has led to the delusional appropriation of individual "freedom" under the prevailing regime of neoliberalism[45]—and this is in contrast to the concentration of wealth in the hands of a few globally operating corporations, which, among other cultural forms, has attained symbolic *visibility* in the emerging needle-type towers soaring in Manhattan and other financial centers of late capitalism. It can be argued that this typological shift from the Heideggerian bridge—a horizontal construct—to the fashionable soaring thin towers says something about the political regime of architecture in the age of global capitalism. Paradoxically, "some of the world's most powerful corporations, like Apple, Microsoft and Walmart, have their headquarters in rustic (though well-connected) locations and are characterized by a pronounced horizontality."[46] These architectonic developments, along with the present political turmoils taking place around the globe, coincided with Frampton's decision to add a new section to *A Critical History* in 2017. In the forthcoming fifth edition (2020),[47] Frampton intends to explore architectural projects produced in countries that have entered the process of modernization in different time zones.[48] The new edition is expected to include a critical assessment of the state of architecture in different cultures that, unlike "modern architecture," confront a state of production, consumption and appropriation of the culture that is wall-to-wall commodified and distributed globally. It is worth looking forward to seeing which architect's or thinker's statement will be quoted on the opening page of the recent edition of the book!

The quotation from Benjamin's text did not violate Frampton's project as discussed in the short introduction to the 1980 edition of the book. The quotations used in the forthcoming edition should be important because the historicity of the "course of two actions"—a Miesian "almost nothing" and an Aaltoesque sense of "placemaking"—are transformed drastically. The technical shift from mechanical to digital reproducibility (to stay with a Benjaminian notion of periodization) has pumped new blood into the old, well-known Marxian idea of commodity fetishism to the point that the fluidity of *image* has put behind itself both the physical and metaphysical content of the Renaissance perspectival regime, which aimed to sustain a balance between the visual and the spatial, among other things. Armed with the latest digital preprogrammed visuality, and disregard for locality, most architects today have chosen to enjoy the given *freedom*, manipulating form for the sake of self-indulgent pleasure, and the possibility of tossing architecture into the orbit of spectacle to be consumed instantly through digital media networks such as Facebook, Instagram and Twitter.

These reflections on the state of contemporary architecture were made to shed a different light on Frampton's decision to omit a number of architects in the first edition of *A Critical History*. The omission was reasoned on the conviction that their work stopped short of addressing the dialectics between space and *place* but also type-tectonics central to the scope of architectonic possibilities that separate Mies from Aalto. These remarks also underline the significance of his take on critical regionalism, a strategic project of resistance against dichotomies internal to modernization and the culture of building beyond the centers identifiable with the dark side of the Enlightenment. Frampton's critical regionalism suggests a vision of historiography that is also concerned with the architecture produced in geographies whose past and present do not synchronize with the temporality experienced in the Western hemisphere, particularly in the context of the Classical versus Modern paradox. Therefore, it is safe to speculate one more time that with the upcoming edition, Frampton has once again tried to locate the stakes of architectural ideology in the conflict between the globalization of capital and information, and the "uneven development" of modernism unfolding in different countries.[49] As we will see later in this volume, the suggested unevenness is indeed fundamental to the dialectics between the two notions of autonomy and semi-autonomy that are central to Frampton's critical reading of the protagonists of the ideology of modernism then and now.

Notes

1 Walter Benjamin, "One Way Street," in *Reflections*, ed. Peter Demetz (New York: Harcourt Brace Jovanovich, 1978), 61–96.
2 For the critical importance of the concept of montage in 1920s avant-garde artistic work, see Martino Stierli, *Montage and the Metropolis* (New Haven, CT: Yale University Press, 2018).
3 https://www.google.com.au/?client=safari&channel=mac_bm&gws_rd=cr&ei=etSzWOWhOIqB8wWQgLWACA#channel=mac_bm&q=constellation+meaning& (accessed February 10, 2017).
4 Giorgio Agamben, "The Melancholy Angel," in *The Man without Content*, trans. Georgia Albert (Stanford: Stanford University Press, 1999), 104. The essay's title recalls A. Dürer's engraving *Melencolia*.
5 Walter Benjamin, "Paris, Capital of the Nineteenth Century," in *Reflections*, 146–62.
6 Walter Benjamin, "Theses on the Philosophy of History," in *Illuminations*, trans. H. Zohn (New York: Schoken, 1969), 253–64.
7 "My wing is ready for flight, / I would like to turn back. / If I stayed timeless time, / I would have little luck."
8 Manfredo Tafuri, *Architecture and Utopia: Design and Capitalist Development* (Cambridge: MIT Press, 1976), 2.
9 The literature on the subject is vast. For the most recent reading of Walter Benjamin's philosophy of history, see Stuart Jeffries, *Grand Hotel Abyss: The Lives of the Frankfurt School* (London: Verso, 2017), 19–21; and Fredric Jameson, *The Benjamin Files* (London: Verso, 2020). The entire book is recommended!
10 Kenneth Frampton, *A Critical History* (London: Thames & Hudson, 1980), 9.
11 Ibid.
12 Harry Harootunian, *History's Disquiet* (New York: Columbia University Press, 2000), 19.

13 Giorgio Agamben, "The Melancholy Angel," 111.
14 Fredric Jameson, *A Singular Modernity: Essays on the Ontology of the Present* (London: Verso, 2002), 161–66.
15 Jürgen Habermas, "Modernity—An Incomplete Project," in *The Anti-aesthetic: Essays on Postmodern Culture*, ed. Hal Foster (Washington, DC: Bay, 1983), 3–15.
16 Fredric Jameson, *Postmodernism, or, the Cultural Logic of Late Capitalism* (Durham, NC: Duke University Press, 1991).
17 Kenneth Frampton, "On Reading Heidegger," *Oppositions* 4 (October 1974): 6–9.
18 In a meeting with Kenneth Frampton in Manhattan, he briefly explained why he had resigned from the journal. The ideological gist of disagreement among the editorial group is suggested in K. Michael Hays, "The Oppositions of Autonomy and History," in *Oppositions Reader*, ed. M. Hays (New York: Princeton Architectural Press, 1998), ix–xv.
19 Kenneth Frampton, "Labour, Work & Architecture," in *Meaning in Architecture*, ed. Charles Jencks and George Baird (London: Barrie & Jenckins, 1969), 151–70. Reprinted under the title "The Status of Man and the Status of His Objects," in *Modern Architecture and the Critical Present*, ed. Kenneth Frampton (London: Academy Editions, 1982), 7–19. This issue of *Architectural Design Profile* was published on the occasion of the publication of Frampton's *Critical History* (1980). Frampton would use *Labour, Work & Architecture* as the title of his collected essays, published in 2002.
20 Frampton, "Labour, Work & Architecture," 163.
21 On this subject, see Howard Caygill, "Benjamin, Heidegger and the Destruction of Tradition," in *Walter Benjamin's Philosophy*, ed. Andrew Benjamin and Peter Osborne (London: Routledge, 1994), 12–31.
22 See Sokratis Georgiadis, "Introduction," in *Building in France, Building in Iron, Building in Ferro-concrete*, ed. Sigfried Giedion (Los Angeles: Getty Center Publication Program, 1995), 53.
23 Todd Gannon, *Reyner Banham and the Paradoxes of High Tech* (Los Angeles: Getty Research Institute, 2017), 3.
24 Ibid., 11.
25 Kenneth Frampton, *Studies in Tectonic Culture: The Poetics of Construction* (Cambridge: MIT Press, 1995).
26 See Gannon, *Reyner Banham*, Chapter 5. The idea of *bricoleu* is introduced in Charles Jencks and George Baird (eds), *Meaning in Architecture* (London: Barrie & Jenckins, 1969). In addition to the continuity and discontinuity of the present views of the authors who contributed to the book, rereading it today sheds light on the historicity of postwar architecture.
27 Charles Jencks, "Preface," in Jencks and Baird, *Meaning in Architecture*, 7.
28 In France, during the late 1930s, Martin Heidegger's discourse opened the door to seeing in "phenomenological dialectic" the entire business of the Marxian philosophy of history. Alfred Schmidt, "Henri Lefebvre and Marxism: A View from the Frankfurt School," https://thecharnelhouse.org/2017/02/10/henri-lefebvre-and-marxism-a-view-from-the-frankfurt-school/ (accessed February 11, 2017).
29 Walter Benjamin, "The Work of Art in the Age of Mechanical Reproduction," in *Illuminations*, 217–52.
30 Jacque Rancière, *The Politics of Aesthetics* (London: Continuum, 2006), 31.
31 Hannah Arendt, *The Human Condition* (Chicago: University of Chicago Press, 1958), 88.

32 See, for example, Maria Gough, "Tarabukin, Spengler, and the Art of Production," *October* 93 (Summer 2000): 76–108.
33 It is worth recalling that a dialectical understanding of the rapport between type and tectonics was the pedagogical cornerstone of the architecture program at Columbia University when Frampton was the director.
34 The subject is discussed in Kenneth Frampton, *The Evolution of 20th Century Architecture: A Synoptic Account* (New York: Springer Wien, 2007), 123–36.
35 The consequence of these exclusions for the "linear" quality of history is discussed in Manfredo Tafuri's review of Frampton's book. See Tafuri, "Architecture and 'Poverty,'" in Frampton, *Modern Architecture and the Critical Present*, 57–58.
36 Albert Prez-Gomez, *Architecture and the Crisis of Modern Science* (Cambridge: MIT Press, 1983).
37 Ibid.
38 Paraphrasing John McCole in *Walter Benjamin and the Antinomies of Tradition* (Ithaca, NY: Cornell University Press, 1993), 171–80. The author makes these claims based on Benjamin's remarks on "Experience and Poverty." For a comprehensive exploration of Benjamin's concept of "experience," see Andrew Benjamin, "Time and Task: Benjamin and Heidegger Showing the Present," in *Walter Benjamin's Philosophy: Destruction and Experience*, ed. A. Benjamin and P. Osborne (London: Routledge, 1994), 216–50.
39 Wolfgang Schivelbusch, *Railway Journey: The Industrialisation of Time and Space in the 19th Century* (Berkeley: University of California Press, 1986), 15. Also see Sigfried Giedion, *Mechanization Takes Command: A Contribution to Anonymous History* (New York: Oxford University Press, 1948).
40 One year after the publication of *A Critical History*, in discussing "regionalism," Frampton extended the list of architects to include Alvaro Siza and Mario Botta, among others. See Frampton, *Modern Architecture and the Critical Present*, 77–83.
41 Ibid., 10.
42 Paraphrasing from Gevork Hartoonian, *Modernity and Its Other* (College Station: Texas A & M University Press, 1997), 49.
43 Fredric Jameson, *Representing Capital: A Reading of Volume One* (London: Verso, 2011), 146.
44 For the classic account of this historical development, see Manfredo Tafuri, *Architecture and Eutopia* (Cambridge: MIT Press, 1976).
45 On neoliberalism, see the Introduction in Douglas Spencer, *The Architecture of Neoliberalism* (London: Bloomsbury Academic, 2016), 1–10.
46 Goran Therborn quoted in Owen Hatherley, "Comparing Capitals," *New Left Review* 105 (May–June 2017): 129.
47 The reader should take note of the fact that this volume was completed before Kenneth Frampton's publication of the fifth edition of *A Critical History*, which was released late 2020.
48 This issue came up in the author's conversation with Kenneth Frampton sometime during January of 2017.
49 Fredric Jameson, *A Singular Modernity* (London: Verso, 2002), 165.

Chapter 2

A TRILOGY

Kenneth Frampton's historiographic taxonomy is essential for the project pursued in *Modern Architecture: A Critical History*, first published in 1980. The previous chapter demonstrated the extent to which a well-known passage from Walter Benjamin's "Thesis on the Philosophy of History" (1940) set the theoretical premises of Frampton's brief introductory remarks, notable aspects of which he elaborates on in the subsequent chapters of the book. It is to Frampton's credit that he writes the history of modern architecture while criticizing the Enlightenment idea of progress. His text also critiques the stakes involved in the avant-gardist failed attempt to catch up with the wind of progress (in artistic terms) that pushes Benjamin's angel of history forward. This "failure" speaks to the ideology of modernity, wherein "reality persisted independent of that sentimental and romantic 'sphere of culture.'" Accordingly, it took almost half a century, Fredric Jameson contends, to face the vanishing stage of the suggested mode of separation, at least in the regions of the world that were the bedrock of early modernism.[1] Call it the postmodern condition or the full-moon visibility of an ideology when alternative views are almost nullified, if not tossed to the dark orbit of history, at least for now.

At issue for a historian, among other things, was/is the possibility of maintaining a strategic distance from the Real without isolating historiography from the objective and subjective conditions of the everyday life that capitalism has successfully managed since the middle of the past century. Frampton maps the historicity of the formation of modern architecture in three chapters of the book's Part I. He argues that what makes modernity distinct from the Classical are transformations implanted in the cultural, territorial and technical areas, which are discussed under the rubric of the "trilogy" below. These transformations run the historical gamut extending from 1750 to 1939. In addition to witnessing the emergence of architectonic expressions motivated by technical changes, the last years of the decade of the 1930s designated the end of modernity. This does not mean the literal end of modernity, a singular historical event that has attained global currency since the end of the Cold War (*ca.* 1990), but the loss of the theoretical currency of modernity versus

Classical paradigm. Apropos, modernization has turned into a strategic means for capitalism to expand its territorial domination globally, both culturally and technically, if today we can distinguish between these two realms! Moreover, most early historiographies of modern architecture were written according to the paradigm of Modern versus Classical. Frampton's discussion in Part I of the book expands the landscape of *critical history* to include the regions of the world that, for historical reasons, did not pass through the "Classical" period as we know it in the West, let alone the Renaissance period, a preoccupation for most historians, including Manfredo Tafuri.[2]

Related to the Modern-Classical paradox are themes discussed throughout the book's three-part structure, which set the premises of Frampton's theoretical departure from the orthodox historiographies of modern architecture. Central to his strategy is the historicity of three dates, each marking the end of one of the book's three sections. This chapter argues that the dates 1939, 1967 and 1978 highlight a historical tangent when architecture was traumatized by an *event*. We are reminded of the beginning of the end of bourgeois "civil" society exemplified by the usurpation of the project of Modernity by capitalism and the weakening of international-style architecture by 1939; the departure from modernism and the formation of postmodernism, 1967; and the possibility of critiquing the international-style architecture from *within* disciplinary praxis. This latter development was seen as part of the general reaction against the crisis of modernity, attaining theoretical visibility in the late 1960s. Reflecting on this subject, Hal Foster adds Frampton to the list of critics, including Rosalind Krauss, among others, who formulated a particular critical position against the interiority of a disciplinarity that was framed according to the Enlightenment order both in art and architecture.[3] We will return to the implied idea of the interiority (autonomy) of architecture shortly and map the historicity of ideas and themes central to Frampton's discussion of the three mentioned transformations. For now, we should note that the passage from each of the three aforementioned eventful dates to the next did not follow a linear path. While monitoring history's forward push, Frampton takes two steps backward, casting a critical eye on the contemporaneity of architecture at any given historical moment. Thus, the book's Part III covers the period spanning 1925–78; Part II, 1936–67; and Part I, 1750–1939, to put things in reverse chronological order. This makes his take on periodization different from that of historians who discuss the actuality of the ongoing events in the presumed light of modern spirit(s). A critical and retrospective account of the history of modern architecture is Frampton's major contribution to the historiography of architecture.

Frampton is sympathetic toward Benjamin's approach to history and attempts to highlight the disjunction between architecture and capitalism at every historic turn when the system refueled its engine of progress. If this strategy is central to the concept of critical historiography, a position Tafuri also pursued, what distinguishes Frampton from the Italian Marxist historian is how he subdues a Hegelist claim for the impossibility of *architecture* in modernity. Most historians and theoreticians with Marxian inclination have been, in one form or another, nurtured by German idealist philosophy, while at the same time struggling to surmount the alleged dialectics that cast a shadow over the debate between Max Horkheimer and a group of American thinkers known as the New York intellectuals during the late 1930s.[4] To go beyond the pragmatism advocated by the group, and to plot a critical and *reflective* architectural praxis, Frampton turns to Martin Heidegger. Of particular interest is Heidegger's view of technology as a "standing reserve."[5] This concept has remote associations with a Marxian analysis of capital and the reified subject/object relationship. Although Heidegger intended to alleviate the alienating effects of technology, one cannot but "demand for a sober historical phenomenology that accounts for the body's ever-shifting interaction with its environment," which, according to David Cunningham, "has undergone fundamental and irreversible change in the 'second nature' of capitalist modernity."[6] As Jameson has also noted,[7] in search of an absolute beginning, Heidegger's narrative of modernity hinged on representation, a *construction*, the metaphysics of which runs its full course from the perspectival regime in painting to montage in film. Nevertheless, Frampton's reading of Heidegger was overshadowed by architecture(s) produced in countries with diverse stages of productivity and culture, countries where, beyond philosophical issues, "placemaking" was still an attainable desire. Despite a common Heideggerian subject/object relation, it is important to differentiate Frampton's formulation of the architecture of resistance from the Zevian "organic architecture" that was tagged as "operative history" by Tafuri.[8] Frampton's project also differs from Reyner Banham's overvaluation of technological maximization when architects tried to respond to challenges raised by postwar capitalism.

Frampton's historiography demonstrates that architecture and capitalism did not, or could not, run in parallel tracks after the war. A missed encounter, one consequence of which was to highlight architecture's autonomy, as evident in the typological and formal investigations of architectural theories produced in the 1960s. Working toward two different ends, these methodologies revisited the eighteenth-century discourse on type searching for design methods different from those offered by the "biotechnical determinism" monitored by some circles of early modernists.[9] On the one hand, the most advanced formal analysis available at the time could not but reduce *type* to its pure geometrical origin, re- or deconstructing its elements in the light of various structuralist and post-structuralist theories exemplified in Peter Eisenman's early work, for one.[10] On the other hand, the postmodernist approach to notions such as precedent and typology remained locked in the traditions of rhetoric. These two theoretical unfoldings, and Alan Colquhoun's timely discussion of the typological turn in architecture, were indeed ideological responses to the missed historical encounter alluded to earlier. Consequently, architecture's autonomy was in many ways considered part of the totality that would index a building's dependency on available labor, technique and materiality. Related to this postwar unfolding, and the demise of the political agency of modernity, was the turn to theories that looked at architecture through the lenses of philosophical work, each trying to revisit a wide range of available critical discourses. The spectrum of this theoretical shift included the orthodoxies of Marxism, the negativity of Frankfurt School Critical Theory and the revisionist interpretations of Sigmund Freud inspired by linguistic paradigms. In retrospect, we should map the historicity of postwar architecture in the intersection of theories such as structuralism and post-structuralism, and in the post-Fordist production and distribution tactics that prevailed in the 1980s. Interestingly enough, many symptoms of these briefly noted developments are today conveniently discussed in terms of globalization. The postwar historicity suggests that contemporary historiographies of architecture, including Frampton's, should be revisited accordingly.

In the suggested allegorical "one step backward" move, Frampton succeeded in plotting the vicissitudes of a semiautonomous architectural praxis. He tries to save the past not because of its stylistic merits but because the past—although Frampton does not put it in these words—has not been left behind simply by its unfulfilled purpose. Rather, he does this because the historicity of architecture since the nineteenth century embodied languages associated with the classical period, a disciplinary knowledge that was not yet fully aligned with the prevailing technological regime of the age of mechanical reproducibility. At issue is not even the temporality that stirred the quarrel between the moderns and the ancients[11]—in which, by the way, the claim of the moderns was not just limited to the fact that they were newcomers. They boasted of being armed with a telescopic knowledge of the past. Positivistic as it sounds, these ancients of our global moderns paradoxically could not see the dynamics of the now-time unleashed by the demise of bourgeois civic society, the old regime. They also missed the point that much of the experience of temporality in capitalism is inflected by constant change, best understood in analogy to the state of fashion discussed by George Simmel[12] or Marx's famous claim that "all that is solid melts into the air."[13] To say that the debate between the moderns and the ancients has turned out to be integral to the ever-accelerating experience of time in capitalism is one thing; the conviction to revisit Frampton's book in the matrix of contradictions underpinning the present architectural praxis is another. These observations are important considering the number of editions Frampton has introduced since the book's first publication in 1980. In fact, the book has been expanded several times in anticipation of "World Architecture and Reflective Practice," the title of the last chapter of the third edition (1992), discussed in the concluding chapter of this volume.

If in modernity all products are doomed to be outdated before being fully experienced, then in what ways and to what ends should the culture of building, the interiority of architecture that Frampton so eloquently discusses in *A Genealogy of Modern Architecture* (2015),[14] be given its proper role in the historiography of architecture? Central to this inquiry is that architecture is often late on time or "non-contemporaneous" to recall Ernst Bloch.[15] The untimely modern state of architecture, evident in the work of art Nouveau and Expressionism, had a foot in the ontological dimension of the art of building—the sheer fact that, at each historical turn, architecture is expected to provide spatial, tactile and formal solutions associable with the prevailing temporality, including the available technical know-how, solutions that, paradoxically, are most often modified in the purview of the received traditions of building, lest architecture becomes a by-product of the machine. Therefore, in the savviest technological age, architecture cannot afford to throw the baby out with the bathwater, for the sheer reason that its rapport with everyday life is ontological. Here, we should agree with Mario Carpo that most architects tend to resist accepting technological changes.[16] Turning his focus to digital techniques, Carpo dismisses the fact that, as with the transformation from handicraft to mechanical, the transformation from mechanical to digital reproducibility is also informed by the dialectics of the technical and the ideological. This means that, in each major historical unfolding, technical developments ensure the formation of a particular subjectivity. For instance, the ethos of modernism in architecture was deeply rooted in the replacement of the masonry construction system with the frame, and in consideration of the availability of materials such as steel, glass and concrete, the spatial, formal and aesthetic properties of which Sigfried Giedion mapped in *Building in France, Building in Iron, Building in Ferro-concrete* (1928). However, this technical and perceptual unfolding did not and could not stop the continuity of the architectonics of the masonry construction system either then or today. On the other hand, Carpo correctly associates the emergence of the "architect" as the author of the design with the beginning of Renaissance Humanism. In two different moments, both Leon Battista Alberti and Filippo Brunelleschi conceived of and produced an architecture that secured the architect's authority over those involved in the construction site, directly and indirectly. This schism between design and construction persists, despite the claim of the proponents of parametricism that building information modeling (BIM) will close the gap between them.[17]

This detour is necessary in consideration to the contemporary generation of architects and theoreticians, Peter Eisenman, for example, has been exemplary in upholding the authority of the architect through constant recoding of the ethos of autonomy. Frampton, a member of the same generation, has consistently pondered the importance of the *material* (objective and subjective) dimensions of the culture of the building that has survived in the face of progress. The critical importance of the untimeliness of architecture, dismissed by the advocates of formal autonomy, is evident in Theodor Adorno's reflection on the remains of Paris after the savage war. He wrote, "What survives here may well be condemned by history […], but the fact *that it*, the essence of untimeliness, still exists is part of the historical picture and permits the feeble hope that something humane survives, despite everything."[18] Accordingly, and considering the nuances of architectural ideology, Frampton has not given up resisting the ever-accelerating experience of time, despite the evidence that the march of progress is destined to further enforce the instrumental reason in every design aspect of the built environment. This observation, underpins Frampton's project of the historiography of modern architecture, regardless of whether the reader agrees or disagrees with his interpretation of a particular architect(s)' work discussed in different chapters of the book.

In addition to plotting the historicity of the period integral to the formation of Frampton's critical historiography, the lengthy prelude to this chapter is also intended to set the premises highlighting the significance of Frampton's choice of image for the opening page of Part I of the book, entitled "Cultural Developments and Predisposing Techniques, 1750–1939." The image shows the interior space of the Church of Ste-Genevieve, known as the Pantheon, designed by Jacques-Germain Soufflot, Paris, 1755–90 (Figure 2.1). Frampton's additional note to the figure caption of the same image is worth mentioning; it reads, "Crossing piers strengthened by Rondelet in 1806."[19] The fact that an addition was made to the church after its construction suggests that either the overall tectonic-image Soufflot had sought failed to engineer the gravity forces adequately[20] or it failed to fulfill the expected traditional aesthetics wherein a free-standing column was seen next to a pier and/or a wall.[21] An exception to this tectonic generalization is the Doric temple at Paestum which Soufflot had visited in 1750. Surrounded by free-standing Doric columns on four sides, the temple raised the problem of the corner column, the architectonics of which has been revisited by many architects since then. The tectonic rapport between the aesthetic and the structural (image) is suggested in Barry Bergdoll's observation; he writes, "Soufflot's project was continuously revised and refined over

Figure 2.1 Jacques-Germain Soufflot, Ste-Genevieve, Paris, 1755–90, interior view. Photo courtesy of Wikimedia Commons, the free media repository.

the long years of construction, marking it as the foremost of several experimental buildings where the aesthetic and structural limits of architecture were tested and debated."[22] The design of Ste-Genevieve was also unique for combining its structural clarity with spatial lucidity, even though this was achieved by a system of hidden iron rods reinforcing the building's vaults.

Still, the "free-standing" interior columns of the Church of Ste-Genevieve allude to a fundamental departure from the Vitruvian association of the column with the human body, and from the concept of Orders—the progenitor of the Classical language of architecture—which overshadowed architectural praxis until the dawn of the Industrial Revolution and the subsequent emergence of the need for new and unprecedented building types.[23] The metaphoric use of "free-standing columns" intends to capitalize on the perspectival regime that allowed Brunelleschi to conceive of a building, not as space "enclosed by walls, but as a skeleton made of clearly defined structural line."[24] Even in *Capella dei Pazzi* (1430), where the columns of the facade appear to be free-standing, a closer inspection of the building's plan reveals the extent to which each column structures the grid underpinning the spatial organization of the design. The insistence here on the tectonic dimension of the column, and the resultant gridded spatial organization in the mentioned edifices, are important for several reasons. In addition to Frampton's choice of image for the cover page of Part I of the book, his critical reservation toward Mies, who, interestingly enough, avoided the issue of the free-standing corner column in his later work, also comes to mind. In the New National Gallery of Berlin (1968), he placed a free-standing column in the middle of each bay of a square-shaped plan. Also noteworthy is Frampton's interest in tectonics, a subject that throughout the past hundred years has been recoded according to the available construction systems. Since the rise of industrialization, the vicissitudes of tectonics have been defined and redefined by the building industry, itself a product of the production and consumption system of capitalism. Yet, the historicity of this development is one of the significant aspects of Frampton's discourse on the *critical* anticipated in the title of Part I. In retrospect, the phrase "predisposing techniques" alludes to Frampton's desire for the continuity of masonry construction culture, and its related tactile and tectonic connotations at large. After the war, the emergence and dissemination of the "culture industry" did reduce the relevance of the construction techniques and aesthetics that were dominant before the Industrial Revolution. This development brings us back again to Frampton's proposed second choice of future action, which is, as pointed out in the previous chapter, "patently visible and often takes the form of masonry enclosure,"[25] one of the core principles of Critical Regionalism, discussed in the last chapter of this volume.

I: 1750–1900

In the three short chapters compiled in Part I of *A Critical History*, Frampton maps the formation of cultural themes integral to the Enlightenment, as the everyday life of major European centers faced three unprecedented developments. These were the rise of the industrial bourgeoisie, the migration of peasants to big cities and the realization of astonishing works of engineering. Frampton examines the implications of these "cultural transformations" in the two interrelated areas of "territorial" and "technological" transformation. Like most historiographies of the Modern Movement architecture, Frampton's narrative is also marked by many other significant unfoldings. For example, by the mid-eighteenth century, architects had attained the knowledge necessary to recode architectural languages accumulated throughout Western history, and this is in reference to the prevailing encyclopedic briefs. Frampton also mentions the changes taking place in humanity's rapport with nature, the rise of national identity[26] and aesthetic sensibilities such as the sublime and picturesque. He gives equal importance to the separation of mechanical arts from Christian cosmology, which occurred in roughly the mid-seventeenth century—a decisive step toward the replacement of the Corps des Ponts et Chaussees with the Ecole des Ponts et Chaussees, and the institutionalization of the schism between the two disciplines of engineering and architecture. Interestingly enough, most architects noted and theorized the spatial and aesthetic consequences of this divorce. Even by the time of the publication of his seminal book *Vers Une Architecture* (1924), Le Corbusier was reminding his comrades that if they did not learn lessons from the structures engineers had erected in the agrarian landscape of mid-nineteenth-century Europe, they might lose their historical task of reorganizing the prevailing built environment anew. Considering the precision and beauty of machines and liners, Le Corbusier extended his "anxiety" to the aesthetics discussed in a chapter of the same book, alluringly titled "Eyes Which Do Not See"![27]

In spite of the crack introduced into the singular and holistic norms of Humanism during the Baroque period, by the 1750s, the horizon of historical knowledge was expanded both laterally and vertically. Thus, the reassessment of the antique world did "encourage expeditions further afield, and visits were soon being made to ancient Greek sites in both Sicily and Greece," Frampton writes.[28] In retrospect, diverse historical assessments of the architecture of ancient Rome initiated two tendencies that colored architectural praxis for some time. We are reminded of Johann J. Winckelmann's vision of "historicity," exemplified in his depiction of the classical ruins in their original state while contextualizing aesthetics in the sociocultural conditions of antiquity. His work solidified the stylistic "distinction between an earlier, purer Greek tradition and a later, imitative and inherently inferior Greco-Roman one [that] began to take hold."[29] Even though Winckelmann's idealization of Greek art was noted by diverse thinkers stretching from J. W. Goethe to Hegel to Marx, contemporary attention has remained focused on the strategies that would turn the ruins of the past into a series of delirious imaginaries of the kind depicted in Giovanni Battista Piranesi's reconstruction of Rome. To offset the rococo appropriation of the "sleep of reason," Frampton highlights the rise of neo-Palladianism in England, the home of the Industrial Revolution, which ironically would remain rather reluctant to fully accommodate the most radical aspects of modernism without baptizing them into the country's romantic take on the landscape (the picturesque), and the pragmatism exemplified in practices associated with the Arts and Crafts movement, discussed extensively in the first chapter of Part II of the book. However, we should not forget that the London of 1789 was an urban city with about a million people.[30] At the time, England was one of the first European nations to advance a capitalist agrarian system. Frampton recognizes these particularities of eighteenth-century Britain's contribution in the three areas mentioned below, each playing a significant role in the formation of the discourse of early modernism in architecture. Besides the Arts and Crafts movement, we are reminded of the Garden City movement and the realization of the Crystal Palace. To these, a fourth one should be added: the rise of Neo-Classicism, a widespread movement that exposed the English architecture of the late sixteenth century to radical interpretations, demonstrating the impact of the Enlightenment on art and architecture, a phenomenon that had already taken place in France and Germany.

What concerned Neo-Classicism was to rethink the Classical language afresh. This included the Enlightenment concept of autonomy, which had expanded the scope of the meaning of the work beyond "objectivity." For the first time, the work's rapport with the spectator was upheld anew. In fact, the sublime and picturesque aesthetic experience could not make sense without a theoretical shift from the Vitruvian paradigm to the two concepts of *character* and *type*, both foundational for the formation of modern architecture. In Caroline van Eck's coverage of the subject, also cited by Frampton, we learn that during the age of the Enlightenment, the pleasure associated with the experience of architecture had little to do with the correct handling of the Orders.[31] The sensation that a building aroused was rather seen as part of the architect's conscious selection of elements designed to evoke joy, horror and shock. Call it *architecture parlante*! This was also the moment when architecture entered the realm of ideology, the spectrum of which ran from the French Revolutionary architects to the British architect Sir Christopher Wren, who, interestingly enough, was more explicit about the paradox involved in an earlier understanding of architectural ideology. According to van Eck, Wren saw the Classical Orders as the unchangeable essence of Western architecture, "the interaction of load-bearing and thrust from which spaces are created. The Other is cultural; classical architecture is the building style of the Greeks and Romans, and thereby stands for everything their classical culture implies, ranging from democracy to the idea of Empire."[32] Reading these lines through the lens of critical theory, we are indeed in full agreement with Frampton's long-standing passion for semiautonomous architecture.

Frampton indexes the vicissitudes of Neo-Classicism in a discussion that is centered on the reception of the operative scope of the Enlightenment in three countries, namely Italy, France and Germany. The architects and architectural theories he briefly considers are the regulars cited in most historiographies: Giovanni Battista Piranesi in Italy, the three visionary architects (E. Boullée, C. L. Ledoux and J. Lequeu) and Henri Labrouste in France and Karl Friedrich Schinkel in Germany. On the other hand, the period's coming to terms with the disjunction between the historicization and reconstruction of the Classical heritage is examined through design strategies that would empty the geometry of Vitruvian anthropomorphism. We are reminded of Cordemoy's tendency toward geometrical purity, which had thematic consequences such as autonomy of form, an abhorrence for ornament and typological extractions from history. Above all, it was assumed that architecture should be what it was during the Greek era: "column-and-lintel architecture with rigorous articulations of all elements and little and no ornament."[33] This attitude was pushed to a "modern" state of mind in Claude Perrault's distinction between arbitrary and positive beauties.[34] In retrospect, we should agree with Frampton's taxonomy and his prognosis that these developments would be taken up by architects (discussed in Part II of the book) toward the institutionalization of the two main lines of modern movement architecture plotted below.

To further understand Frampton's examination of these tropes, consider the two sets of illustrations that accompany the text of the first chapter of Part I. On the one hand, there is a section drawing of Boullée's project for Isaac Newton's cenotaph (1785) set next to a drawing from Durand's Precis (1802). On the other is Schinkel's Altes Museum (1823–30) (Figure 2.2) placed next to an image of the stacks of Labrouste's Bibliotheque Nationale (1860), and Auguste Choisy's axonometric projection of the Pantheon (1899). If the first two images anticipate the formal and typological autonomy that would permeate postwar architecture, the latter three images present different takes on tectonics, wherein things are put together or added to each other. We should also give attention to the overwhelming presence of the masonry construction system, the principal material of enveloping and cladding of each illustrated building. This is evident from the cladding of the interior of the Bibliotheque Nationale, a progenitor of the dialogue between iron and the masonry wall essential to the style debate of the nineteenth century, a subject alive even in Louis I. Kahn's hypothetical dialogue with the brick wall. While the brick interlocutor wanted to be seen as an arch, the American architect insisted that, with the help of a steel beam, a straight brick opening could also look beautiful. Central to these developments was the dichotomy between the late nineteenth-century perception of architecture and the city and the challenge posed by the visible intrusion of the railway and the realization of industrial structures erected in the cityscape.

The key to understanding the significance of these transformations is the word *Baukunst* and its particular tectonic connotations advanced by Neo-Classicism. Literally meaning "building art," *Baukunst* "signified a beauty that must be built-in and not applied, an art governed by necessity, construction, and utility."[35] We should also mention the class relations inherent in these transformations, evident in a bird's-eye view of Ledoux's ideal city of Chaux (1804). The design's semicircular form, according to Frampton, "may be seen as one

Figure 2.2 Karl Friedrich Schinkel, Altes Museum, Berlin, 1823–30. Photograph courtesy of the author.

of the first essays in industrial architecture, since it consciously integrated productive units with workers' housing."[36] In addition to rendering the surface of each building according to its *character*, Ledoux's city recalls Charles Fourier's Phalange, a utopian community in anticipation of Le Corbusier's Unite d' Habitation in Marseilles (1952). Similar small communitarian enclaves and civic edifices are evident in most projects that Frampton squeezes into his short text. These were indeed the offshoots of the Enlightenment, which drew "strength primarily from the evident progress of production, trade and from the economic and scientific rationality believed to be associated inevitably with both." Such structural interconnectivity, according to Eric Hobsbawm, "championed the economically most progressive classes," who happened to be the forerunners of communities in which "class distinctions did not count and the ideology of the Enlightenment was propagated with a disinterested zeal."[37] This is the core of what we still desire to discuss under the rubric of the project of Modernity, and Frampton's book presents a retrospective criticism of it.

Frampton discusses these developments in a dense and informative text, outlining two tendencies and an implied third one that we can identify with the realization of modernism in architecture. These are Structural Classicism, Romantic Classicism and the trajectories of avant-gardism implicit in the work of Piranesi. This Italian architect's "nostalgic Classical images," writes Frampton, were treated by Tafuri "as a myth to be contested [...] as mere fragments, as deformed symbols, as hallucinating organisms of an 'order' in a state of decay."[38] Associating Piranesi's reconstructions with Michel Foucault's definition of heterotopia, Tafuri extrapolated from the Italian architect's engravings ideas such as the loss of place and center, and the dissociation of form from history,[39] each of which, interestingly enough, drew the attention of the postmodernist architects of the 1980s. As noted, a different take on autonomy, call it *tectonics*, is evident in Cordemoy's suggestion that the freestanding column is the essence of architecture, anticipating the cast-iron columns of the reading room of Labrouste's Bibliotheque Nationale—and this in consideration of this building's multistory wrought- and cast-iron book stack, where the "precise form of its execution implied a new aesthetic whose potential was not to be realized until the Constructivist work of the 20th century,"[40] and perhaps in the free-standing column of the Pantheon and Mies's later work. We should extend these associations with what Frampton elaborates in the subsequent synoptic account of the book in terms of tectonics, or "the product-form,"[41] depending on the case at hand. As such, the tectonics in architecture had one foot in the characterization of the Doric as a wooden structure to be transposed into masonry construction and another in Auguste Perret's tendency to detail reinforced concrete structures in analogy to traditional wood framing, evident in the Rue de Franklin apartments in Paris (1903).

In contrast to the postrevolutionary events taking place in France, the defeat of Napoleon in 1814 and the triumph of Prussian nationalism opened a space for the return of the Classical, first noted in the work of the German architect Friedrich Gilly but also seen in the great projects designed and executed by Schinkel. The typological modifications implied in the planimetric organization of the Altes Museum Frampton present as a departure from Durand's typological reduction, designed to create "a spatial articulation of extraordinary delicacy and power, as the wide peri-style gives way to a narrow portico containing symmetrical entry stair and its mezzanine (an arrangement to be remembered by Mies van der Rohe)."[42] Thus, given the tendency of a few architects to emphasize structure and the Romantic inclination toward *meaning* (external to the spatial and structural dictates of architecture), we are back once more to Frampton's two possible courses of future action, presented in the introduction to his book. While one course of action would reduce the so-to-speak constructivist agenda of Rational Classicism to the exigencies of the prevailing production and consumption system, the other would retain a critical rapport with the city within a masonry enclosure, a monastic setting capable of "linking man to man and man to nature."[43] This certifies the Mies versus Aalto dichotomy proposed herein and implicit in Frampton's historiography of modern architecture.[44] Highlighting tectonics in Mies's work, Frampton has taken every opportunity to demonstrate the significance, as a major index for critical practice, of a contained space where the occupant might be able to contemplate a Heideggerian sense of dwelling![45]

II: 1800–1909

Frampton's discussion of "territorial transformation" is centered on ideas and forces that changed the state of the preindustrial finite city. Before industrialization, the geometric structure of most finite cities was symbolically integral to the life-world of their citizens. For Françoise Choay, "the citizen in the process of inhabiting his city is integrated into the structure of a given society at a specific moment in time, and every plan that might exist corresponds implicitly to that structure which it both constitutes and controls."[46] The emergence of unprecedented new building types (ur-forms) during the nineteenth century, along with the proliferation of iron and glass structures, drastically transformed the fabric of European cities. With their elongated interior marble-walled passages and glass roofs, the Parisian arcades introduced a major intrusion into the traditional organization of the finite city, tallying with the erosion of the traditional fabric of cities caused by the railway. Following Walter Benjamin's footsteps, Douglas Murphy writes that "the new social world of modern capitalism" took place through the interior spaces of the arcades.[47] For Benjamin, Paris was an archeological site filled with traces and residues that could only be rescued by ideological reconstruction.[48] Still, in anticipation of Baron Haussmann's deconstruction of central Paris, the arcades initiated a surgical urban strategy that most planners have followed since then. Aside from political and aesthetic reasons, the transformation of Paris and other major industrial centers of Europe, including London and Barcelona, to follow Frampton's list, was motivated by technical innovations and the "fever of capitalism," a term coined by Choay. Her observations on the subject were apparently good enough for Frampton to use them for the epigraph of the chapter entitled "Territorial Transformation." According to Choay, "Railway, daily press, and telegraph will gradually supplant space in its previous informative role,"[49] opening the possibility of producing textiles (one of the most consumed commodities of the time) in locations not close to natural resources. Accelerated by the expansion of the railway network, especially in England, similar uprooting and displacements channeled the movement of the population toward job-centers such as factory towns and big cities. Reminding the reader of Charles Fourier's essay "New Industrial World" (1829), Frampton associates Le Corbusier's Unite d' Habitation, built at Marseilles in 1952, with Fourier's phalansteries, an ur-form for contemporary hybrid buildings, though mostly devoid of what Fourier called the "psychological principle of 'passionate attraction.'"[50] Henry Roberts's design for the Streatham Street flats (1848–50) is another mentioned ur-form. Roberts's flats initiated a generic model for stacking apartments in pairs around a common staircase, which, according to Frampton, "was to influence the planning of working-class housing for the rest of the century." As Choay demonstrates, strategic approaches to *regularization, pre-urbanism* and *urbanism* slowly but surely destroyed the finite city and introduced the objectivization of urban space beyond its protective walls, making the landscape *visible* differently. From the English picturesque movement to the French gardens shaped by the Cartesian geometric system to the Olmsted-designed parks in America, the landscape was prescribed an appropriate aesthetic and hygienic remedy for the ills of industrial cities. And yet, even the Garden City movement could not heal the wounds caused by the velocity of the industrial movement, technical innovation and unprecedented population growth. In retrospect, we should say that, under the auspices of capitalism, territorial transformation attained a dialectical dimension; in each stage of urbanization, the logic of capital investment also foreclosed the scope of related remedies to be prescribed by planners, urban designers and architects.

Interestingly enough, what stands out among the images accompanying the chapter's narrative is mostly composed of *line* and linear structures of the kind evident in the geometric configuration of Howard's Garden City, Rurisville (1898), but also Olmsted's plan for Riverside (Chicago), and most obviously in Haussmann's Paris. Frampton places special emphasis on the Catalan engineer Ildefons Cedra's project for Barcelona (1858). To overcome the limits imposed by the geometric nature of the walled city of Barcelona, Cedra created an extended grid, which demonstrates his prioritization of transit as discussed in his "General Theory of Urbanization." Cedra justified his proposed expansion in terms of movement into "the form of a proto linear city where separate zones of accommodation and transportation are organized in bands." Cedra's design, Frampton continues, "anticipated in certain respects the Russian linear city proposals of 1920" and was itself another urban ur-form. And yet, among the aforementioned images, the plan of the town of Pullman in Chicago (1855) stands tall. In juxtaposing an existing factory with the town, the composition looks like a mechanical organism, perhaps an unconscious palimpsest for the eventual fusion of territorial transformation with the technical, evident in the contemporary erosion of the threshold separating the urban from the agrarian landscape. With its gridded property subdivision, and the main railway tracks connecting the city to Lake Calumet on one side, the Illinois Central railway on the other, the plan of Pullman is nothing short of an early optimization of the urban landscape (diagram), combining infrastructural elements with mechanisms of property ownership. The city of Pullman foregrounds the rationalization of space and time beyond Ebenezer Howard's dream for a self-sufficient and larger cooperative synthesis[51] and Frank L. Wright's Acre City, another dream work intended to eliminate property ownership. With its hybrid juxtaposition of territorial and technical lines, Pullman City is unique compared to later diagrammatic representations of the city, such as "figure and ground," and the vehicular circulatory system in Kahn's proposal for downtown Philadelphia. The Pullman plan illustrates the absolute logic of planning available in the era of capitalism yet flexible enough to accommodate the Humanist cultural norms evident in the examples mentioned earlier.

Frampton's discussion of territorial transformation recalls Marx's observation that "all our invention and progress seem to result in endowing material forces with intellectual life, and stultifying human life into material forces."[52] Despite the finite city's defensive walls, what slowly disappeared in the city's encounter with various forces of industrialization and commerce was the dialogical rapport between architecture and the city. The importance of this schism is notable even today, when architecture is mostly discussed in reference to a biotechnical, if not discursive, understanding of form, wherein the city is left open to the interplay of economic and planning incentives. Also unattended is the state of public space,[53] a major theme in Frampton's oeuvre, which at the time was delivered similar to Camillo Sitte *City*'s *Planning According to Artistic Principles* (1889). In the finite city, public squares "formed an entity with the buildings which enclosed them." Today, Sitte continues, "They serve at best as places for parking vehicles, and they have no relation to the buildings that dominate them […] In brief, activity is lacking precisely in those places where in ancient times, it was most intense, near public structures."[54] Obviously, public space has not totally vanished. What has happened is the replacement of *civitas* with spatial configurations that are conceived to accommodate the commodification of *things*, charging architecture and space with the phantasmagoria of commodity fetishism. Gone in this metamorphosis are the organizational and spatial forces instrumental in raising concerns about issues such as the state of social housing for workers, who had left the agrarian landscape for the cityscape in search of jobs. Equally important was the housing of a Siedlung block typology, designed for the urban middle classes. Frampton also reminds us of the English Park Movement and the collaborative work carried out by Humphry Repton and John Nash in Regent's Park in London. Let alone ideas and projects, most of which were intended to amend the ills of the industrial urban environment but either failed or could not deliver on their full promises.

What the reader might take away from these briefly outlined projects is the Blumian projection that the integration of nature into a "healthy and open city would be the generator of a healthy and open people: the creation of a new environment would result in the emergence of a new man."[55] The failure of these projects results from the fact that they were not conceived fully in alliance with the exigencies of the process of the modernization of space and time and the commodification of consumer goods. Another reason can be traced in the Adornosque suggestion that "the object does not go into its concept without remainder."[56] Thus, even Ledoux's progressive resolve to "transplant mountains, drain the marshes surrounding Paris, build new grand boulevards, and construct monumental architectural symbols of new social virtues, thereby reconstructing society itself" could not clean the slate along the lines of Enlightenment Reasoning.[57] No wonder that Saint Simon dreamed of a grand alliance between industry, science and the arts, a harmonious phalanx proposed by Charles Fourier. In retrospect, we can trace aspects of the logic of Pullman's plan in Le Corbusier's early and late visions of the city and in Ludwig Hilberseimer's Hochhausstadt project (1924) where infrastructural elements emptied architecture of any figural elements. Call it humanist or post-humanist, but these projects were symptomatic of a period the historicity of which still overshadows the historiographies of modernism in architecture. Frampton instead takes a critical position on these and similar proposals elucidated in different chapters of the book—and this in anticipation of his formulation of an interventionist urban theory of resistance, "Megaform as Urban Landscape," put forward after the publication of the first edition of *A Critical History*. Without reflecting on this subject as fully as it deserves, what should be noted in passing are two things: first, that megaform differs from the megastructure formulated by Banham. Second, megaform by definition is topographic, given the "horizontal thrust of its overall profile together with the programmatic place-creating character of its intrinsic program."[58] Here, too, Frampton directs his criticism toward the concept of autonomy at work since the three French revolutionary architects were reinterpreted during the 1970s in purely formal terms. For Frampton, the idea of semiautonomy is critical because it reactivates architecture's two archaic purposes: its public stature, which is tied to program and scale, and the fact that architecture is rooted in the landscape.

III: 1775–1939

Whatever of the Classical was still operative in the monuments of Structural Classicism was obliterated by the construction of John Paxton's Crystal Palace in 1851 (Figure 2.3). Designed in eight days and built in four months, Paxton's work offered an alternative to most industrial structures and technical inventions that Frampton chases throughout the third chapter of Part I. With its prefabricated and identical iron members, the in-between filled with glass; the Crystal Palace was the first industrially produced *container* to precede the modernist architecture of steel and glass. Compared to most examples elaborated on in the third chapter, the Crystal Palace exemplifies two important architectonic characteristics associated with the rising industrial bourgeoisie: the drive to combine an infrastructural typology, that is, the exhibition hall, with an uncharacteristic monumentality that had no historical precedent. Whereas "the free-standing structure presented none of the problems of the terminus, for where the issues of cultural context could scarcely arise the engineer reigned supreme," the Crystal Palace, a large space housing the strolling spectators among the exhibited industrial products and exotic artifacts from nonindustrialized cultures, could not remain immune to environmental issues such as comfortable air movement.[59] As a container for both industrial products and construction techniques that would soon constitute the major elements of modernism in architecture, the Crystal Palace glorified the exchange value of the commodities, creating a "framework in which its use-value becomes secondary." Excluded from consumption, "masses are imbued with the exchange value of commodities to the point of identifying with it." Walter Benjamin concluded his observations on world exhibitions in full anticipation of the current culture of spectacle. He wrote that these building types "provide access to the phantasmagoria which a person enters in order to be distracted."[60] The Crystal Palace was unique compared to the railway terminus, a building type that also had no historical precedent, and yet its entrance faced the city and was most often dressed-up (cladding) with classical garments, as was the case with Gare de Nord in Paris (1864). Again, whereas the terminus called for strategies to conjugate an industrial structure with a city that was wall-to-wall covered by the garments of premodern styles, the all-glazed enclosure of the Crystal Palace, built in an open landscape, raised a unique historical issue: the recoding of the greenhouse as a proper ur-form for light and well-tempered structures, exemplified in the architecture of the glasshouse, the best examples of which were also built outside of cities.

To put these observations in a theoretical context, it is important to note that Frampton opens this chapter with another famous quotation from Walter Benjamin, "Paris, Capital of the Nineteenth Century" (1930).[61] Benjamin's

Figure 2.3 John Paxton, Crystal Palace, London, 1851, the nave. Photographer, Philip H. Delamotte. Image courtesy of Getty's Open Content program.

text should be considered a generic outline of the historicity of modernism in architecture and the city. This much is evident from the six short subtitles of the essay (Expose of 1939) where Benjamin associates particular building types with related social figures; thus, we have, for example, Charles Fourier and the arcades, where the French social theorist sees in the latter the architectonic canon of his utopia, the phalanstery. Benjamin makes a similar association between the glorification of "exchange values of the commodities" displayed in world exhibitions and the fantasies depicted in Grandville's cartoonish delineations.[62] What stands out in Benjamin's analogical reading of these works is how technology and the bourgeoisie hand in hand "produced" and motivated these figures to make excursions into the past, each with a different strategy, the outcome of which was wish-images where the new is fused with elements of the immediate past. If the 1867 World Exhibition was the ultimate phantasmagoric state induced by the emerging capitalist culture, Haussmann's technique assured Benjamin that architecture was to make something new in the image of "constructional engineering." These unfolding, he wrote, "worked to emancipate the forms of construction from art, just as in the sixteenth-century sciences freed themselves from philosophy."[63] His observation is convincing in recollection of Carl Botticher, a nineteenth-century German architect cited by Benjamin. According to Botticher, architects had exhausted the tectonic potentialities of stone, and the new style would rise out of new materials such as iron. Even though these issues are central to Frampton's discourse, he neither fully pursues Benjamin's assessment that, for the master builders of Napoleon's time, "construction fills the role of the unconscious" nor gives due attention to the centrality of the notion of wish-images, a concept essential for Benjamin's understanding of how the past resurfaces in the *new*, aspects of which he had noticed in Sigfried Giedion's *Bauen in Frankreich, Bauen in Eisen, Bauen in Esienbeton* (1928).

Instead, Frampton shares Benjamin's account of the impact of iron rails as the "first prefabricated iron component, the forerunner of the girder."[64] We could trace Benjamin's shadow in Frampton's observation that the Naval Dockyard at Sheerness, a four-story cast- and wrought-iron framed building, is the ur-form of "modern steel-frame construction." In the same line of consideration, Frampton associates the experience of traversing the "aerial matrix of the space" of the Eiffel Tower with Vladimir Tatlin's monument to the Third International (1919–20), "the prime symbol of a new social and technical order."[65] Recalling Giedion's association of Tatlin's project with the soaring lantern of Borromini's Sant' Ivo,[66] it is not farfetched to differentiate the formal problem-solving criteria of Giedion from Frampton's political agenda. The analogy Frampton makes between the Eiffel Tower and Tatlin's work suggests that social and technical orders constitute major lines of investigation along which he peruses the sociopolitical impact of the Industrial Revolution on architecture. In any event, writing in the late 1970s, Frampton could not but express his skepticism toward the "hope" Benjamin and Giedion had invested in "the new technological possibilities" that the nineteenth century "was incapable of responding to."[67] Equally important for Frampton is the architectural culture, the historicity of which was overshadowed by what he would later give critical consideration, the Arendtian notion of "the human condition."[68] Nevertheless, the exploitative velocity of capitalism unleashed since the 1980s not only differed from the situation of the late 1920s but has also deepened the dialogue between architecture and the city, the many facets of which have shaped our past and present understanding of the human condition.

Still, a constructive complement to the aforementioned Structural Classicist notion of the free-standing column would obviously be Le Corbusier's Domino frame (1914), the constructive potentialities of which, in the manner of

Marc-Antoine Laugier's primitive hut, could not be avoided by modern architecture. Accordingly, Frampton provides a detailed account of the evolution of the use of concrete in architecture, first in projects that explored the architectonic implications of concrete in different building types, and second in industrial buildings such as factories (Fiat Works in Turin) and exhibition halls such as Luigi Nervi's Turin Exhibition Hall (1948), a rather recent date example. In addition to Frank L. Wright's preoccupation with the design of reinforced-concrete structures such as his unrealized Village Bank project (1901), and the E-Z Polish factory and Unity Temple, completed in Chicago in 1905 and 1906, respectively. We are also reminded of Auguste Perret's Rue de Franklin apartment block and the Théâtre des Champs-Élysées (1913). The Turin Fiat Works complex, built from 1915 to 1921, is exemplary as it *exhibits* the materiality of concrete as such, an aesthetic of massing and volumetric resolution different from what can be expected from a steel frame and masonry construction systems. This much is also evident from the particular way in which the Fiat Works expands the scope of the Corbusian idea of ramp extended to the rooftop. The Fiat project further showcases the French architect's esteem for making a conjecture between the logical beauty of automobiles and the work of engineering. Nevertheless, the ultimate formal and aesthetic properties of concrete would be realized in the late work of Le Corbusier; a style termed Brutalism by the Smithsons and Reyner Banham, a postwar architecture least highlighted in Frampton's oeuvre.[69]

The proposed trilogy was not intended to rehearse the historical development of capitalism that has touched every sphere of contemporary technical and cultural domains. The aim, at a general level, was the conspicuous (ideological?) introduction of the formation of the mental life and subjectivities that capitalism enforces and, in particular, the tabling of issues related to the technical and territorial transformations unfolding during the early decades of modernity that were essential for Frampton's formulation of "critical history," explored in the last two main parts of the first edition of the book. In discussing issues associated with the changes taking place in the three areas of the cultural, technical and territorial, Frampton attempted to highlight themes that have seemingly amused architects, designers and planners for some time, at least until 1939, until the creation of networks aimed at interconnecting these three areas more conspicuously than ever before. This is a plausible conclusion because the intellectual courses of action evolving in Europe and America in the early twentieth century demonstrate the tendency toward handing over most organizations of the old regime to production and consumption systems that were essentially different from those established through various crafts and the prevailing apparatus governed and nurtured by palaces, kings and popes. The newly emerging geopolitics of the nation-state, on the other hand, slowly but surely accelerated the processes of modern industrialization in the western hemisphere, cementing the economic system of capitalism, which in retrospect we can claim has prevailed as an autonomous system since 1939. However, it only became tangible two decades after the horrible war.

Frampton's discussion of the historical gamut of territorial and technical transformations was essential to his two major theoretical contributions to date and we are reminded of his idea of "mega-form" and tectonics. A *linear* and continuous urban intervention, the mega-form seeks to resist colorful urban planning strategies and utopic proposals. It is also believed to stand in stark contrast to the proliferation of tall building typologies soaring today in most cosmopolitan centers of Western origin or otherwise. As for the ongoing imposition of *technique* on architecture, the tectonic culture draws from traditions vested in the preindustrial moments. In a nutshell, Frampton's critical historiography cannot be fully comprehended without the theoretical triad of tectonics, mega-form and Critical Regionalism mapped in advance along with the three above analyzed transformations. Critical Regionalism is discussed in the last chapter of this volume, which addresses aspects of the other two themes as the occasion arises.

Notes

1 Fredric Jameson, "Postmodernism and the Market," in *Mapping Ideology*, ed. Slavoj Zizek (London: Verso, 2012), 585.
2 These issues have been discussed further in "Towards a Retrospective Criticism: How Not to Historicise the Past," presented in the July 2020 Society of Architectural Historians Australia, New Zealand, University of Sydney, Australia.
3 Hal Foster, "Postmodernism: A Preface," in *The Anti-aesthetic: Essays on Postmodern Culture*, ed. Hal Foster (Washington, DC: Bay, 1983), xiii.
4 Stuart Jeffries, *Grand Hotel Abyss: The Lives of the Frankfurt School* (London: Verso, 2017), 199–203. Sidney Hook, an active member of the group, saw pragmatism as "offering an intellectually respectable Marxism that dispensed with the determinism and fitted better with American sensibilities" (201).
5 Martin Heidegger, "The Question Concerning Technology," in *The Question Concerning Technology and Other Essays*, trans. W. Lovitt (New York: Harper & Row, 1982), 3–35.
6 David Cunningham, "Marx, Architecture and Modernity," *Journal of Architecture* 11.2 (April 2006): 169–85.
7 Fredric Jameson, *A Singular Modernity: Essays on the Ontology of the Present* (London: Verso, 2002), in particular, 42–52.
8 Manfredo Tafuri, *Theories and History of Architecture* (New York: Harper & Row, 1980).
9 Alan Colquhoun, "Typology and Design Method," in *Essays in Architectural Criticism: Modern Architecture and Historical Change* (Cambridge: MIT Press, 1981), 43–50.
10 On the postmodernist abuse of tradition, see Robin Middleton, "The Use and Abuse of Tradition in Architecture," *Journal of the Royal Society of Arts* 131.5328 (November 1983): 729–39.
11 Joseph Rykwert, *The First Moderns: The Architects of the Eighteenth Century* (Cambridge: MIT Press, 1983).

12 George Simmel, "Fashion," *International Quarterly* 10.1 (October 1904): 130–55.
13 In addition to the *Communist Manifesto*, also see Marshall Berman, *All That Is Solid Melts into Air: The Experience of Modernity* (London: Verso, 2010), first published in New York City in 1982.
14 Kenneth Frampton, *A Genealogy of Modern Architecture*, ed. Ashley Simone (New York: Lars Muller, 2015).
15 Ernst Bloch, *Heritage of Our Times* (Los Angeles: University of California Press, 1991). Also see Harry Harootunian, *Uneven Moments: Reflections on Japan's Modern History* (New York: Columbia University Press, 2019).
16 Mario Carpo, *The Second Digital Turn: Design beyond Intelligence* (Cambridge: MIT Press, 2017), 1.
17 Pedro Frori Arantes, *The Rent of Form: Architecture and Labor in the Digital Age* (Minneapolis: University of Minnesota Press, 2019).
18 This is Theodor Adorno's reflection on what had survived in Paris, writing to his friend Horkheimer upon returning from fifteen years of exile in America. Jeffries, *Grand Hotel Abyss*, 261; original emphasis.
19 Kenneth Frampton, *Modern Architecture: A Critical History* (London: Thames & Hudson, 1980), 10.
20 The "tectonic-image" has been discussed in Gevork Hartoonian, *Ontology of Construction: On the Nihilism of Technology in Theories of Modern Architecture* (Cambridge: Cambridge University Press, 1994), especially the chapter "Montage: Recoding the Tectonic" (5–28).
21 On this subject, see Gevork Hartoonian, "Mies van der Rohe: The Genealogy of Column and Wall," *Journal of Architectural Education* 42.2 (Winter 1989): 43–50.
22 Barry Bergdoll, *European Architecture, 1750–1890* (Oxford: Oxford University Press, 2000), 24. Also see Antoine Picon, "The Freestanding Column in Eighteenth-Century Religious Architecture," in *Things That Talk: Object Lessons from Art and Science*, ed. Lorraine Daston (Brooklyn, NY: Zone, 2004), 67–100.
23 Joseph Rykwert, *The Dancing Column: On Order in Architecture* (Cambridge: MIT Press, 1996).
24 Pier Vittorio Aureli, "Do You Remember Counterrevolution? The Politics of Filippo Brunelleschi's Syntactic Architecture," *AA Files* (2016): 147–65.
25 See "Introduction" in this volume.
26 On this subject, see Benedict Anderson, *Imagined Communities: Reflections on the Origin and Spread of Nationalism* (London: Verso, 1983).
27 Le Corbusier, *Towards a New Architecture* (New York: Dover, 1986).
28 Frampton, *Modern Architecture*, 13.
29 Alex Potts, "Introduction," in *History of the Art of Antiquity*, trans. H. F. Mallgrave and Johann Joachim Winckelmann (Los Angeles: Getty Research Institute, 2006), 3.
30 E. J. Hobsbawm, *The Age of Revolution, 1789–1848* (New York: A Mentor Book, 1962), 26.
31 Caroline van Eck, *Classical Rhetoric and the Visual Arts in Early Modern Europe* (Cambridge: Cambridge University Press, 2007).
32 Ibid., 102–3.
33 John Summerson, *The Architecture of the Enlightenment Century* (London: Thames & Hudson, 1986), 14.
34 On this subject, see Joseph Rykwert, *The First Moderns*, 1986.
35 Fritz Neumeyer, "Iron and Stone: The Architecture of the Grobstadt," in *Otto Wagner: Reflections on the Raiment of Modernity*, ed. ed. Harry F. Mallgrave (Santa Monica: Getty Center for the History of Art and Humanities, 1993), 115.

36 Frampton, *Modern Architecture*, 16.
37 Hobsbawm, *The Age of Revolution*, 37.
38 Frampton, *Modern Architecture*, 13. For Manfredo Tafuri's full account of Piranesi's *Campo Marzio*, see Tafuri, *Architecture, and Utopia: Design and Capitalist Development* (Cambridge: MIT Press, 1976), 14.
39 Manfredo Tafuri, "The Wicked Architect," in *The Sphere and the Labyrinth* (Cambridge: MIT Press, 1987), 40.
40 Frampton, *Modern Architecture*, 18.
41 Kenneth Frampton, *The Evolution of 20th Century Architecture: A Synoptic Account* (New York: Springer Wien, 2007), 123.
42 Frampton, *Modern Architecture*, 17.
43 Ibid., 10. See Gevork Hartoonian "Violence of Quotation," SAHANZ17 (2017).
44 See Chapter 6 in this volume.
45 Kenneth Frampton, "On Reading Heidegger," *Oppositions* 4 (1975).
46 Françoise Choay, *The Modern City: Planning in the 19th Century* (New York: George Braziller, 1969), 7.
47 Douglas Murphy, *Last Futures: Nature, Technology and the End of Architecture* (London: Verso, 2016), 207.
48 For contemporary urban implications of Walter Benjamin's reading of Paris, see Martino Stierl, *Montage and the Metropolis: Architecture, Modernity and the Representation of Space* (New Haven, CT: Yale University Press, 2019), Chapter 6 in particular.
49 Françoise Chaoy, quoted in Frampton, *Modern Architecture*, 20.
50 Frampton, *Modern Architecture*, 22.
51 Robert Fishman, *Urban Utopias in the Twentieth Century* (Cambridge: MIT Press, 1989), 25.
52 Karl Marx, "Speech at the Anniversary of the People's Paper," https://www.marxists.org/archive/marx/works/1856/04/14.htm (accessed December 22, 2017).
53 These issues are also discussed in Anthony Vidler, *The Scene of the Street and Other Essays* (New York: Monacelli, 2011), 6.
54 Frampton, *Modern Architecture*, 25.
55 Vidler, *The Scene of the Street*, 245.
56 Jeffries, *Grand Hotel Abyss*, 327.
57 Vidler, *The Scene of the Street*, 245.
58 Kenneth Frampton, *Megaform as Urban Landscape* (Chicago: University of Illinois, 2010).
59 Frampton, *Modern Architecture*, 34. On Crystal Palace, see Dan Smith, *Traces of Modernity* (London: Zero, 2012).
60 Walter Benjamin, *The Arcades Project* (Cambridge: Harvard University, 1999), 18.
61 Walter Benjamin, *Reflections* (New York: Harcourt Brace Jovanovich, 1978), 146–62.
62 Associations are also made between Louis Philippe and the interior space, Baudelaire and the streets of Paris, and Haussmann and the barricades. See Benjamin, *The Arcades Project*, 14–26.
63 Ibid., 13.
64 Benjamin, *Reflections*, 147.
65 Frampton, *Modern Architecture*, 36.
66 Sigfried Giedion, Space, *Time and Architecture* (Cambridge: Harvard University Press, 1962), 113–17.
67 Benjamin, *The Arcades Project*, 26.

68 On this, see Kenneth Frampton, "The Status of Man and the Status of His Objects," in *Modern Architecture and the Critical Present*, a special issue of *Architectural Design*, ed. Kenneth Frampton (London: Academy Edition, 1982), 6–19.
69 On Brutalism and proper references to the subject, see Gevork Hartoonian, "On Brutalism: The Crisis Postponed," in *Time, History and Architecture: Essays on Critical Historiography* (London: Routledge, 2017), 130–50.

Chapter 3

THE VICISSITUDES OF A CRITICAL HISTORY

Opening

Under the umbrella title of "A Critical History," Part II of Kenneth Frampton's *Modern Architecture* (1980) comprises 27 chapters, each of which focuses on the work and contribution of a particular architect or architects and thinkers associated with a tendency or a movement. The present chapter neither presents a detailed discussion of each chapter of this section of Frampton's book nor examines the extent to which the two major architectural trajectories of modernism outlined in the introduction to the book inform Frampton's take in each chapter. What it does instead is to present a close reading of the ways that a few protagonists cast light on the proposed "Aalto contra Mies" paradox. Central to this inquiry is the ideology of architecture, especially in the politics of public space, the Arendtian "space of public appearance," that Frampton has even pursued its dialectical relevance for the private nature of domestic space. Following this line of consideration, ample attention is given to Frampton's discussion of Giuseppe Terragni's Casa del Fascio (Figure 3.1), a project charged with civic and political connotations—and this concerning the concept of "monumentaliazation" introduced in connection with the late work of Mies van der Rohe and Le Corbusier, discussed in the next chapter. What is involved here is a constellation of themes, if you wish, that anticipate Jürgen Habermas's annunciation of "Modernity—an Incomplete Project."[1] To start with, the historicity of the annotated period is mapped at the expense of exceeding the scope of disciplinarity, keeping in mind that autonomy is a grey zone informed by history and the contingencies of the present time, the Benjaminian "now-time" (*Jeztzeit*).

At the outset, the importance of the epoch-making decade of the 1930s is highlighted. During this time, the revolutionary specter haunting Europe since the end of World War I culminated in *crisis*, aspects of which Walter Benjamin unpacks in his famous essay "The Work of Art in the Age of Mechanical Reproduction," first published in 1936. Conversely, this is also the moment

Figure 3.1 Giuseppe Terragni's Casa del Fascio, Como, Italy, 1932. Photographed by Luigi Mazzoletti, 1936, courtesy of Archivio NodoLibri.

when the architecture of Europe and America cultivated the formative ethos of modernism. In retrospect, the ideological apparatus of the contingencies of the project of modernism did foreground various stages of contemporary architecture. The dialectical approach to periodization, if you wish, is hinged on the idea of the "loss of aura" and the emergence of the notion of *image* as part of the reproducibility of artwork contemplated in analogy to filmic and photographic techniques as discussed by Benjamin, a subject taken up recently by Martino Stierli.[2] In addition to its historical importance, the subject of an image and its photographic reproduction is, surprisingly enough, integral to Frampton's portfolio.

In his 2018 plenary talk at the 71st Annual International Conference of the Society of Architectural Historians in Saint Paul, Minnesota, Frampton presented his book as an attempt to hold on to some aspects of the vanished project of modernism in architecture. However, he went further, associating the decline of the contemporary conceptualization and reception of architecture with the advent of high-speed filming techniques. Frampton's interest in the subject of photographic and filmic techniques goes back to his short-lived career as the technical editor of the British magazine *Architectural Design* (*AD*; 1962–65) before he moved to the States.[3] This much is also evident from the long hours he would spend in the slide room of the Avery library searching for appropriate images for a scheduled lecture. In a retrospective account of his experiences as the technical editor of *AD*, Frampton wrote:

> I was one of the first editors to publish pictures of Stirling and Gowan's Leicester Engineering Building. Most of the photographs we used on that occasion were taken by Richard Einzing with a plate camera. The difference between Einzing's images and several high-speed alternative shots we had in hand was very marked. As opposed to the dramatic darks and lights of the latter, the specific textures of metal, glass, and brick were almost palpable (tactile) in Einzing's almost shadowless pictures.[4]

Frampton was convinced that, alongside the narrative, a photographic image helps in understanding the architect's design strategy and how a historical moment leaves its traces on architecture. It went well with Walter Benjamin's reflection on photography. Discussing the two faces of the *gestus*, its visual form and the "underside of an interminably glossed set of possible meanings," Benjamin wrote, "The invention of the film and the photograph came in an age of maximum alienation of men from one another, of immeasurably mediated relationships which have become their only one. Experiments have proved that a man does not recognize his gait on the screen or his voice on the photograph"[5] The implied unconscious dimension of photography is taken to its next logical step. In addition to the title of each of the three major parts of Frampton's book, equally important is the cover-page image he selected for each of the three main parts—a "postcard," as mentioned in the introductory remarks to this volume.

Despite technical differences between them, what is raised by most reproductive images is the issue of representation, which, beyond its general connotations, attains a particular dimension in Frampton's formulation of the two pillars of his criticism, tectonics and Critical Regionalism. Hence, there is no need to elaborate on the representational dimension of *image*, a subject extensively explored by art and architectural historians. Instead, the reader's attention is drawn to Neil Levin's insightful reading of Leon Battista Alberti, in conjunction with his analytical reading of the photomontages Mies produced in his American tenure.[6] Levine's reflection on technology, architecture and ideology, as in the next heading, sheds a different light on Frampton's take on the rationalist architectural agenda, Terragni's work included.

It is commonly held that the column-looking incisions in the main facade of the Palazzo Rucellai (1446–51) were for Alberti nothing but ornament. And yet, the distribution and how these columns are stacked upon each other evokes a perceptual grid system that in retrospect can be considered a plausible precedent to the skeletal frame structure used in most buildings a century later. Alina Payne similarly writes that the sculpted surfaces divided into the vertical and horizontal members of the Palazzo Vitelli by Cristofano Gherardi (1534) are "an embellishment as a representation of a fictitious structural system at work rather than the actual makeup of the building (the carrying elements were invariably walls and not columns)." Further refinement of this tradition "provided the predominant semiotic expression of architecture as tectonic/sculptural build-up thereafter."[7] Still, notable in the surface embellishment of both Palazzo Rucellie and Capella dei Pazzi is the tectonic dialogue between column and wall.[8] Notwithstanding the *necessary* separation of the column from the wall for the theorization of tectonics, Frampton sees the genesis of the structural rationalists' discussion of tectonics in the light of split between the liberal and mechanical arts that led "to the rise of *homo faber* as a man of invention and speculation; of which the architect and *uomo universal*, Filippo Brunelleschi, was one of the earliest examples."[9] Accordingly, for Frampton, tectonics is not centered on technique alone but on how particular "poetics" initiate phenomenal experiences bringing together the three realms of the cultural, technical and territorial, discussed in the previous chapter. Likewise, Frampton's appropriation of photographic and filmic images is not technical but representational, that is, ideology as such.[10] The triad of image, representation and ideology will structure the interpretative reading of Casa del Fascio in this chapter and other significant projects that, in addition to their historical significance, help us understand Frampton's historiographic agenda.

Architecture and Ideology

As an overture to what follows, it is essential to note that the architectural project was able to sustain a relative balance between the cultural, technical and territorial triad during the first two decades of the past century. The intensive technological transformation, heralded by the 1930s, dragged architecture slowly but surely away from its regional and cultural roots, tossing *building* into the broader orbit of the "technification" of culture.[11] The acceleration of this process and its overwhelming visibility in the contemporary situation convinced Frampton to make two observations: that the loss of welfare society coincided with the end of the 1930s; and that the "aggressive face of global capitalism that we have entered lately is a very ruthless landscape, and the techno-sciences, our pride, and joy, are the one thing we seem to have lost all control over."[12] The diachronic observations here and throughout this volume suggest that Frampton's criticism of contemporary architecture is in tandem with his critical approach to the historiography of modern architecture and that the 1930s plays a significant role in understanding what the critical stands for in Frampton's historiography of modern architecture.

Consider this: if the Miesian tectonics of column and wall was a feat in the development of modernism in architecture, then, following Hannah Arendt, "the space of public appearance" in modernity was to "serve not only to house the public realm but also to present its reality."[13] Frampton's juxtaposition of "public" with "reality," where architecture plays both a constructive and an ideological role, demands attention. Consider the illustration Frampton chose for the cover page of Part II of his book; it shows a famous photomontage of Giuseppe Terragni's Casa del Fascio, Como (1932–36), where architecture's public "appearance" coincided with the mass demonstration of the populace. The political implied in the juxtaposition of the crowd of people in front of Terragni's building was representationally effective due to the design's original purpose: to house the headquarters of the Fascist Party. The montage of masses gathering in front of a technically and aesthetically advanced building brings to mind "Convention Hall," one of the three photomontages Mies produced in Chicago (1954). Like Terragni's photomontage, Mies also combined an advanced tectonic structure with a marble wall to foreground space for the public, most likely in analogy to one of the Republican conventions in Chicago around the 1950s. Aside from spatial and tectonic considerations, in this and another photomontage called "Concert Hall," Mies "made one of the most provocative moves in the history of twentieth-century architecture, provocative both in its formal and its political implications," writes Neil Levine.[14]

Using the avant-garde technique of photomontage, these images encapsulate the hegemonic presence of the political in two different historical moments: the Nazi takeover of most parts of Europe in the 1930s and Pax Americana in the 1950s. Taking into consideration the architectonic differences between Mies's work and Casa del Fascio, it is reasonable to agree with Levine that Mies's definition of technology as a "fact" had both "dangerous" and "expressive" promises. This was part of the consensus among a few European architects who looked to America "for a vision of modernity in the 1920s and 1930s" without realizing that the steel frame used in America "was not a neutral, value-free material."[15] Mies's "Convention Hall" montage represents an absolute space with no room for the public—the masses indeed had already occupied the space! The implied nihilism might be one reason why Frampton has been critical of Mies's notion of *almost nothing*—an absolute space that disengages the public in advance of its "appearance." On the other hand, in Terragni's photomontage of Casa del Fascio, despite or because of its instrumental grid structure, the building's internal space, as we will see shortly, leaves enough room for programmatic flexibility. With this difference in mind, Terragni's building has not only been read like a textbook for formal autonomy[16] but, more importantly, it is considered exemplary of what Walter Benjamin meant by the "aestheticization of politics," a term he coined in the work of art essay. In discussing these two photomontages, Frampton's interest in the reproductive image concerning criticism is emphasized. Moreover, the essentiality of the 1930s and 1950s (the dates when these photomontages were produced) for Frampton's take on the critical is also considered; as is his Arendtian insistence on the phenomenal correlation between being and appearance despite or because of the disappearance of the demonstrative dimension of public space during the 1970s when Frampton drafted the main argument of *A Critical History*.

This is also the moment when the rapport between architecture, technology and ideology attained visibility. This triad has been triangulated since the rise of modernization and reached a projective stage in the early twentieth-century avant-garde work, Futurism in particular. Throughout modernity, architects have oscillated between either taking a neutral position toward technological maximization or critically reviewing its potentialities to recode the culture of building. In this spectrum of doubt and certainty, there have been moments in history when a change in construction techniques had a political connotation. One of these rare occasions was when Filippo Brunelleschi designed the dome of the Florence Cathedral. It caused the masons to stand "against the master mason who had become 'architect' or 'engineer.'"[17] Frampton agrees with Giulio Argan's assessment that the dome of this cathedral was a precursor for making a distinction "between ideative techniques—activities of thinking and translation into precise projects—and the work of execution, whose sole task was to put such plans into effect."[18] Having put behind the institutionalization of the schism between design and construction, it is not far-fetched for us today to say that Casa del Fascio (now called Casa Popolar) was politically neutral if the historical destiny of the masses is not equated with Mussolini's Fascist agenda. This claim is supported by the fact that architecture in itself has no political color. However, its language could be abused for a particular political agenda, as was the case with the architecture of postrevolutionary Russia and the Nazi's rejection of modern architecture in Germany. It took some time for the activist artists and architects of the 1960s to realize that form does not have any intrinsic political and/or revolutionary values but can be *used* toward either end.[19] This might be one reason why this particular work of Terragni is considered a fertile site for the formalistic interpretation of architecture. In addition to analyzing the building's "appearance" in the public domain, Frampton's reading underlines the significance of its internal spatial grid organization for tectonics. Similar to Capella dei Pazzi, Casa del Fascio also enjoys the congruity between space and the building's columnar grid system. Seemingly, Terragni took advantage of the compositional system associated with civic architecture to describe an imaginary correspondence between the logic of the exposed grid of the main facade and the raison d'être of the masses gathered in front of the building's main entry facade.

In a related chapter, Frampton maps what he calls the "ideal symbolization of Fascism" in the Italian postwar ideological polarity fixated on the heritage of Futurism and Classicism. Setting this historical background, he plots the Italian Rationalist movement in a rather long and dense paragraph. Ironically, what the reader takes away from his discussion is Le Corbusier's esteem for the logical precision integral to the machine and the French architect's prioritization of geometry for the language of architecture elaborated in *Vers une Architecture* (1924). Frampton also reminds his reader that the surface layering of Casa del Fascio is manipulated in "such a way as to express the presence of the internal atrium," and this is in regard to traditional palazzo typology. More importantly, and this is in connection to the revolutionary aspirations of Constructivism, Frampton writes:

> The original political purpose of the structure is expressed in almost literal terms through the battery of glass doors which separates the entrance foyer from the piazza. These, when simultaneously opened by an electrical device, would have united the inner agora of the cortile to the piazza, thereby permitting the uninterrupted flow of mass demonstrations from street to interior.[20]

Despite the flow of the political atmosphere from the inside to the outside, Casa del Fascio's placement on top of a masonry base with an oblique position against the central axis of the Domo alludes to Classical traditions of civic building and monumentality. This topographic image is also evident in Mies's Barcelona Pavilion (1929), Friedrich Schinkel's Altes Museum in Berlin (1830) and Gunnar Asplund's addition to the Gothenburg Law Courts (1937).[21] The reference to Mies speaks for the spatial implications of the tectonics of columns and walls. However, I would like to expand on Frampton's insightful comparative analysis of Casa del Fascio and Schinkel's Altes Museum, two important civic works with significant implications for tectonics and the idea of public "appearance." Noteworthy in these two buildings is the tectonics of a row of free-standing columns with a loggia behind them, a transitional space leading to the main entrance and the public atrium. Featuring a vertical blank marble-cladding wall at the far-right corner of the main facade, Terragni's design for Casa del Fascio challenges the uniformity of the classical syntax. Like a "mask" with two connotations, the blank wall covers up the uneven distribution of the building's structural frame, a pair of wider bays compared with the equal bays of the rest of the entry facade. On the other hand, the alignment of this blank wall with the face of the front columnar bays is seen as a strategic device to mask the daily entrance to the building and the custodian room behind. Yet, the wall's extension up to the building's full height provides a surface-like banner for propaganda announcements. It has an honorific character (Framptonian terminology) that stands for the horizontal bay behind the volume's four floors. This composition secures a distinction between served/service spaces, between the administrative wings of the brief, and the spaces allocated to the state authorities on the opposite wing of the volume. The main entry facade is emblematic of the functional and the representational; the tall wall next to an orderly columnar system; the Roman versus the Greek if you wish. Related to this ideologically informed organization of the volume is the atrium located in the middle of these two wings, which establishes the overall formal vigor of the design. This latter articulation is indeed a tour de force; it creates a correspondence "between the space of public appearance in the atrium and the quasi-public roof terrace that, like tiered balconies, overlooks the plaza and the Duomo."[22] Frampton goes further, associating the authoritarian discipline of the Fascist Party with the choice of materials and the design of furniture, especially those allocated to the meeting rooms and the building's main stairs. He writes, "The status of the stair is expressed through its profile and material treatment," and the fact that it serves only the first three tiers, is another allusion to the separation of served and service spaces.[23] In any event, and considering the earlier statements on the suggested neutrality of architecture, it is useful to put the trabeated spatial organization of Casa del Fascio next to the skeletal frame implied by the interior space of Brunelleschi's Santo Spirito (1436). Nothing short of this hypothetical juxtaposition assures the ideological dimension of representation and the skeletal system's use and abuse. Still, whereas Frampton sees a correspondence between "ideology" and the hierarchical organization of Casa del Fascio's internal volume, Peter Eisenman, instead, highlights the skeletal nature of the design for the formalistic agenda evident in the architect's "cardboard architecture."

Criticism: Traditions of Modernism

The dialectics of modernism and Classicism implied in the reading of Casa del Fascio do indeed subdue and at the same time complement the design's ideological dimension. In addition to the building's placement in the city's historic core, Frampton also directs our attention to how its facing throughout in "Bolticino marble and its use of glass block to designate its honorific space, combine to create a work which is at once tectonic, meticulous and monumental."[24] This appraisal should be taken cautiously: first, in consideration of the proposed theoretical paradigm, Aalto contra Mies, discussed in Chapter 6 of this volume and considering Frampton's sympathy with the "monastic" dimension of architecture rooted in the premodern forms of masonry enclosure; second, due to the fact that neither the "rationalism" of the period under consideration (1926–43) nor the neo-rationalism of the Rossian brand had secured a significant place in Frampton's long-standing advocacy for critical praxis. On the Italian *Tendenza* group and Aldo Rossi's architecture, Frampton wrote, "This return to 'reason' has meant, at least in part, a return to the concerns of the pre-war Italian Rationalist movement."[25] The rhetorical and typological returns to classical elements that had attained currency in the architectural discourses of the late 1970s were seemingly alarming to Frampton. Of concern was the disappearance of regional cultures (placemaking?), the reconstruction of which, along with tectonics, was essential for his appropriation of Alvar Aalto's work. Particular to Aalto is the resilience to emulate concepts such as abstraction and autonomy, most often discussed among the orthodoxies of the 1970s, including the neo-rationalist's tendency toward aesthetics associated with the Enlightenment. The "closure" frequently attributed to Mies in this author's writings was, obviously enough,[26] not a productive concept for late 1970s architecture. At the time, the future of architecture was plotted in an "expanded field," which in retrospect should be considered the tip of the iceberg of "world architecture and reflective practice," a chapter Frampton introduced in the third edition of the book.[27]

To further elucidate the importance of these observations, it is helpful to turn once again to the classificatory mode of Frampton's book, the core of which has not changed since the first edition. For instance, the chapter on Terragni precedes and is followed by chapters on the work of Alvar Aalto and what is called "Architecture and the State: Ideology and Representation 1914–43," respectively. The latter chapter draws from the historicity of a period encapsulated in Sylvia Danesi's claim that the demise of the Rationalist approach culminated in the "total integration of conceptual, structural and symbolic form." He notes that in the crisis of the middle class's loss of ground and the rise of "the new State bourgeoisie that was being formed on the strength of the 1920 crisis, [...] a class who got on fine with big capital interests and felt at ease with the totalitarian regime." Apropos, Frampton's interest was the ways that Terragni's project responded, relatively speaking, to the historical separation of building from architecture, and the work's analogical attainment of an Arendtian life of "action," that is, architecture speaking politically! By the 1940s, however, architecture had no choice but to remain "silent" even with one of its main causes, the res publica. The book's organization also recognizes modernism in architecture as a fait accompli as Europe entered the dawn of the first three decades of the twentieth century. Since then, and to follow the thematic additions Frampton has introduced in every edition of the book, the history of architecture has witnessed nothing but the failures and successes of modernism, a phenomenon acknowledged in the title of a chapter introduced in the third edition of the book. Interestingly enough, the first two chapters of Part II discuss the early reception of modernism in England amid the Arts and Crafts period, and in America, which was dominated by the Chicago School architecture. Ordered chronologically, these two chapters provide a portrait of the contextual contrast between the two continents, one burdened by the historicity of the debate between the ancients and the moderns, a subject taken up differently, and in a critique of modernization, in Britain, with autobiographical implications for Frampton's critical discourse. However, following Arendt, Frampton could not but remain sympathetic to John Ruskin's criticism of the labor status at the dawn of the industrialization of the workforce. In parenthesis, the progressive aspects of the Arts and Crafts movement had a major bearing on Frampton's positions on labor and the ethical dimension of architecture, and the distance he maintained from formative themes of Classical architecture. On the other side of the Atlantic, the Chicago of the Henry Sullivan era grew out of the post-fire city (1871), a tabula rasa exerting formal logic derived from "the land prices from the pressure of population growth, and the pressure of population from external pressure." Thus, the emergence of the tall building was due to the invention of the passenger elevator, itself part of sequences of *pressures* and *necessities*, to put it in terms of Sullivanesque dialectics of the mechanic and the organic at work in nature. Moreover, the implied negativity in American modernism, the absence of the Classical as such, was emulated by modernist architects as diverse as Adolf Loos, Eric Mendelsohn, Le Corbusier and our contemporaries such as Rem Koolhaas and Bernard Tschumi, among others.

Historical Hinge

Frampton's historiography takes both critical and complementary positions toward previous historiographies of modern movement architecture. The *critical* in his historiography draws from the instrumental role the 1930s played in reskilling capitalism, an unprecedented change with enormous sociopolitical and cultural consequences for postwar architecture. No wonder that in an already mentioned chapter, "Architecture and the State," Frampton would pick up the trail of Fascist Italy (1931–42) one more time, alongside the post-revolutionary situation of the Soviets and the America of the 1930s. We can follow a detailed account of Frampton's consideration in Eric Hobsbawm's *Age of Extremes*.[28] For Hobsbawm, the 1930s was unique because it had to digest two contesting ideological families: the specter of radical and sometimes revolutionary sentiments informed by the dissemination of Marxism among working-class and intellectual groups, and the emergence of the radical Right after World War I. Both were true "descendants of the eighteenth-century Enlightenment and great revolutions, obviously, the Russian revolution."[29] Specific to architecture, the decade witnessed two unfolding phenomena with particular bearing on Frampton's historiography. These were (1) the eclipse of the hope for "social realism" in Germany and the Soviets, and (2) the closure of both the Bauhaus school by the Nazi state and the avant-garde institutions in Russia by the Stalinist regime. Whereas in its early formative years, the Bauhaus was able to attract the forerunners of both radical and conservative groups, the rise of Fascism in Germany, in contrast, had no tolerance for the school, shutting it down in 1933. Among other reasons, the Bauhaus was shunned because its curriculum pursued radical (modernist) design agendas, and the fact that a few core teachers of the school were openly collaborating with the members of Russian constructivism, most notably, Laszlo Moholy-Nagy with El Lissitzky. However, the demise of the Bauhaus was symptomatic of the fall of liberalism and the ideological nakedness of the Nazi state in its confrontation with an institution founded on the principle of collaboration among various trades and interest groups, artists, craft and business sectors. Frampton writes that the Bauhaus was a composite institution "consisting of the Academy of Art and the School of Arts and Crafts, an arrangement that was to divide the Bauhaus, conceptually, throughout its existence."[30] It had a portfolio structured to achieve goals such as "programmed art production," close affiliation with the *Neue Sachlichkeit* and an inclination toward a more "socially responsible" design program, at least under the leadership of Hannes Meyer. Frampton's observation leaves little room for the reader to doubt if it was because of Meyer's particular ideological agenda that the Bauhaus of 1932 was considered a threat to the Nazi regime. Or was the downfall of the Bauhaus due to the instrumental reasoning permeating the period, which happened to be more comfortable with a culture intertwined with patriotism, race and conventions that were deeply rooted in the old regime? Even though architecture was the profession Hitler had shown some interest in during his youth, the Nazi Party's dislike of modern architecture and the move "to bring conservative architects into the forefront of the Kampfbund's propaganda" was, according to Barbara Miller Lane, the tip of the iceberg in the party's sentiment for "blood and soil." It was also part of the Nazis' yearning for the "disappearance of a tradition of monumental buildings." The Bauhaus was indeed branded as the "cathedral of Marxism" and an advocate of "the bolshevisation of architecture" in the German homeland, to follow Miller Lane.[31]

Even though Terragni's architecture was well received, the conflict between modernity and the Classical remained a major concern for the architectural ideology pursued by the Italian Fascist movement. Frampton argues that this was the case from the famous March on Rome in October 1922 to 1931. During this time, "the government-backed Union of Architects withdrew its support from the newly founded Movimento Italiano per l'Architecture Razionale (MIAR) and relied on the leadership of Marcello Piacentini to support the cause of reconciling rival factions into a single ideological formation, the Raggruppamento Architetti Moderni Italiani."[32] Surprisingly enough, the suggested factional conflict had roots in two interpretations of "rationalism," each emboldened by different Italian traditions, the Classical and the Futurist movements, respectively. Even though Fascism could not fully invest in Futurism's "machine culture," De Chirico's work was seen as the amalgamation of these two traditions. For Frampton, the painter's *The Enigma of the Hour* (1911), for example, anticipated the realization of the Palazzo della Civilta (1942), presenting a sense of monumentality "divorced from social reality." Again, and this time concerning his British background, Frampton detects the problematic conflict between modernity and the Classical in Augustus Pugin's distinction between "the utilitarian, universal standards of industrial production (reified in the Neo-Classical form) and a basic Christian desire to return to the *rooted* values of an agrarian craft economy."[33] As noted earlier, the German Nazi state reapproached the traditions of conservatism in the name of "blood and soil," turning the implied organicity into an ideological state apparatus. Frampton pursues the conflict as mentioned above in Herbert Rimpl's workers' housing and factory designs (1936), one articulated in a neo-classical reading of the cottage-type also advocated by Heinrich Tessenow, the other drawing mainly from the functionalism of the time. In retrospect, the conflict between modernity and the heritage of the premodern culture of the building remained essential for the architecture of various countries, Italy and the Nordic region in particular. It would also stay a basic theme for the historiographies of modern movement architecture, Frampton's included.

Theorizations!

Considering what has been said so far—that the conflict between modernity and Classical traditions peppered Italian postwar architecture—I want to make two speculative observations that might shed further light on certain aspects of Frampton's positions. First, consider his long-lasting collegiality with Vittorio Gregotti of the *Casabella* years, which enticed Frampton to navigate the intellectual corridor between Manhattan and Milan at any opportunity. Frampton's major published essays were, most likely, inked with an eye to the ideas circulating among Gregotti's circles before their wide dissemination. Obviously, by the late 1970s, the intellectual rapport between architects and scholars had attained a global scale thanks to scholarly journals, symposiums, exhibitions and the emergence of independent institutions. Of these, it is important to mention the collaboration between the Institute for Architecture and Urban Studies (IAUS), New York City, and the *Europa-America* exhibition of 1976. According to Gregotti, the exhibition aimed to establish a tradition of contemporary architecture. This event also pumped new blood into the generational conflict between the emerging architects from both sides of the Atlantic and the second generation of architects whose work and aspirations were still overshadowed by mainstream modern movement architecture.[34] Second, the contact between Italian and American architects showed a game of a different type that Peter Eisenman announced in the Lido debate. Eisenman claimed that, as Americans, "we have, I believe, the hope of bringing for the first time some ideas from America; that is possible today because, in this period of transformation of the modern movement, we feel less deeply marked by the weight of functionalism and modernism, which do not belong—as occurs in your case—to our cultural history."[35] A member of the New York Five Architects and one of the founding members of IAUS, Eisenman embraced a structuralist approach to history, putting behind him the aforementioned conflict that had overshadowed Europe in the postwar era. By contrast, an active member of IAUS, Frampton interpreted these unfoldings through the intellectual lenses of the work of two German thinkers, Hannah Arendt's discourse in *The Human Conditions* (1958) and Jürgen Habermas's "Modernity—an Incomplete Project."[36] Nevertheless, Frampton's rapport with Italy remained part of a general commonality trend shared among American and European architects on several issues that were relevant to the postwar reconstruction project, or the "crisis of renewal" of art and architecture.[37] Of particular interest was the work of Aldo Rossi and Manfredo Tafuri's take on issues such as the city and the historiography of architecture,[38] and the push for "artistic realism" advanced by the Italian communist party, which enjoyed large membership and was home to most radical Italian intellectuals of the 1970s. Even though Frampton had expressed reservations about the work of the two aforementioned prominent Italian architects/historians, in an interview, he suggested that every first-year graduate student of architecture must read Tafuri's *Architecture and Utopia* (1973).[39]

There were two sides to Frampton's particular comradeship with Gregotti. Both men were interested in a phenomenological reading of how aspects of the past culture of the building could contribute to contemporary architectural praxis beyond high modernism and the assimilation of semiology and structuralism prevalent in architectural theories of the time. Both figures had also engaged and collaborated, to different degrees, with a series of public events and committees that culminated in the 1980 Venice Architecture Biennale, *The Presence of the Past*, and their eventual criticism of the work paraded in the *Strada Novissima*. According to Lea-Catherine Szacka's account of the exhibition, after attending three meetings in Venice,[40] Frampton resigned and withdrew from the organizing group of the exhibition. The background to his resignation and criticism of what was displayed in the exhibition as "collage-pastiche" relates to Frampton's critical review of the by-now famous book *Learning from Las Vegas* (1977), a summary of which was published in *Casabella*. In a letter to Robert Stern, a committed member and stunt supporter of the content and aims of *The Presence of the Past*, Frampton wrote: "I have written a text which is categorically critical of this position, and I had until recently intended to submit this text for the catalogue." He also admitted to Paolo Portoghesi that "I entertained the illusion that it would be possible for me to keep my distance from the overall ideology of the show by simply writing a critical article and allowing this to go forward in the catalogue."[41] The story circulating was that the text mentioned in Frampton's letter was the draft of his core argument presented in "Critical Regionalism." This subject will be discussed in the last chapter of this volume. Emphasizing Frampton's rapport with the Italian intelligentsia is for the purpose of demonstrating his continuous political and critical stance in his historiography of modern movement architecture and the ways he has positioned himself alongside and against events and organizations that had a crucial bearing on contemporary architectural criticism.

Consider this: to highlight Terragni's neutral take on the ideological dimension of fascist state politics, Frampton points to various manifestations and disseminations of the architecture of *Neue Sachlichkeit*, the new objectivity movement, throughout Europe. We have already noted El Lissitzky's collaboration with several Dutch architects gathered under the umbrella of the left-wing ABC Group. Their goal was not limited to reacting against traditional architecture; they also wanted to criticize the theoretical work of Van Doesburg and Van Eesteren. Despite Lissitzky's disapproval, the group's emphasis on the essentiality of economics for modern building technology (absolute utilitarianism) sums up their "distaste for massive architecture demonstrated in the equation 'building x weight' = monumentality." Nothing short of Hannes Meyer and Hans Wittwer's collaborative design for the Palace of the League of Nations Building, Genova (1926–27), and the Petersschule (1926) demonstrates their drive to put aside aspects of the culture of the building that were central to the conflict between modernity and Classical traditions. Their work was a perception of *objectivity* centered on "lightness" and "utility," a mirror image of the work produced by a few circles of the Russian Constructivists. Frampton's deliberate note on the caption of Meyer's project for the League speaks for itself; it reads, "Compare Le Corbusier's entry." He continues, "One might question the architect's claim for 'objectivity' when elevator shafts are glazed (after Russian Constructivist models) to reveal the 'machine aesthetic' in action."[42] Highlighting the ideological differences between these two entry projects with Arendt in mind, Frampton claimed, "The Utilitarianism of Meyer leads to the idealization of the appearance of utility. The idealism of Le Corbusier, instead, leads to the idealization of the *appearance* [my italic] of man. His Palais des Soviets was rejected for its functionalism—yet it was he who provided the ideal space of public assembly, his open-air tribune or agora for 50,000 people." Frampton concludes his critical reflection on Le Corbusier's and Meyer's entries for the 1929 competition with Arendt's statement: "What makes mass society so difficult to bear is not the number of people involved, at least not primarily, but the fact that the world between them has lost its power to gather them together, to relate and separate them."[43] Still, in an interview with this author, Frampton had this to say about Meyer's entry: "The ingenious shape and structure envisaged for his auditorium was rather irrational from the point of view of both structural resolution and acoustics; all the more so when compared to the auditorium projected by Le Corbusier, which was more hierarchical in its structural concept and also more appropriate acoustically." He continued, "Although I admired the objectivity of the left-wing German and Swiss-German architects of the period, I nonetheless felt one had to give credit to the more balanced rationality of Le Corbusier's proposal."[44] Interestingly enough, in his Arendtian conclusion anticipated in an earlier cited paragraph, Frampton writes, "Today the problem of idealism versus utilitarianism re-emerges not only in the capitalist West but also in the socialist East, under conditions that are even less propitious for its resolution than they were 40 years ago. Then the millennium was a distant possibility; today, at least technically, it is within our grasp."

Surprisingly enough, Frampton's reservation benefited from Lissitzky and Mart Stam's project *Wolkenbugel* (anti-skyscraper), where, despite the design's elementary composition, it made a distinction between "the horizontal (the useful)" and "the vertical (the support, the necessary)."[45] Whether or not this had anything to do with the distinction Louis Kahn would make between service and served spaces, Frampton recalls Yona Friedman and Kenzo Tange's proposition that the construction of "additional accommodation, for both the maintenance of density and the alleviation of congestion in urban centers, employing either space frames or wide-span bridge structures erected on pylons over the pre-existing street system."[46] In addition to Lissitzky's skills in combining typography with Suprematist-Elementarist work (Proun), what makes Lissitzky relevant to Frampton's text is the Russian artist/intellectual's radical rethinking of modernity's rapport with premodern traditions. Contrary to the Corbusian vision of the city, what Lissitzky postulated was somehow in line with Lenin's idea that "there will be no 'tabula rasa,' and that proletarian culture will ultimately emerge from the vestiges of bourgeois art."[47] New building proposals similar to Lissitzky's anti-skyscraper and Leonidov's project for the Lenin Institute were indeed expected to transform the city engineered by capitalism. Theirs was part of Walter Benjamin's sentiment in a short but important essay entitled "The Destructive Character" (1931). According to Pier Vittorio Aureli, the article should be read as a "paradoxical ode to the same aggressive forces—capitalism and fascism—that would threaten the lives of people, and especially the working class, in 1931."[48] The article also says something about Benjamin, who lived in rooms almost empty of any accessories during his visit to Moscow in 1926. Benjamin wrote,

> Weekly the furniture in the bare rooms is arranged; this is the only luxury indulged in with them and at the same time a radical means of expelling "cosiness"—along with the melancholy with which it is paid for—from the house. People can bear to exist in it because they are estranged from it by their way of life. Their dwelling place is the office, the club, the street.[49]

Without sentimental or destructive approaches to the existing city, the aforementioned *Constructivist* projects had the potential to open *room* for architecture as a background to the Arendtian notion of action. This brief digression demonstrates Frampton's intellectual caliber in weaving together complex works of different origins, foregrounding a critical vision of the historicity of the 1930s, the "crime scene" of contemporary architectural failures and successes.

Throughout related chapters, Frampton's observations demonstrate the difficulty involved in grounding the operative dimension of Arendt's notion of "the space of public appearance" in a state of modernity that had already yielded its critical edges to capitalism under reconstruction during the late 1930s. Obviously, architecture's inevitable rapport with various institutions of capitalism had roots in the formation of the language of modern architecture. In a chapter dedicated to the Werkbund, Frampton highlights the a-tectonic shift in Peter Behrens's work while collaborating with the AEG in Berlin. This much is evident from the design of the Turbine Factory (1909);

in an attempt to reconcile German cultural mystics with the cold reality of industrialization, the roof's profile projects forward in the image of Classical temples. Throughout chapters leading to the New Objectivity, Frampton attends to various architects' work and ideologies, and the essentiality of the emerging contradictions as industrialization began conquering the cultural realm bit by bit. Of these contradictions, mention should be made of the distinction between Norm and Form, or between *type* and *individuality*. This distinction colored the famous 1914 debate between Hermann Mathesius and Henry van de Velde. Paradoxically, the 1914–18 war refueled the old cultural mystics with premeditated subjectivity nurtured by a totalized spirituality. This development had as much to do with the premodern mentalities as with the mystics delivered in Richard Wagner's music, the writings of Fredrick Nietzsche and Alois Riegl, and the general public's nostalgia for the medieval spirituality adhered to even by major figures of the British Arts and Crafts movement, not to mention Behrens himself. Frampton writes that despite the war, Behrens's dedication to Riegl's "will to form" found a different outlet. For the design of Hoechst AG (1920) "a brick and stone structure" tried to reinterpret "the lost syntax of medieval civic architecture." At its core, Frampton continues, a faceted five-story hall of corbelled brickwork, capped by a crystalline roof-light, was to wrap a mystic space of public ritual and renewal, that "theatrical space of public appearance which had inspired" Behrens's youth.[50] Despite the work and manifestos propagated by the historical avant-garde, the reactionary forces of the old regime successfully rechanneled the constructive forces of modernization into the militarization of the production forces. This development created a militant atmosphere ready to be taken over by Fascism. This reading aligns well with Frampton's aspiration for the incompleteness of the project of Modernity. However, the earlier-mentioned chapter maps many key conceptual dualities formative for Frampton's later writings. The debate between Gottfried Semper and Riegl on tectonic matters[51] and the latter's drive for "the evolution of a civilized Norm," to quote Frampton, are important points to consider. More importantly, the two notions of "product object" and "tectonic object" that Frampton attributes to Semper were taken up again in the fourth edition of *A Critical History* (2007) under the subheadings of "product-form" and "place-form." Still, the chapter on the Werkbund is important because Behrens was the practitioner who institutionalized the marriage between the architect and the capitalist forces of production and consumption, a key subject for Frampton's vision of critical history.

Considering Frampton's take on the *critical*, it is not far-fetched to say that nothing short of Lissitzky's strategic approach to the city approximates Frampton's discourse on megaform, a schematic edition of which was plotted in 1979.[52] In what reads like a montage of short reflections on various themes and figures (architects and thinkers), Frampton maps the vicissitudes of his critical stand on important subjects such as architecture and the city. In discussing the impact of the technification of architecture, Frampton postulates that to open a space for the actualization of the Arendtian idea of "action," we need to keep in mind Martin Heidegger's differentiation between *spatium* (the Latin word for "space") and the German word *Raum*, which also means "room," an enclosed space similar to Loos's notion of *Raumplan*. Putting aside the problem of a phenomenologically informed "enclosed space," Loos is important for Frampton because of the architect's belief that architecture "is only appropriate where memory and representation are involved." Frampton writes, "Architecture for Loos is restricted to the idea of permanence in the Arendtian sense."[53] Considering the expected physical durability of artifacts, Arendt's notion of "permanence" is important for Frampton because of the durability and memorability of architecture and its existential connotations for humanity, despite the thinker's distinction between work and labor. Having an eye on the expansive implications of the universal dimension of space beyond the domestic space, and into the Western megalopolis, Frampton proposes "the city within the city," a contained space similar to the organization of the projects underpinning his vision of megaform. Despite the basic differences between contemporary megaforms and historical examples of the city within the city, these projects, according to Frampton, "constitute valid points of departure for the reorientation of the profession, not only toward the creation of concrete, bounded places at whatever level they might occur, but also toward the creation of places as increments of built culture, limited by definition, within a global condition which is otherwise totally dominated by process and the economy of consumption."[54] Central to the idea of megaform and its horizontal trajectory is the likelihood of the disappearance of the privatization of land ownership, and megaform's capacity to push the envelope of the "collective" beyond what Le Corbusier had conceived in his major housing projects. To this end, Frampton postulated what for Lissitzky was "typically the civic buildings of the new Bolshevik state."[55] By the time of the economic depression of 1929, however, the advocacy for social housing had already lost its political and economic agency in most of the western hemisphere. Concomitantly, with the rise of right-wing politics, the ground was prepared for the main provocateurs of the ABC Group to migrate to the Soviets. Whatever else Habermas's claim for the incompleteness of the project of Modernity might mean, the fact remains that even the most radical architects of the postwar era were not able to make *room* for the continuity of the political agency of the project of Modernity, even when it came to channeling the historical avant-garde's ideas to the shores of Manhattan: the simulation of historical forms had already conquered America of the late 1970s!

At the risk of overemphasizing the 1930s as the turning point in the destiny of the project of Modernity, we need to recall the distinction Arendt makes between the "modern age" and the "modern world."[56] Her distinction hinges on the scientific discoveries and technological developments that were instrumental in transforming the collective dimension of the "human condition," the permanence of which was shaken by the specter of *progress* she associates with the first atomic explosions. Thus, the permanent aspects of the human condition still retrievable at the dawn of the modern age (roughly the seventeenth century) came to an end at the threshold of the twentieth century. The timing suggested in Arendt's account of the Enlightenment's faith in technological determinism is relevant to Frampton's position on a few issues: the conflict between modernity and premodern traditions of architecture, which attained different visibility during the 1930s; his reserved criticism of the abstract radicalism pursued by the avant-garde architects; and the conservative politics wanting to "synthesize" the conflict between modernity and premodern traditions in the postmodernist simulation of Classical styles. It is against this background that the reception of Terragni's work by the Italian Fascist state, highlighted in previous pages, draws attention for two additional reasons: first, because the language of monumentality—call it civic architecture—delivered by Casa del Fascio was consequential for the design's attempt to establish a tight rapport between space and structure, a major modernist duo; and second, because of the ever-presence of architecture in Italian everyday life in general, and the role Italian Futurist movement played in charging art and architecture with politics along with technologically driven vision of progress. No wonder, then, that, pursued by the optimization of economics involved in American consumer culture, let alone by the Venturiesque "Learning from Las Vegas" (1972), Italy found itself celebrating "The Presence of the Past," the Venice Architecture Biennale (1980).[57] Frampton's *A Critical History* (1980) should be read as a timely response to these two historical moments, in addition to its critical account of the work associated with modern movement architecture.

In closing, the significance of the 1930s for Frampton's critical approach to the historiography of the modern movement architecture needs to be reiterated. To assess the historicity of this epoch-making decade, it is worth noting that seven out of the twenty-seven chapters of Part II of *A Critical History* (1980) cover architectural events that took place during the rise and fall of Nazi Germany (1933–47). These seven chapters are dedicated to the Bauhaus, De Stijl, Mies, "The New Collectivity," Le Corbusier, Giuseppe Terragni and "Architecture and the State." Frampton's critical analysis in these chapters demonstrates genealogies of the crisis of architecture in modernity. In making this claim, Frampton's take on historical unfoldings that preceded or succeeded the period stretching from 1933 to 1947 cannot be discounted. In addition to benefiting from the shared historical knowledge of the world economic crisis of the 1930s, a vision of history that does not envision events in their singularity needs to be presented. History, according to Reinhart Koselleck, "indicates the conditions of a possible future that cannot be solely derived from some individual events. But in the events which it investigates, there appear structures which condition and limit room for maneuver in the future."[58] Of these *structures*, mention should be made of the 1914 debate between Mathesius and Van de Velde (Chapter 9 in Frampton's book), and the two chapters that mark the beginning and the end of the seven chapters devoted to the 1930s, namely Chapter 14, "The Bauhaus: The Evolution of an Idea 1919–32," and Chapter 24, "Architecture and the State: Ideology and Representation 1914–43." To further highlight the complex rapport between state and architecture during the postwar era, the subject is taken up in the next chapter in association with Frampton's formulation of the concept of "monumentalization," which he attributed to the late architecture of Mies and Le Corbusier, covered in Chapters 25 and 26 of Part II of the book.

Notes

1. Jürgen Habermas, "Modernity—an Incomplete Project," in *The Anti-aesthetic: Essays on Postmodern Culture*, ed. Hal Foster (Washington, DC: Bay, 1983), 3–15. The essay was originally delivered as a talk in September 1980.
2. For a comprehensive understanding of the evolution of modern architecture along with film and photography, see Martino Stierli, *Montage and the Metropolis: Architecture, Modernity, and the Representation of Space* (New Haven, CT: Yale University Press, 2019).
3. See Zachary Edelson, "Kenneth Frampton Isn't Done Changing Architecture," *Metropolis Magazine*, March 2018. Also Sally Farrah, "Representation as Quotation: The Verbal and Visual Languages of Kenneth Frampton in *Architectural Design*, 1962–1964," the proceedings of SAHANZ17 Conference, University of Canberra, 2017.
4. Kenneth Frampton, "A Note on Photography and Its Influence on Architecture," *Perspecta* 22 (1986): 40.
5. Quoted in Fredric Jameson, "Benjamin's Readings," in *The Ideologies of Theory* (London: Verso, 2008), 227–28.
6. Neil Levine, "The Significance of Facts: Mies's Collages Up Close and Personal," *Assemblage* no. 37 (December 1998).
7. Alina Payne, "Wrapped in Fabric: Florentine Facades, Mediterranean Textiles, and a-Tectonic Ornament in the Renaissance," in *Histories of Ornament: From Global to Local*, ed. Gulru Necipoglu and Alina Payne (Princeton, NJ: Princeton University Press, 2016), 274.
8. I have discussed this subject on many occasions, and in Gevork Hartoonian, "On Mies," in *Time, History and Architecture: Essays on Critical Historiography*, ed. Gevork Hartoonian (London: Routledge, 2018), 91–114.
9. Kenneth Frampton, "The Status of Man and the Status of His Objects: A Reading of The Human Condition," in *Labour, Work and Architecture* (New York: Phaidon, 2002),

31. The essay was first published in *Hannah Arendt: The Recovery of the Public World*, ed. Melvyn A. Hill (New York: St. Martin's, 1979).
10 Here and throughout this volume I use ideology as an imaginary construct facilitating the subject's domestication of his/her stance within a given production and consumption system.
11 Theodor Adorno, "Music and Technology," in *Sound of Figures* (Stanford: Stanford University Press, 1994), 199. I will take up this subject again in the chapter discussing Critical Regionalism.
12 Kenneth Frampton, interviewed by Cynthia Davidson, *Architectural Records*, May 29, 2018.
13 Frampton, "The Status of Man and the Status of His Objects."
14 Neil Levin, "The Significance of Facts," 84.
15 Ibid. Martino Stierli makes a similar assessment in *Montage and the Metropolis*, 158.
16 I am also thinking of Peter Eisenman's formalistic reading of the Casa Fascio. See Eisenman, *The Formal Basis of Modern Architecture* (New York: Lars Müller, 2018).
17 Giulio C. Argan, *The Renaissance City* (New York: Braziller, 1969), 25–26.
18 Kenneth Frampton, "The Status of Man and the Status of His Objects," in *Modern Architecture and the Critical Present*, a special issue of Architectural Design Profile guest edited by Frampton (1982): 6–19. See also Gevork Hartoonian, *Ontology of Construction* (Cambridge: Cambridge University Press, 1994), 5.
19 Fredric Jameson, *The Seeds of Time* (New York: Columbia University, 1994), 203.
20 Kenneth Frampton, *Modern Architecture: A Critical History* (London: Thames & Hudson, 1980), 203–9. Subsequent references are from the same pages.
21 The following remarks benefits from Kenneth Frampton's comparative analysis of Giuseppe Terragni and Gunnar Asplund's buildings mentioned in the main text. See Kenneth Frampton, *A Genealogy of Modern Architecture: Comparative Critical Analysis of Built Form*, ed. Ashely Simone (New York: Lars Müller, 2015), 186–203. For this author's review of the book, see *Domus* (February 2017): 18–21.
22 Frampton, *Genealogy of Modern Architecture*, 192.
23 Ibid., 200.
24 Frampton, *A Critical History*, 206.
25 Ibid., 290.
26 On this subject, see the chapters on Mies van der Rohe in Hartoonian, *Ontology of Construction* (1993); and *Time, History and Architecture* (2018 and 2020).
27 Mark Jarzombek has recently discussed the same phenomenon in "The Identitarian Episteme: The 1980s and the Status of Architectural History," in *Theories and Methodologies in Architectural Research*, ed. Sten Gromark and Jennifer Mack (Barcelona: Actar, 2019).
28 Eric Hobsbawm, *The Age of Extremes: The Short Twentieth Century, 1914–1991* (London: Abacus, 1994), particularly Part I, entitled "The Age of Catastrophe."
29 Ibid., 144.
30 Frampton, *A Critical History*, 123.
31 Barbara Miller Lane, "The New Architecture and National Socialism," in *Architecture and Politics in Germany 1918–1945* (Cambridge: Harvard University Press, 1985), 147–68.
32 Frampton, *A Critical History*, 214.
33 Ibid., 216. See also Chapter 1, 42–50.
34 Lea-Catherine Szacka, *Exhibiting the Postmodern: The 1980 Venice Architecture Biennale* (Venezia: Marsilio Editori, 2016).

35 Ibid., 74.
36 Hal Foster, *The Anti-aesthetic: Essays on Postmodern Culture* (Washington, DC: Bay, 1983), 3–15.
37 On these issues, see Luca Molinari, "Between Continuity and Crisis: History and Project in Italian Architectural Culture of the Postwar Period," *2G: Revista Internacional de Arquitectura* 3.5 (2000): 4–11.
38 The differences between the two Marxist historians Manfredo Tafuri and Kenneth Frampton await a comprehensive and in-depth study. See Gevork Hartoonian, *The Mental Life of the Architectural Historian* (Newcastle: Cambridge Scholars, 2013).
39 See note 27 above.
40 Szacka, *Exhibiting the Postmodern*, 233–41.
41 Ibid., 233–34.
42 Frampton, *A Critical History*, 134.
43 Kenneth Frampton, "The Humanist versus Utilitarian Ideal," in *Labour, Work, and Architecture* (New York: Phaidon, 2002), 119. The essay was originally published in *Architectural Design* 38.3 (March 1968): 134–36.
44 "Kenneth Frampton Interviewed by Gevork Hartoonian," in *Global Perspectives on Critical Architecture: Praxis Reloaded*, ed. Gevork Hartoonian (London: Routledge, 2017/15), 43.
45 Quoted in Kenneth Frampton, "The Work and Influence of El Lissitzky," in Frampton, *Labour, Work and Architecture*, 132. Frampton's article was first published in *Urban Structure: Architects' Yearbook*, no. 12 (1968): 253–68.
46 Frampton, *Labour, Work, and Architecture*, 132.
47 Matthew Critchley, *Continuity or Crisis? A Brief History between the Polemics of Aldo Rossi and Reyner Banham*, unpublished thesis, 2013, 5.
48 Pier Vittorio Aureli, "The Theology of Tabula Rasa: Walter Benjamin and Architecture in the Age of Precarity," *Log 27* (Winter/Spring 2013): 111–27.
49 Walter Benjamin, "The Moscow Diary," *October 35* (Winter 1985). For an insightful reflection about the Dom-ino house and Hannes Meyer's Co-op Zimmer, see Aureli, "The Theology of Tabula Rasa," 111–27. See also Michael K. Hays, *Modernism and the Posthumanist Subject* (Cambridge: MIT Press, 1992).
50 Frampton, *A Critical History*, 115.
51 For the present author's take on the subject, see Hartoonian, *Time, History and Architecture*, specifically the chapter "On Mies" (91).
52 Kenneth Frampton, "Reflections on the Status of Architecture and Building," *MODULUS* (1979): 4–13. This essay seems to be an early draft for Frampton's most famous text, "The Status of Man and the Status of His Objects: A Reading of The Human Condition," first published in *Hannah Arendt: The Recovery of the Public World*, ed. Melvyn A. Hill (New York: St. Martin's, 1979).
53 Frampton, "Reflections," 8. See also Chapter 8, "Adolf Loos and the Crisis of Culture," in Frampton, *A Critical History*, 90–95.
54 Frampton, "Reflections," 13.
55 Frampton, *Labour, Work, and Architecture*, 133.
56 Hannah Arendt, *The Human Condition* (Chicago: University of Chicago Press, 1998), 6.
57 Szacka, *Exhibiting the Postmodern*.
58 Reinhart Koselleck, *Future Past: On the Semantics of Historical Time* (New York: Columbia University Press, 2004), 114.

Chapter 4

IN DEFENSE OF ARCHITECTURE

Even though architecture's engagement with modernization was momentarily interrupted by the outbreak of war in the late 1930s, the sociopolitical outcomes of the war had drastic consequences for the building art. As noted in previous chapters, since the advent of modernity, architecture had to revise its lexicon according to the emerging new building types, most of which had no precedent in the premodern era. This development reached a decisive point in the architecture of postwar years, and Frampton outlines its profile in a chapter of *A Critical History* (1980) with the telling title "Architecture and the State: ideology and representation 1914–1943." At stake was, among other issues, architecture's civic purpose under the auspices of a state apparatus, at least in America, the accelerative engine of which left almost no room for ideas such as *civitas*. Not only was the prospect of returning to the ideals of the Roman Republic shattered a long time ago but the postwar sociopolitical map differed from that of the 1920s and was in many ways colorful like a kilt. By the end of World War II, the theme of the culture of building, discussed alongside the modernist notion of autonomy, for example, had been redefined. This was not according to the exigencies of a single and coherent totality (*res publica*) but rather according to diverse sociopolitical and cultural regimes tagged "advanced," "developing" and "underdeveloped," each with a specific understanding of the stakes involved in nation-state ideals. The question haunting most committed architects was: to what extent and at what price can architecture and the city be, once again, part of a *totality* that plans its path to success and failure within a network of decision-making with no constructive role assigned to architecture? Mostly considered as a means toward definitive ends, architecture faced a situation that had the least relevance to its disciplinary history, speaking relatively. Despite the unfavorable conditions of the 1950s, architects and historians did try to reenergize tropes such as civic architecture and monumentality.

Before getting to the bottom of these observations, a few words about the organization of Frampton's book, particularly its general ordering principle and the chapters compiled in Part II, are in order. It is worth noting that the text of "Architecture and the State" precedes a chapter that focuses on the architecture of Giuseppe Terragni and Italian rationalism. The two chapters following Frampton's presentation each explore the late architecture of Le Corbusier and Mies, respectively. The political message in this line-up is evident not only in the title of the last chapter of Part II, "The Eclipse of the New Deal," but also in the image used for its cover page. As noted in the previous chapter, the image shows a photomontage of Terragni's Casa del Fascio (designed initially for the headquarters of Mussolini's Fascist Party), in which the building's entry facade is surrounded by masses. A juxtaposition that allegorically anticipated the endgame of architecture in late capitalism, the rise of consumer culture in America after 1945 and its worldwide dissemination. This unfolding not only concerned architecture's rapport with the state—although architecture had already lost its symbolic and communicative dimension—but, more importantly, was abused by the German Nazi state and Stalinism in Russia. The public appropriation of architecture developed through the centuries-long practice of classical traditions (speaking in the context of Europe) was also gone. This phenomenon's disappearance is echoed in Hannah Arendt's call for the "space of public appearance." What characterized the architecture of the postwar era was not a stylistic issue or the will-to-form as such. All of these things were in a situation where the masses were already indoctrinated by the objective and subjective products of the "culture industry," a concept coined by Theodor Adorno and Max Horkheimer (1947), the founding thinkers of the Frankfurt School of critical theory. This was the time when committed architects and critics began formulating critical positions against architecture's reduction to a commodity form. It is against this historical background and its impact on contemporary architecture that Frampton's critical take on the history of modern architecture should be weighed.

In light of these trajectories of postwar architecture, this chapter explores the two notions of "monumentalization" and "monumentality." Their differences elucidate Frampton's reading of the late work of Le Corbusier and Mies discussed in two consecutive chapters of Part II of the book. Frampton's short examination of monumentality in American architects such as Frank Lloyd Wright, Buckminster Fuller, Louis Kahn and Philip Johnson helps to underline the importance of monumentalization. To consolidate, "The Eclipse of the New Deal," the title of the last chapter of the book's Part II, Frampton examines Kahn's work next to Johnson and Fuller. To single out the state of postwar architecture in America, he differentiates the notion of *objectivity* in the work of these three architects from the *Neue Sachlichkeit* movement of the 1920s. Tectonics is another essential theme in Frampton's differentiation. While Mies's tectonic centered on the column, Kahn and Johnson emphasized cladding at the expense of hiding the column behind a brick wall or a transparent glass enclosure. These observations disclose Frampton's conscious attempt to rewrite the history of modern architecture from the exigencies of the *present* that by the 1970s had put behind it the project of Modernity, ushering in modernization at a global scale. This latter development is the central focus of Frampton's later editions of the book.

The following pages argue that the Miesian "monumentalization of technique" and the Corbusian "monumentalization of the vernacular" were strategies conceived in defense of architecture under the hegemonic operation of postwar capitalism. It also suggests that Frampton's formulation of "monumentalization" anticipated his departure from "building review" essays for an ideological critique of architecture.

Monumentality

I

The paradox implied in the two subtitles of this chapter confirms the usefulness of the late work of Le Corbusier and Mies for a different understanding of Frampton's approach to periodization. Through the lens of monumentalization, Frampton explores significant shifts in the work of these two prominent figures of modern movement architecture, presented in Chapters 25 and 26, respectively. Frampton's notion of monumentalization is convincing if we agree with the proposition that with two different interpretations of events coloring the late 1930s, Le Corbusier and Mies departed from their earlier advocacy for architecture coincident with the main lines of the project of Modernity. In a retrospective account of modernism, monumentalization offered a strategic choice "in defense of architecture," to recall the title of a 1933 letter Le Corbusier wrote in response to Karel Teige's criticism in 1929 of the former's proposed Mundaneum museum. Frampton's attribution of the monumentalization of technique to Mies and the monumentalization of vernacular to Le Corbusier is an analogical recalibration of the beginning of the end of modernity. The importance of these two classificatory strategies will be taken up in the closing section of this chapter.

At the outset of his critical remarks compiled in Chapters 25 and 26, Frampton introduces Henry-Russell Hitchcock's notion of the "New Tradition." This concept was a tactical "relief" from the modernist abstraction, the language of which could hardly deliver the expected visual and tactile experience of monumentality advocated by the state ideologies of the time. Hitchcock took Frank Lloyd Wright's reinterpretation of both formal and tactile aspects of the Richardsonian tradition (the masonry brick wall, in particular). He presented the New Tradition to highlight the contribution of many other countries, particularly the Netherlands, that were directly or indirectly influenced by Wright and the culture of a building whose formal and volumetric expressions debunked those of the Dom-Ino frame system.[1] The New Tradition prevailing in Wright's work and Chicago School architecture, however, was part of the historicity of modernism in America, where technological innovations made inroads into the art and architecture disciplines, surpassing classical traditions, as was the case in Europe.[2]

One may agree or disagree with Frampton's interpretation of Hitchcock's "New Tradition." However, with the demise of the historical avant-garde agenda, government agencies in different countries took the opportunity to revitalize a state-sponsored "monumentality" that most often relied on the civic connotations of classical languages of architecture. Frampton observes that the neoclassical monumentality "was not restricted to, as Speer noted, to totalitarian states, but could be seen in Paris, [...] and in the United States." The reader also notices the "official style of the World's Columbian Exposition of 1893, Lincoln Memorial of 1917, and the opportunities raised by the emergence of the high-rise office building types using Gothic elements for cladding." Beyond the century's enthusiasm for historicism, the America of the 1930s embraced Art Deco styles in most famous tall buildings. Frampton describes "a sense of stylistic propriety comparable to that which obtained according to 'party line' in totalitarian countries,"[3] each style used for a particular institution, be it urban, domestic or commercial. Eclecticism was indeed part of America's interpretation of the received traditions of Classicism and modernism. Developed in Europe, these traditions were "found objects" devoid of historicity in their new. Upon transplantation in the New World, these empty signs were utilized for ideological "games," from the Jeffersonian organizational drive for democracy to contemporary Eisenmanesque "cardboard" architecture.[4]

Within this gamut of fact-finding pragmatism, Frampton highlights both the singular and the residual openings that had significant public and urbanistic consequences. This goes beyond the ideology of design and various forms of rationalization embedded in the process of the allocation and distribution of space, program and capital under the auspices of the capitalist production system. Conceived during the Depression years (1932–39), the Rockefeller Centre integrated numerous high-rise buildings with the hub of emerging communication industries. Next to its public arenas, "one artistic work after another, be it sculpture or mural, took as its subject matter themes such as light, sound, radio, television, aviation, and progress in general." Among these is Diego Rivera's *Man at the Crossroads*, a revolutionary iconography "placing his patrons in an impossible public position, in which politically they had no choice but to insist on its removal." Frampton continues: this "contradictory

New Deal gesture of monopoly capital consciously commissioning an emblematic work from a communist artist seems now, almost half a century later, to be as remote and fictitious as Hugh Ferriss's vision of Manhattan transformed into an endless repetition of skyscraper ziggurats, in his book, *The Metropolis of Tomorrow* of 1929."[5] In retrospect, we should say that the black-and-white-toned drawings of Ferriss allude to Rivera's "man at the crossroads," a figure that by the end of the war would slowly but surely be channeled into the abbeys of Herbert Marcuse's *One-Dimensional Man*, a book first published in 1964.[6]

This much is also evident from Frampton's short but essential conclusion to the chapter at hand, entitled "The New Monumentality 1943." Unlike most chapters of the book, the general argument of Chapter 24 is delivered through three subtitles. Each elaborates on different aspects of turning points in the history of modern movement architecture. These are: (1) the failure of the utopian dreams in the context of the Europe of the late 1930s; (2) the coincidence of a few independent movements in British colonies due to the dissemination of the architectonics of the New Tradition; and, perhaps the most important one, (3) the American New Deal, the tip of the iceberg of modernity in America, soon to be hijacked by late capitalism, which was retooling itself since the end of World War II. This chapter of Frampton's presents a cohesive outline of research waiting to be taken on board, perhaps under the title of "the incomplete project of modernity," to paraphrase Jürgen Habermas's famous essay of 1980.[7] The same goes for the last section of the same chapter. Frampton highlights the significance of the urban vision delivered in Manhattan and calls it raw modernity. The absence of "history" allowed buildings to comply with the city's gridiron pattern and with the fact that the entire fabric of the city turned into the index of capital accumulation, of the *future* at a global scale and in the wake of the failure of the historical avant-garde. We should extend the scope of these associations to include the rise of the new media, the modern mass production of RCA and the Hollywood of the Depression years. Each offers convincing points of differentiation for Frampton's claim that "the manipulatory advantages of less permanent but cheaper, more flexible and more penetrating modes of ideological representation were soon seen as far surpassing the effectiveness of architecture."[8] Interestingly enough, aspects of this unfolding in the metropolitan centers of America, particularly New York City and Chicago, were already noted in Sigfried Giedion's *Nine Points on Monumentality*, coauthored by Fernand Leger and Jose Luis Sert in 1943. Drawing conclusions from Le Corbusier's ill-fated 1927 design for the Palace of the League of Nations, Giedion largely blamed politicians and bureaucrats for architects' distance from what he called "the emotional life of the community." He believed the latter to be a lost perspective seen "from the humanist point of view."[9]

In between the lines of Frampton's chosen seven points, reiterated out of the nine listed in the original text, is Giedion's approach to history. The mainline of this approach pursues "the spirit and collective feeling of modern times," arguing that the architecture of both the New Tradition and functionalism stopped short of responding to people's aspiration for the collective. Giedion's implicit dedication to the ongoing nature of modernity's spirit in conjunction with the demands of "common man," a term popularized by James M. Richards,[10] were convincing to Frampton such that he claimed that Giedion's main point "seems to be as valid today as first written." However, in a later interview, Frampton explains why he had acknowledged the New Deal architecture and Giedion's text on monumentality. What was convincing in highlighting these two events had something to do with "Soviet Realism and the Indian architecture of British imperialism. Indeed, for the entire interwar period, that aspect of modern building culture that was not tied to Rationalism, Nordic Doricism, Lutyen's New Delhi." Interestingly enough, Frampton recalls the extent to which he was at the time "indirectly influenced by Clement Greenberg's 'Avant-Garde and Kitsch' of 1939."[11] Not fleshed out are aspects of modernity that did not occur as expected during the first three decades of the past century.[12] It is not clear why the failure of modernism received such wide currency during the 1970s in America, including the emerging interest in the meaningfulness of architecture for its ordinary users, and the fate of modern architecture after the war. The reader is also kept in darkness as to whether the visibility of semantics such as "people" and "ordinary users" in architectural discourses was symptomatic of the prevailing mass culture and America's cultural turn to populism. Alternatively, these were part of a "collectivity" motivated by many factors, including the student uprising of the 1960s, the dissemination of linguistic theories and the yearning for an organic situation similar to the classical, when architectural language was seen as everlasting, as were the body, language and nature. In her epilogue to *The Invention of the Historic Monument*, Françoise Choay recalls Melvin Webber's essay "The Urban Place and the Nonplace Urban Realm" (1964). She argues that the architecture of the late 1950s was already charged with "patrimonial inflation," enticing the cultural realm with the narcissistic recollection of historical images.[13]

These queries make sense if reconsidered in the late 1960s, when capitalism had usurped the culture of modernism, disseminating it as part of the emerging consumer-oriented culture. The system could provide the postwar generation of architects with the ammunition to position themselves if they had chosen to do so against the modernist faith in technology and the aesthetic of abstraction. Despite or because of its turn to historicism, postmodernism was indeed an umbrella movement. It embraced tendencies as diverse as "pattern language," "do-it-yourself" and "participatory design," most of which to various degrees were inspired by the rise of phenomenology, a prominent theoretical contender to "neo-rationalism." In addition to questioning the modernist tendencies for an abstract notion of space and time, architectural phenomenology, Jorge Otero-Pailos writes, "played a central role in setting into motion what we now call theory—not only intellectually, through the expansion and re-articulation of architecture's modes of scholarship, but also socially, by staking out a new position for architect-historians within the academy as the custodians of architecture's peculiarly ambiguous mode of intellectuality."[14] Here lie a few traces of Frampton's intellectual genealogy, searching for an alternative to the "decorated shed" seen through the lenses of Martin Heidegger and Paul Ricoeur. Each has theoretical handbooks popular among certain circles of architects and critics then and to some extent today. In anticipation of the argument presented in Chapter 7 of this volume, it is reasonable to say that Frampton's discourse on critical regionalism and tectonics meaningfully articulated the schism between building and architecture (representation). It was an alternative to the postmodernist simulation of historical forms.[15] Against the line of architectural phenomenology, which would put the importance of practice over theory, Frampton's love affair with critical theory could not but entice him to pursue a dialectical approach to praxis. Nevertheless, during his long-standing advocacy for critical practice, Frampton exposed himself to criticism launched by radical advocates of the French theory. His phenomenological pendulum swung back and forth between Walter Benjamin and Heidegger.

II

It should be clear that Frampton penned most of his manuscript during the 1970s when architectural praxis in America framed two significant camps of postmodernism and the formalism of the New York Five architects. It is not far-fetched to say that *A Critical History* presents a retrospective view of modern architecture enlightened by the postwar state of architectural praxis. Frampton writes, "In the year since 1943 the issue of representation—the fundamental problem of meaning in architecture—has recurred again and again, only to be met by repression and denial, or by escapist withdrawal into the supposedly spontaneous and hence popular significance of advertising and media in the consumer economy." This much is also evident from his chapter essay contribution to the timely book *Meaning of Architecture* published in 1969, a foreword to the much-needed critique of the populist position advocated by Robert Venturi et al. in *Learning from Las Vegas* (1972). To further cement his critical position at the time, Frampton would occasionally recall Manfredo

Tafuri of *Architecture and Utopia: Design and Capitalist Development* (1976). For this Italian Marxist historian, architecture has already lapsed into "silence." He argued the impossibility of "architecture convincingly" in modernity and that "the crisis of modern architecture is not the result of 'tiredness' or 'dissipation.' It is instead a crisis of ideological function of architecture."[16] Frampton instead was keen to formulate the particulars involved in the architecture of the postwar era, knowing that the rise of capitalism and the dissemination of the "culture industry" weakened institutional support for architecture's engagement with the "true" needs and demands of the public (the collective). He was conscious that "the political institutions that would be capable of re-articulating this particular form of significance are today as fragile as the culture of architecture itself." Nothing short of this prognostic language, written almost 40 years ago, tallies with Tafuri's position. Their differences aside, these two historians critiqued contemporary architecture's love and lust affairs with the culture of spectacle.

To further elucidate the importance of these observations, it is useful to reconsider the New Deal advocacy for "public work" and Kahn's take on the subject in 1944.[17] If the idea of monumentality was central to the nineteenth-century discourses on heritage conservation and national identity, it attained different currency in postwar America. To nurture the public with a sense of "belonging" to a community, but also to camouflage the barbaric side of history written by the victors (Walter Benjamin), the humanistic ethos such as monuments and civic were called upon to conceal the divide introduced by the war and the emerging consumer culture. Thus, Kahn wrote, his generation "is looking forward to its duty and benefits to build for the masses with its problems of housing and health […] the nation has adopted the beginnings of social reform." Kahn urged architects to give "full architectural expression" to public buildings such as schools and community centers. Most buildings conceived and built for schools and other institutions stood out because of their distinctive fenestrations, materiality and detailing. A desire to return and reactivate the congruity between sign and signifier is implied in Kahn's design strategies such as "what the building wants to be" and the "society of rooms." Kahn's particular attention to historical typologies and the tactile sensibilities of brick architecture also says something about the dialogical rapport he wanted to establish between monumentality and authenticity. However, it was hard to draw the line, sketching the grey zone where the recoding of capitalist institutions coincided with Kahn's advocacy for community centers. America's timely "desire" for civic architecture arose along with the need to reconcile worn-out institutions with the demands of the rising mass culture. This sentiment is perhaps what "situated modernism" is meant to be.[18] The point is not to discuss the sociopolitical history of the postwar era but to highlight how architects, especially Kahn, would capitalize on the notions of civic and monumentality at the threshold of postmodernism. He was to formulate the theme of architecture after the New Deal's short tenure. The time-bound calls for "monumentality" and civic architecture were indeed an unconscious expression of a moment when these ideas were slipping out of architects' hands! Frampton's investigation of the subject in Mies and Le Corbusier, and Kahn and, to some extent, Wright sheds light on the privatization of civic space paramount today.

III

To contextualize these developments, Frampton maps the emerging postwar theoretical work in the two-institutional axis of the Harvard Graduate School of Design and New York's Museum of Modern Art (MoMA) on the one hand, and schools of architecture at Yale University and the University of Pennsylvania on the other. The former axis played a major role in the institutionalization of functionalism championed by European migrant architects. Kahn, a regular at the latter axis, had already established American postwar monumentality, exemplified in the design of the Yale University Art Gallery in 1953.[19] Although Kahn used the word "monumentality" occasionally, he was less concerned about the issue of size. He was rather keen to weave the *message* into the representational capacity of architecture. A proto-phenomenologist, Kahn dispensed with the arbitrary populist association of sign and signifier. Instead, he kept his work connected to modernism and the French revolutionary architects discussed by Vittorio Gregotti and Frampton, respectively.[20]

Frampton's essay on Kahn is vital for two additional reasons. First, it chases the idea of tectonics in Kahn's mature work regarding the building's structural support system and cladding. Mention is also made of the French structural rationalist discourse and Paul Philippe Cret, Kahn's professor at Penn. Second, Frampton contextualizes Kahn's architecture, along with Wright's appropriation of "the New Tradition." He also contextualizes Kahn's rapport with historical typologies and the materiality of brick—an ordinary, tactile and sensual material—and, of course, his recourse to monumentality. Frampton associates Kahn's mature work with Wright's Unity Temple and Larkin Building, hinged on the notion of an "introspective" public realm and the Kahnian idea of "room," with two additional connotations. The first is the influence of these two works detected in the concept of void permeating Robert Le Ricolais's structural design with specific tectonic connotations for Kahn.[21] The other is the implied conceptual marriage between tectonics and public gathering space, another subject awaiting architects and historians. Here is what Frampton has to say on this subject:

That which Kahn seems to have taken from the Enlightenment—and which Wright strictly left alone—was the possibility of deconstructing classical Roman elements to such a point that they became nothing more than thin tensile screens (empty shells of their origins, so to speak). These devices could be used to simulate the presence of an absent mass and could readily serve to engender a series of buildings within buildings.[22]

Frampton offers a radical interpretation of the tectonics of void in analogy to the Miesian notion of "almost nothing." He highlights its essentiality for the architecture of postwar America, when most progressive ideas, including Wright's organicism, had failed to make room for the realization of the "frontier" that after the war was informed and charged by constant technological innovations. In response to this and to "the unexpected rejection of functionalism in the United States rather than elsewhere," Kahn's phenomenological and disenchanted "afunctionality" explained

> the perennial frontier conditions obtaining in the cultural ethos and socio-psychology of the United States: the fact that North America has always felt itself to be on the frontier, not only because of the progressive thrust that it has always made into the future [but] because of its ever-receding frontier of an abandon culture and history, which by definition was the condition of its foundation.[23]

Here, Frampton expands his critical position beyond architecture to include American culture, the transitory nature of which left no space for the durability necessary for reflective practice. It is to Frampton's credit that he solidifies the chapter under consideration here as a dense account of a turning point in architectural history, the historical conditions of the postwar era and architects' drive to recode their praxis accordingly. This much is also evident from the two preceding chapters, both titled with the adjective "monumentalization" rather than monumentality. These chapters explore the late work of Le Corbusier and Mies, respectively. The architecture of these two protagonists of modern movement architecture is discussed earlier (Chapters 17 and 18, Part II), confirming the significance of Frampton's periodization of the postwar architectural practice hinged on the events of the 1930s unfolding on both sides of the Atlantic.

IV

Frampton reiterated the seven points from Giedion's essay on monumentality (1943), advocating an organic unity between people and institutions. It was a holistic affair not heard of since the dawn of modernization, and Giedion's proposal stopped short of offering a proper protocol for its actualization. He calls for alternatives to Russian new realism and the de-political intellectual life of the America of the 1940s and 1950s, when "avant-garde and modernism had been realigned with the conservative liberalism of the times."[24] In the tradition of the 1920s manifestos, the content of Frampton's chosen seven points calls for monuments to express the cultural needs and the collective consciousness of the time. Interestingly enough, the representational dimension of monumentality was taken up in a symposium entitled "What Is Happening to Modern Architecture?" held at the MoMA in February of 1948.[25] Dismissed in Frampton's book, the symposium aimed at addressing the future of architecture thriving under the rubric of late International Style architecture.

By the time of the MoMA symposium, new architectural directions were already questioning the linguistic monologue and the machine analogies pursued by early modernists. During the symposium, the advocates of both British New Empiricism and Lewis Mumford's regionalism, discussed in his "Bay Region Style" article, emphasized the importance of "expression" and the need to "humanize the theory on its aesthetic side and to get back to the earlier rationalism on the technical side."[26] Theirs was neither the expressionism delivered in Eric Mendelsohn's work nor did it allude to the ideal Giedion had in mind. It was instead a response to the aesthetic of the matter-of-factness solidified by the *Neue Sachlichkeit*. Hitchcock, one of the speakers at the symposium, raised the issue of expression and monumentality in general and connected with the proposed United Nations projects. Regardless of size and scale issues, Hitchcock remained skeptical as to whether these buildings "will have a strong, symbolic expression of their significance." He speculated that "pseudo-monumental" expression was perhaps one of the reasons why these projects did not succeed. He was also doubtful that a "new monumentality will find its expression there."[27] However, Hitchcock left it unclear whether it is a hopeless affair to expect "expression" from Giedion's idea of new monumentality, or whether it was the fact that the United Nations buildings had failed to achieve the due expression. Most speakers addressing the three tendencies of New Empiricism, Bay Region Style and International Style architecture stopped short of articulating what was happening to architecture beyond the desire to have buildings expressing their purpose, as was the case with the cottage style. In retrospect, it is fair to say that it took almost two decades for architects and historians, including Frampton, to formulate architecture in the "postmodern condition" as the fog camouflaged the emerging new state of capitalist production and consumption systems cleared away.

In any event, Mumford, the last speaker at the 1948 symposium, reiterated Giedion's points, suggesting that architecture should relate to its social conditions in the future. He claimed that "society is now in the process of a very profound transformation. It may either commit suicide on an inconceivably large scale or develop the foundations of a new civilization." He hoped that architecture "will be seen as the indication of a greater humanism and universalism."[28] One year later, he indexed the promised future in the following words: "a moment when the whole ideology of the machine is in dissolution, for culture is passing now from an ideology of the machine to an ideology of the organism and the person."[29] He was perhaps anticipating Reyner Banham's ecological turn and that the mainstream architecture of modernism would be recoded anew. Between Giedion's ideological association of monumentality with the state and Mumford's romantic yearning for the individual, Frampton chose to drop the subject of "expressionism" and Art Deco from his historiographic taxonomy. Seemingly Frampton was following in the footsteps of a Benjaminian "strategist" who "acts" in consideration of "the advent of 19th century l'art pour l'art, i.e., art as the *ersatz*, sublimated sphere where the values denied in material life *per se* can be harmlessly realized, and more importantly enjoyed."[30] Instead of a "naive appreciation" of the art and architecture of the past, Frampton had decided to intervene in the political ramifications of the work within a given production and consumption system, presenting a different approach to periodization championed by art historians.

Monumentalization

To shed further light on Frampton's interventionist approach to historiography, we should turn to Wright's esteem for "introspective public space" and the aesthetic of his later work, placed next to the work of Le Corbusier and Mies. There are several reasons why these three architects are put on the same page. Aside from the chronological issue, it is noteworthy that Frampton dedicates two chapters to Mies and Wright and three to Le Corbusier, among other architects discussed throughout Part II. Another reason is the importance of monumentalization, under which heading Frampton examines the late work of Mies and Le Corbusier. A third one is contextual, the historicity of the postwar era in America and Europe and the aesthetic implication of technology that by the late 1940s had already infused into the American mass culture.[31]

It is helpful to recall Frampton's choice of title chapter for Wright's work, "The Disappearing City." It might be that the absence of the historical city in America enticed Wright to deconstruct the classical investment in platonic geometry, reconstructing it according to the concept of organic architecture, which in retrospect reads like the Secessionist "total work of art." Instead, most European architects were thriving under the prevailing ideology of modernity, witnessing the erasure of the threshold separating the historic city from the countryside. Wright's ideals stepped "outside" of history as such, despite his will to individualism. To settle this picture, Frampton draws from a 1938 article by Meyer Schapiro. The American Marxist art historian wrote that Wright "could not bring himself to acknowledge that architecture and planning must, of necessity, address themselves to the class struggle."[32] Evident in this charge is the language Wright employed for the Usonian vision, be it a house or a civic building, let alone his vision of the city that Frampton correctly describes as "science-fiction architecture." One thinks of the image of the Guggenheim Museum (1943), a project that "combines the structural and spatial principles of the Falling Water with the top-lit containment of Johnson Wax."[33] However, to describe the architectonics of the Marin County Civic Center (finished in 1962 and after Wright's death), Frampton had no better word than "ultra-kitsch": an aesthetic sensibility that preceded the postmodern turn to pop and kitsch culture. It took place in the context of Hollywood postwar Art Deco productions, the latest image-making techniques and electrification and mechanical mobilization, which, interestingly enough, Wright praised. In *The Living City* (1958), Wright wrote, "Miracles of technical inventions which our hit and run culture has nothing to do are—despite misuse—new forces with which any indigenous culture must reckon."[34] These observations also say something about the shift in Wright's design strategy, which is evident in "the masterpieces of 1904–06, a house, a church, and an office building." Apart from being "a monumental variation of the same architectural *parti*," what prevails in the Martin house (1905) is a "gridded articulation of support and void," a syntax prevailing in the main volume of the Unity Temple and Larkin Building.[35] The concept of repetition also prevails in Mies's late work, which makes one speculate whether Frampton's overly expressed sympathy with Alvar Aalto's work was not subduing the dialectics hinged on the tectonics and the *negativity* paramount in Mies's later work.

In addition to monumentalization, another distinctive thread running through the work of Wright, Le Corbusier and Mies is their conscious attention to tectonics. Mies never relinquished the tectonics of the steel frame structural system, especially after immigrating to the States. Using a concrete structural system, Le Corbusier and Wright conceived their later work in sculptural tectonics. There is no need to reiterate the centrality of Le Corbusier's postwar architecture for Banham's formulation of the idea of New Brutalism.[36] Instead, following Frampton's footsteps, we should turn to Wright's Johnson and Son Administration building (1936) (Figure 4.1). Of interest is the tectonic rapport between this building's enclosure, its concrete

Figure 4.1 Frank L. Wright, Johnson and Son Administration Building, Racine, Wisconsin (1936–39), interior view. Image courtesy of "SC. Johnson."

columnar system and the artificially illuminated ceiling that make Wright's notion of "introspective public space" meaningful. The theatrical ensemble set in the interior space and the workplace of this project is evident in its tendril-shaped columns with mushroom-shaped endings connected by a short beam. The composition creates a floating perforated surface beneath the artificially lit ceiling as if supporting nothing. Le Corbusier also used columns to punctuate the interior space in the Japanese National Museum of Western Art (1959). Of course, an artificially illuminated ceiling is evident in Otto Wagner's Austrian Postal Savings Bank (1906). Nevertheless, the theatricalization permeating this work of Wright's draws from both the visual sensibilities of the Art Deco spectacles and a phenomenological sense of grounding and forward projection that Frampton identifies with Fallingwater, itself an analog to the phenomenon of support and suspense evident in nature. The image in Wright's Midway Gardens, built in 1914, evokes "a social response to the dance craze" and speaks for the early entertainment culture exemplified in the design's "exotic references," which, according to Frampton, would become a "theatrical formula in Wright's Hollywood houses of the 1920s."[37] In addition to highlighting Frampton's critical assessment of Wright's radical and eccentric work, these observations underline the historicity of Wright's architecture, which differed from that of

Mies and Le Corbusier. This line of consideration justifies Frampton's decision to discuss the work of these three architects in more than one chapter. Frampton's chapters on Wright demonstrate, among other things, the evolution of modernity in America, where the entertainment industry had the upper hand over any aspiration for the political and historical demonstration of the forces of modernization.

Wright's "introspective interior space" was a metaphoric response to the absence of the historical city. In Berlin's New National Gallery (Figure 4.2), Mies left no room for art lovers to escape the urban anguish experienced through the building's glass enclosure, which stands free of the columns supporting the roof. Frampton's following observation suggests an implied dichotomy between the historicity of architecture and the nihilism of technology. He writes of the New National Gallery: "Mies's black-on-black aesthetic returns us to the tradition of the modernist avant-garde." Mies also "achieved a highly accomplished architectonic integration of two primary aspects of within the Western building tradition: structural rationalism on the one hand, and romantic classicism on the other." He reasserted "the sublimity of the avant-garde, as it appears in the paintings of Ad Reinhardt or Kazimir Malevich's Suprematist White-on-White paintings of the late teens."[38] Hence Mies's unique take on technology compared to Wright, who incidentally maintained a similar position. He wrote that one could not deny the machine's agency, and the architect should come to terms with it.[39] In practice, Mies took on board the nihilism of technology in the spirit of the 1920s avant-garde agenda while questioning the established values without turning to analogies such as organic (Wright) or vernacular (Le Corbusier). While none of these three architects denied the facticity of technology, each tried to accommodate it for a particular utopian ideology—the will to individuation (Wright), the choice to the collectivity of humanism (Le Corbusier) and the will to constructive negativity (Mies).

Therefore, the historicity of architecture and the city was central to Mies's and Le Corbusier's turn to monumentalization, although Frampton does not put it in these words. Monumentalization was not intended to reiterate the civic dimension of architecture; instead, it was a strategy in defense of architecture that had divorced from the city. The content of chapters that Frampton dedicated to these two architects demonstrates the depth and diversity of the genealogies informing Le Corbusier's evolution as an architect as he tried to stay in touch with the traditions of the architecture of humanism without dismissing the sociopolitical, aesthetic and technical dimensions of modernization.[40] Even though the office of Peter Behrens happened to be the crossing site of Le Corbusier and Mies, the former got more out of Auguste Perret's experimentation with a concrete frame structure. According to Frampton, it could resolve the conflict between the centrality of the construction system for Gothic structures and that of the humanist values implied in Renaissance architecture. Here lies the key to Le Corbusier's admiration for the work of engineering in the light of the poetry of the Acropolis, addressed in *Vers une Architecture* (1923). He wrote: "All this plastic machinery is realized in marble with the rigor that we have learned to apply in the machine. The impression is the bare, polished steel."[41] The first part of this quotation suggests a retrospective historicization that would be taken up by Giedion and further elaborated on in Walter Benjamin's concept of dialectical images, in which the past and the present intermingle with each other as if in a dream. The second part anticipated Mies's monumentalization of architecture wherein technique is apprehended without intermediaries, collective or otherwise. Mies considered technology "truth revealing" if considered as the "intrinsic nature" of the art of building, a position that led him to extract the column and the wall from their classical syntax, elevating both into tectonics essential for his later work. Echoing Frampton, Fritz Neumeyer wrote, "It was the desire

Figure 4.2 Mies van der Rohe, New National Gallery, Berlin, Germany, view from Sigismunds Street. Photo by Simon Menges, courtesy of David Chipperfield Architects.

for a more profound traditionalism" that led Mies to formulate the idea of classical modernism around 1930.[42]

On page after page in the three chapters dedicated to Le Corbusier's work, Frampton highlights the architect's pursuit of humanist architecture. The Villa at Garches is presented as a successful example of domestic architecture among Le Corbusier's Four Compositions of 1929. The scheme combines "the comfort and informality of the Arts and Crafts plan with the asperities of geometrical, if not the Neo-Classical form—how to reconcile the private realm of modern convenience with the public façade of architectural orders."[43] Having established this, Frampton reminds us of Le Corbusier's failure to achieve the same level of unity in his public projects. Le Corbusier's failed competition entry for the League of Nations Building, Geneva (1927), was a turning point in the architect's career. His Purist period gave way to paintings with hefty organic and figurative objects and bodies echoing his emulation of symmetrical compositions in civic projects. This transformation culminated in the classical monumentality evident in Mundaneum's design, which triggered a debate with Karel Teige. Frampton's monumentalization does not concern the civic function of a building. It indirectly alludes to Le Corbusier's realization of the impossibility of creating an ensemble "making up for the unrealizable whole through the projection of representational elements on a monumental scale."[44] The profundity of this observation sets up a dialectical rapport between object and subject. As discussed in terms of "retrospective criticism" elsewhere,[45] this meant that Frampton reads the following projects in the context of an incomplete modernity and strategies discussed in "Critical Regionalism," a remedy for the implied loss. Among these strategies and related to Le Corbusier's work is the use of "primitive technical elements" such as timber and stone and the pitched roof of Maison Errazuriz House in Chile (1930), the cabinets of Le Maison de Mandrot a Le Pradet (1930) and the concrete vaulted Weekend House (1937) but also the lightweight and canvas Pavillion des Temps Nouveaux (also 1937). Other examples are Casa en Les Mathes (1935) and Le Petit Maison (1935). Le Corbusier conceived these projects with an eye on the architectonics of local materials: stone or brick load-bearing walls, used in analogy to Mediterranean architecture as the architect remained ambivalent toward machine architecture. The elements drawn from vernacular architecture were discussed in terms of the late modern turn to regionalism,[46] a springboard for Frampton's "Critical Regionalism."

In a chapter focused primarily on Le Corbusier's later work, Frampton introduces techniques of monumentalization such as recoding the Renaissance dome (Ronchamp, 1955) or using local Indian parasols in different shell forms (Chandigarh, 1951). Most historians have also noted these developments in Le Corbusier's long career. Frampton's concept of monumentalization stands out in the genesis of his discourse on *critical* evidence in many subjects elucidated in various chapters of his book and his take on regionalism. This much is clear from Frampton's closing statement on Chandigarh:

> The emerging crisis of Western Enlightenment, its inability to nurture an existing culture even to sustain the significance of its Classical forms, its lack of any goal beyond constant technical innovation and optimum economic growth, all seem to be summed up in the tragedy of Chandigarh—a city designed for automobiles in a country where many, as yet, still lack a bicycle.[47]

Another way to plot the significance of Mies's and Le Corbusier's careers is to show how each approached the idea of progress centered on "constant technical innovation." To elucidate this point, we need to turn to the diachronic parallelism underpinning Mies's and Le Corbusier's appropriation of the frame structural system and materiality. This diachronic temporality helps to clarify Frampton's notion of monumentalization as attributed to these two architects. While the Dom-Ino worked toward Le Corbusier's formulation of the Five Points of architecture (1926), Mies experimented with the formal, spatial and tectonic of brick, concrete and glass. When Le Corbusier turned to his sculpted tectonic phase (Figure 4.3), Mies repetitively explored the tectonics of steel frame and glass enclosure, resisting expressionism and formal playfulness induced by technical innovations. Whereas Le Corbusier attempted to recode the architectonics ethos of humanism, Mies's work benefited from diverse sources, including Hendrik Petrus Berlage's interest in clarity of construction, the pre-1910 work of Wright filtered through De Stijl syntax and Kazimir Malevich's Suprematism.[48] We are reminded of the Concrete Office building project published first in *G* magazine. Frampton associates the design's cantilevered concrete trays with Wright's Larking Building of 1904. On the one hand, the project presents another facet of Mies's portfolio of material experimentation. In 1933, Philip Johnson claimed that the Reichsbank project "will satisfy the new craving for monumentality."[49] On the other hand, Frampton considers the project a turn away from Mies's early exploration of asymmetrical compositions to "symmetrical monumentality." His tendency for "the monumental eventually culminated in the development of a highly rationalized building method that was widely adopted in the 1950s by the American building industry and its corporate clients." Considering other implications of Mies's take on technology, Frampton recalls the architect's address at the Illinois Institute of Technology. He compares the matter-of-factness of technology with singular historical events such as the "classical discovery of man as a person, the Roman will to power, and the

Figure 4.3 Le Corbusier Unite de'Habitation, Marseilles, 1947–52. Image courtesy of Adagp, Paris, France.

religious movement of the Middle Ages."[50] Mies did indeed recognize the singularity of the column, the wall and the roof as constructive elements to be recoded in the light of modern techniques and material sensibilities. He was to reconcile the two opposed systems, the heritage of romantic Classicism, with the authority of a trabeated system inherited from the ancient world. The Miesian skeleton of the steel frame "pointed towards the materialization of architecture, of the mutation of built form into shifting planes suspended in diaphanous space—the image of Suprematism," Frampton writes. These unique design processes support Frampton's notion of monumentalization of technique in the simultaneous expression of transparency and corporality, a combination of glass and fabric evident in the best work of Mies.

Addendum

There are two additional attributes to the Miesian monumentalization of technology that need attention. First, Mies's formulation of the steel frame and curtain wall architecture responded to the nineteenth-century search for style. The abstract and white architecture of the International Style inspired by Le Corbusier's Five Points, on the other hand, did not last long. It was not because of the early modernist utilitarian mandate but because the idea was not flexible enough to accommodate the unequal development nested in the postwar culture and nurtured by capitalism's drive for a totality, unlike the Zeitgeist of modernity. Mies's approach to the free plan, a frozen spatial whole different from Le Corbusier's plan libre and, perhaps more importantly, from Wright's and Aalto's aspiration for an enclosed domestic interior space comes to mind. By the end of World War II, however, the technological forces of capitalism had successfully conquered the cultural realm as well, a state of subject and object dialectics critically unpacked in Theodor Adorno's chapter "The Culture Industry" in *Dialectic of Enlightenment* (1947). This opening was a significant force for the institutionalization of architecture in a different system of production and consumption. The development of what could be called corporate architecture short-circuited the 1920s umbilical cord between technology and the centrality of architecture for the project of Modernity in general and social housing in particular. Among other correlated sociopolitical developments, the crisis of architecture unfolding during the 1960s is analogically suggested in Mies's tendency toward repetition, using steel and glass tectonics for any building type, from a house to an office or civic building. The strategy of repetition adhered to, among other things, the incompleteness of dwelling and the futility of charging the building art with individual expression.

When Mies arrived in America, the "house" had already become a fetish. The idea of homeownership has been widely popular since the 1930s. However, with the rise of the new conservatism in the late 1970s, the dream of house ownership in America "was discovered to be an arena in which social inequalities could be made durable enough to outlast the achievements of political equality."[51] Nothing short of the steel and glass architecture of the 50x50 House (1951) could echo Adorno's dialectics of incompleteness and contradiction launched against the Heideggerian regressive idea of "to be at home" when "the moment of its realization was missed."[52] Mies's work was responding to the search for a forgotten dwelling. More importantly, it was an attempt to induce a theoretical closure ahead of the "third generation" of architects' search for "meaning" without substantial alternatives on the horizon except cashing in ideas formulated outside of the disciplinary history of architecture, phenomenology as it relates to Frampton's later writings. Another matter related to the first is the singularity of Mies's monumentalization of the tectonics of steel and glass, which tallies the monumentalization of stone and brick in Greek columns and Roman walls, respectively. The three proposed epoch-making approaches to monumentalization discussed in this chapter highlight the essentiality of the poetics of construction. By contrast, the architecture preceding or following these three architects was stylistic work in favorable terms and made a reasonable attempt to reterritorialize architecture, making it culturally relevant to the status quo of capitalism at best.

It is worth recalling the coincidence between the institutionalization of postmodernism in architecture (Venice Biennale, 1980) and the publication date of Frampton's book. The dissemination of postmodern architecture is not discussed in the first edition of the book; for Frampton, postmodernism was one manifestation of the loss of the utopian dimension of the project of Modernity. The genealogy of this missed encounter can be associated with the broader and lasting consequences of World War I, viewed from the vantage point of the post-political affairs of the late 1930s. The 1918 De Stijl manifesto made a distinction between the so-to-speak old and new consciousness: "The conflict of the individual and universal is reflected in the World War and as well as in art today."[53] Beyond the issue of periodization hinging on the decade of the 1930s, the implicit evidence of the suggested "conflict" in the chapters that succeed Frampton's take on the art and architecture of the Russian constructivism discussed under the rubric of "the new collectivity" needs to be emphasized. Of these previously noted contradictions, the structural affiliation of modern architecture with capital, land and technology was central to the slow banishment of the ethos associable with humanism, not to mention the demand for the humanization of architecture raised by Alvar Aalto, Le Corbusier and Mies.

While throwing light on the differences between a revolutionary and a bourgeois-liberal interpretation of modernity's confrontation with the old regime, what "monumentalization" connotes is the coincidence between the failure of the October Revolution (*ca.* 1932) and the rise and dissemination of Fascism in Europe. This observation is convincing as far as we establish historical corollaries between collectivity and monumentality. Thus, implied in Frampton's attribution of monumentalization to the late work of Le Corbusier and Mies is the failure of both "the new collectivity" (Russian constructivism) and the project of Modernity (the new objectivity). This is true in the context of the collaboration between Russian constructivist artists and architects known as the international constructivist movement in Europe—a cohort of the De Stijl, the Novembergruppe and artists and architects affiliated with *G: Material zur elementaren Gestaltung*, a constructivist magazine published between 1923 and 1926.[54] In retrospect, these relatively short-lived collaborations were promising despite the divide between East and West—a host of events that ended in the institutionalization of the classical language of architecture in Germany and Russia of the late 1930s. At the same time, critical interventions during postmodernism frequently relied on the reinterpretation of this collaboration. As we will see in the final chapter of this volume, Frampton tailored

"Critical Regionalism" to reinterpret the historicity of the avant-garde from the tangent view of the politics securing the divide between developed and underdeveloped nations, the tip of the iceberg of global capitalism. In addition to Frampton's periodization of modern architecture, these observations offer the key to the proposed "Mies Contra Aalto: A Conundrum?" taken up in Chapter 6.

Notes

1 For this author's take on the subject, see Gevork Hartoonian, *The Mental Life of the Architectural Historian* (Newcastle upon Tyne: Cambridge Scholars, 2013), 68–85.
2 On this difference, see Alan Colquhoun, "Regionalism and Technology," in *Modernity and the Classical Tradition: Architectural Essays 1980–1987* (Cambridge: MIT Press, 1989), 207–12.
3 Kenneth Frampton, *A Critical History* (London: Thames & Hudson, 1980), 220.
4 Here we consider Manfredo Tafuri's criticism articulated in *Architecture and Utopia* (Cambridge: MIT Press, 1976).
5 Frampton, *A Critical History*, 220.
6 Fredric Jameson argues that even a Marxian hermeneutic cannot do without "symbolism." He writes, "Between the image of the triumph of the collectivity and that of the liberation of the 'soul', […] between a 1920 Leninist formulation of communism as 'the soviets plus electrification' and some more properly Marcusian 1960s celebration of an instinctual 'body politics.'" Fredric Jameson, *The Political Unconscious: Narrative as a Socially Symbolic Act* (Ithaca, NY: Cornell University Press, 1981), 73.
7 For Jürgen Habermas's essay and various responses, see *New German Critique*, no. 22, Special Issue on Modernism (Winter 1981).
8 Frampton, *A Critical History*, 222.
9 Sigfried Giedion, "The Need for a New Monumentality," in *New Architecture and City Planning: A Symposium*, ed. Paul Zucker (New York: Philosophical Library, 1944), 547–604. As a corollary to Le Corbusier's project for the League of Nations, Giedion sees Picasso's *Guernica* of 1937 as a work that responds to the community's emotional life. He also reminds his readers that architecture could follow the contemporary art of painting, which, according to him, announces the "rebirth of the lost sense of monumentality."
10 James Maude Richards was the editor of the British magazine *Architectural Review* from 1935 to 1971. See Eric Paul Mumford, *The CIAM Discourse on Urbanism 1928–1960* (Cambridge: MIT Press, 2000).
11 "A Conversation with Kenneth Frampton," an interview conducted by Stan Allen and Hal Foster, *October* 106 (Fall 2003): 47.
12 It was a common lecture subject for some critics during the 1970s: "the promises that the Modern Movement did not keep." See Colin St. John Wilson, *The Other Tradition of Modern Architecture* (London: Black Dog, 1995), 14.
13 Françoise Choay, *The Invention of the Historic Monument* (Cambridge: Cambridge University Press, 2001).
14 Jorge Otero-Pailos, *Architecture's Historical Turn: Phenomenology and the Rise of the Postmodern* (Minnesota: University of Minnesota Press, 2010), xiii. Also see Bryan E. Norwood, "Disorienting Phenomenology," *Log* 42 (2018): 11–22. For a review of the contents

of this issue of the journal, see Matthew Allen and Kian Hosseinnia, "Stranger Thoughts: *Log*'s 'Disorienting Phenomenology,'" *Avery Review* 34 (October 2018): 1-9.
15 This subject is exhausted in Otero-Pailos, *Architecture's Historical Turn*, Chapter 5, 183–250, in particular. See also Chapters 5 and 6 in this volume.
16 Manfredo Tafuri, *Architecture and Utopia: Design and Capitalist Development* (Cambridge: MIT Press, 1976), 181.
17 Louis Kahn, "Monumentality," in *Architecture Culture 1943–1968*, ed. Joan Ockman (Cambridge: MIT Press, 1993), 48–53. This and the following cited article were originally published in Paul Zucker (ed.), *New Architecture and City Planning: A Symposium* (New York: Philosophical Library, 1944). Sarah Williams Goldhagen provides two reasons for architects' interest in monumentality. One was in anticipation of the need for monumental memorials at the end of World War II. The other was that America felt left behind in the esteem for monumental buildings that had permeated Nazi Germany and the Soviet Union. Sarah Williams Goldhagen, *Louis Kahn's Situated Modernism* (New Haven, CT: Yale University Press, 2001), 25–26.
18 See Goldhagen, *Louis Kahn's Situated Modernism*.
19 Refer Kenneth Frampton's Chapter 27, where he takes up the New Deal one more time in a discussion focused on Buckminster Fuller, Philip Johnson and Louis Kahn. See Frampton, *A Critical History*, 242.
20 See Kenneth Frampton, "Louis Kahn and the French Connection," in *Labour, Work and Architecture* (London: Phaidon, 2002), 169–85. The article first published in *Oppositions*, no 22 (1980). Vittorio Gregotti, "The Modern Connection," *Rassegna* 21 (1979): 4–5.
21 For George Robert Le Ricolais's rapport with Louis Kahn, see Lorenzo Ciccarelli, "Philadelphia Connections in Renzo Piano's Formative Years: Robert Le Ricolais and Louis I. Kahn," *Construction History* 31.2 (2016): 201–22.
22 Frampton, "Louis Kahn and the French Connection," 180.
23 Ibid., 181–82.
24 The idea is discussed in Serge Guilbaut's essay "The New Adventures of the Avant-Garde in America," *October* 15 (Winter 1980): 61–78. Here it is quoted from Andreas Huyssen, "The Search for Tradition: Avant-Garde and Postmodernism in the 1970s," *New German Critique*, no 22, Special Issue on Modernism (Winter 1981): 33.
25 For the report of the symposium, see *The Bulletin of the Museum of Modern Art* 15.3 (Spring 1948): 4–20. For the related subjects discussed in the symposium, also see Stanford Anderson, "The 'New Empiricism: Bay Region Axis': Kay Fisker and Postwar Debates on Functionalism, Regionalism, and Monumentality," *Journal of Architectural Education (1984–)* 50.3 (February 1997): 197–207.
26 Ralph Erskine, Sven Gottfrid Markelius et al., "The New Empiricism: Swedish architecture of the 1940s," *Architectural Review* 101/601 (June 1947): 199–204. Quoted in Anderson, "The New Empiricism."
27 *The Bulletin of the Museum of Modern Art* (Spring 1948): 9.
28 Ibid., 19.
29 Lewis Mumford, "Monumentalism, Symbolism, and Style," *Architectural Review* 105/628 (April 1949): 174–80. For further elaboration on Mumford's essay, see Anderson, "The New Empiricism."
30 See Richard Wolin's brilliant essay "From Messianism to Materialism: The Later Aesthetics of Walter Benjamin," *New German Critique*, no. 22, Special Issue on Modernism (Winter 1981): 92–93.

31 The date is about the publication of "The Culture Industry," a chapter of Theodor Adorno and Max Horkheimer, in *Dialectic of Enlightenment*, ed. ed. Gunzelin Schmid Noer (Stanford: Stanford University Press, 2002), first published in 1947.
32 Quoted in Frampton, *A Critical History*, 191.
33 Ibid., 190.
34 Quoted in ibid.
35 Ibid., 61.
36 On this subject, see Gevork Hartoonian, *Time, History and Architecture: Essays on Critical Historiography* (London: Routledge, 2018), Chapter 7, 130–50.
37 Frampton, *A Critical History*, 63.
38 Kenneth Frampton, "Modernism and Tradition in the Work of Mies van der Rohe, 1920–1968," in *Mies Reconsidered: His Career, Legacy, and Disciples*, ed. John Zukowsky (New York: Rizzoli International, 1986), 53.
39 Frampton, *A Critical History*, 190.
40 Mary McLeod, "Le Corbusier and Algiers," *Oppositions* 19/20 (Winter/Spring 1980): 55–85. Kenneth Frampton was the editor of two issues of the magazine (the other was *Oppositions* 15/16 (Winter/Spring 1979)), which focused on Le Corbusier's career from 1933 to 1960.
41 Frampton, *A Critical History*, 152.
42 Fritz Neumeyer, *The Artless Word: Mies van der Rohe on the Building Art* (Cambridge: MIT Press, 1994), xviii.
43 Frampton, *A Critical History*, 158.
44 Ibid., 183.
45 Hartoonian, *Time, History and Architecture*, last chapter in particular.
46 Lewis Mumford, "The Bay Region Style," in *The South in Architecture* (New York: DaCapo, 1967), 21–32.
47 Frampton, *A Critical History*, 230.
48 Ibid., 163.
49 Ibid., 231.
50 Ibid., 232.
51 Matt Waggoner, *Unhoused: Adorno and the Problem of Dwelling* (New York: Columbia University Press, 2018), 15.
52 Theodor Adorno, *Minima Moralia* (New York: Verso, 1985), 38–40.
53 The text continues, "The war is destroying the old world with all that it contains; the pre-eminence of the individual in every field." Quoted in Kenneth Frampton, *A Critical History*, 142.
54 See Detlef Mertins and Michael W. Jennings (eds), *G: An Avant-garde Journal of Art, Architecture, Design, and Film, 1923–1926* (Los Angeles: Getty, 2010).

Chapter 5

THE AGENCY OF THE CRITICAL

Preamble

Starting with the cover page of Part III of Kenneth Frampton's *A Critical History* (1980), this chapter proceeds to unpack the semantics of the title of the last part of the book, "Critical Assessment and Extension into the Present 1925–78," a period ending two years before the publication of the first edition of the book. The argument presented in this chapter benefits from the cover page of Part III of the book, a photo of the Willis-Faber & Dumas Building by Foster Associates (1974) (Figure 5.1). The chosen angle of the daytime image of this project draws attention: Was it intended to mirror the building's surroundings on the surface cladding at the expense of masking the architecture's vitality?[1] However, like an X-ray, the nighttime image of the same project reveals the building's skeleton. The dual representative nature of these two images suggests a critique of postmodern architecture wherein quotations from historical languages camouflage the building's structural system. On the other hand, the daytime image highlights an a-tectonic interpretation of Miesian steel and glass architecture. Considering Frampton's definition of the "product-form," the dual nature of the cover-page image suggests the decline of craft in favor of utilizing a Taylorized process of making that had been in the mind of modernists as early as the 1920s. We are reminded of Walter Gropius's Torten Seidlung Dessau (1926–28), among other examples, that Frampton enumerates in another manuscript where he unpacks the concept of product-form.[2] The title and the suggested two interrelated readings of the cover-page image set the stage for the present exploration of the themes and architects discussed in the four chapters compiled in Part III of Frampton's book. Special attention will be focused on several works necessary for the stakes involved in postwar architecture and on how Frampton's analysis sharpens his critical agenda. The discussion begins with Chapter 4, "Place, Production, and Architecture: Towards a Critical Theory of Building." This chapter reads like a postscript to "Mies contra Aalto conundrum" and a prelude to Frampton's signature essay

Figure 5.1 Foster Associates, Willis-Faber & Dumas Building, Ipswich, 1974, daytime exterior view. Photo courtesy of Nigel Young/Foster + Partners.

"Critical Regionalism," much discussed then and now.[3] These two subjects are discussed in the last two chapters of the present volume.

The architects and buildings investigated in the chapters of *A Critical History* do not follow a chronological order. However, there is an exception to this rule, which opens this chapter's discussion. A quick look through the pages of Part III supports the idea that this section of the book primarily covers the architects' active theories and the architectural theories pronounced during the years leading to the publication of the first edition of the book, 1964–78. This time frame raises questions relevant to the year 1925, and the ideological dimension of Part III hinted at the second part of the title, "and extension into the present." Accordingly, we should ask, what is the designatory nature of 1925, the ghost of which overshadows the work produced between 1964 and 1978? Searching for clues, we should turn to the contents of the book's first edition one more time. As noted in previous chapters, in addition to the title, each chapter of Frampton's book designates a time frame, eleven of which cover the year 1925 and two of which end with it—Chapters 11 and 13, titled "Auguste Perret: The Evolution of Classical Rationalism 1899–1925," and "The Glass Chain: European Architectural Expressionism 1910–1925," respectively. In hindsight, both titles suggest the end of a particular tendency, "Classical rationalism" and "Expressionism," in Europe's architecture. The title of the first chapter of Part III, "The International Style: Theme and Variations 1925–65," provides another clue to the semantics of 1925. Putting this title next to the previous eleven chapters, it makes sense to assume that the year 1925 designates the formulation of the idea of the *Neue Sachlichkeit* (new objectivity); a reductive reinterpretation of Le Corbusier's Five Points, the genesis of the International Style architecture at best and "functionalism" at worst.

Perhaps the most crucial clue to the historical significance of 1925 is the title of Chapter 8 from Part II of the same edition of the book, "Adolf Loos and the Crisis of Culture 1896–1931." In previous chapters, the significance of the historicity of the 1930s for Frampton's critical rapprochement to modern movement architecture was mentioned. Another dimension of the "critical" informing Frampton's historiography draws from Loos's work and writings, which in retrospect anticipated what modernity had in store for architecture, if due attention is given to issues outlined in Loos's essay "Architecture," published in 1910. Frampton restates ideas from this essay on several occasions discussing Loos's work. Highlighting the tentative balance between inner and outer walls permeating vernacular dwelling, Loos had no illusion about the fact that, by 1910, the phantasmagoria of bourgeoisie culture had conquered the Viennese public arena. In Frampton's words, by the time of the publication of "Architecture," "Loos had already begun to sense the full force of the modern predicament, which persist today."[4] The emerging rift between culture and civilization was one reason why Loos's interior spaces of his early residential work feel *cozy* in contradistinction to what was happening outside its enclosing walls. However, extending the implied "cultural crisis" to the contemporary situation, Frampton intertwines Loos's reading with his positions to address issues such as the ethics and aesthetics of materiality and labor and productivity.

As noted previously, Frampton's ideas on labor and productivity had two ancestors; he has been sympathetic to the specific views of the foremost proponents of the British Arts and Crafts movement. His thorough appreciation of Hannah Arendt's writing remains vast, with no need for further emphasis here. In addition to introducing the concept of the "degradation of the operative into a machine," a Ruskinian concern for the state of productivity in nineteenth-century England, Arendt provided Frampton an aperture to read the British movement's romantic enthusiasm critically for the pleasure of handwork and its totalized view of architecture and society. In the opening epigraph of the first chapter (Part II) of the book, "News from Nowhere: England 1836–1924,"[5] Morris writes, "History taught us the evolution of architecture. It is now teaching us the evolution of society."[6] Frampton revisits the implied historicism in the light of a Marxian concept of history.

Accordingly, the seeds of the utopian were already nested in contradictions essential for the emergence of the early bourgeois industrial production system. Frampton considers this unfolding to be the movement's unconscious internalization of the century's longing to associate style with national identity, though plotted along two problematic poles. On the one hand, we have the old medieval guild system aligned with the logic of Taylorization through the Werkbund school. On the other, we have the failed Morrisian "News from Nowhere," epitomized in the architecture of Lutyens's Thiepval Arch, Picardy (*ca.* 1924). The building was to raise "the memory of a martyred generation, and in a Baroque vista opening onto an empire that was already on the edge of being lost." Nothing short of this complex reading of the dialectics between past and present speaks for Frampton's reservations about any prescribed or "single-minded" vision of the complexities pertinent to a critical assessment of architecture even in the infancy of capitalism, during the late nineteenth century. No wonder the flip side of the image used for the cover page of Part II was the famous photomontage of Terragni's Casa del Fascio. The image heralded the beginning of the end of what one might take away from the title of the earlier mentioned chapter of Frampton's book, "News from Nowhere"!

The following two conjectures can be made here: first, Frampton recognizes the main features of the Red House (1859) in the design's "structural integrity" and the building's "integrity into the site and the local culture." These anticipated the dichotomous polarity he establishes between Mies and Aalto and his recognition of Loos's amphibian critique of modernity. Second is Loos's resistance to drawing a clear-cut distinction between structural and nonstructural elements. Rather, he would combine "the propriety of Platonic mass with the convenience of irregular volumes," a typological genre otherwise dear to Le Corbusier's Five Points. In light of Loos's typological modifications, Frampton considers the *Raumplan* to be an "architectural strategy for transcending the contradictory cultural legacy of bourgeois society which, having deprived itself of the vernacular, could not claim in exchange the culture of classicism."[7] Without being explicit, Frampton seems sympathetic to Loos's position concerning the historicity of modernization, particularly the inevitability of architecture landing in the orbit of the technification of culture, an idea formulated by Theodor Adorno half a century later. In an essay written in 1986, Frampton presents the aforementioned dissonance between inside/outside as part of Loos's attempt to "temper the aura of coziness and stability with an underlying feeling of alienation and irrationality."[8] In discussing his own experience as the technical editor of *Architectural Design* magazine, Frampton brings forth Loos's position on photography and other representation techniques, including bricolage as practiced by the historical avant-garde. Frampton's occasional association of Loos with Duchamp, and the fact that the architect was acquainted with surrealist circles in Paris, had convinced him that Loos's disdain for photography did not prevent him from exploiting illusionistic spaces and from challenging "the authenticity of the real." In the Schwarzwald Apartment (1905), Loos used multiple mirrors to generate "a continuous oscillation between illusion and reality" and/or perhaps to mislead the observer, as if "the actual void was a mirror and the real mirror a void."[9] Loos utilized these design strategies along with the concept of *Raumplan* to critique the hermetic of "total" interiors advocated by a number of his contemporaries. This might be another reason why Frampton excluded expressionism and the *art pour l'art* movements in *A Critical History*'s first and subsequent editions.

The untimely turn to Loos intended to highlight Frampton's mixed penchant for the visual and virtual techniques of the avant-garde artists of the 1920s, despite his critical stance toward postwar avant-garde architecture. More importantly, the nature of the affinity between Frampton's critical discourse and ideas popularized by John Ruskin, William Morris and other affiliates of the Arts and Crafts movement needs to be clarified. Despite the movement's romance with the old guild system, what seemed enlightening to Frampton was the state of labor at the dawn of modernization seen through lenses tinted by the work of Arendt and thinkers affiliated with the Frankfurt School of Critical Theory, Walter Benjamin in particular. We will address the triad of Arendt, Benjamin and Frampton shortly. For now, it is argued that, for constructive criticism and praxis of the duality between modernity and tradition and the continual devaluation of labor within the capitalist production system, the scope of Frampton's intellectual caliber embraced issues expressed in Loos's writings and buildings. What justifies this association is that Loos and Frampton, each to different ends, have pursued a critical discourse aiming to disclose the extent to which the cultural ideologies of capitalism have been infused into the, so to speak, most advanced theorizations of architecture produced since then. The historical schism introduced by the project of Modernity has been the driving force of these theorizations. And yet, Frampton's historiography stubbornly insists on revisiting the architectonic consequences of the schism of modernity grafted into the traditional culture in general and the culture of the building in particular.

I

The title of Part III alludes to Frampton's critical assessment of attempts made during the 1970s to decode the International Style architectural ethos. As for the image used for the same title page, a Foster Associates building, we should first consider Frampton's overview of the project provided in the book's last pages and then discuss the preceding pages of the same chapter. This backward reading demonstrates the actual state of architecture wherein the Miesian "almost nothing" was pushed to its literal dimension, a crisis anticipated in Martin Heidegger's 1954 essay "Building, Dwelling, and Thinking."[10] Well known in phenomenological circles, Heidegger's essay played a central role in Frampton's formulation of "critical regionalism," the core ideological framework implicit in the title of the last chapter of the first edition of the book, "Place, Production, and Architecture: Towards a Critical Theory of building." To contextualize the title, we should start with Frampton's comparative analysis of Foster's Willis-Faber & Dumas Offices and Hertzbeger's Central Beheer Building, both completed in 1974. Setting aside the apparent differences between these two projects, both pursued strategies to create a new office building type. Frampton observes that nothing less than the internal circulatory system of these projects anticipated a model later to be copied by commercial developers. This observation has little to do with the old type/model dichotomy; it is instead a reminder of G. C. Argan, for whom "building types embody certain values which were inherent at their inception and which survive any subsequent transposition."[11] Whereas the Central Beheer's internal organization benefits from both the nineteenth-century arcades and the Middle Eastern casbah, the Willis-Faber "with its central escalator access hall lies somewhere between the 20th-century office tower and the 19th-century department store," Frampton notes.[12] The particular attention given to both schemes' internal spatial organization is reflected in their massing, to the point that both buildings look like solid objects, the Central Beheer assembled from several 9x9 meter cube-form modules expandable along two axes. With its glass curtain enclosure hung from the ceiling, the Willis-Faber covers its internal volume, without any articulation of, for instance, the whereabouts of the main entrance. Highlighting the design's distinctive emphasis on "the elegance of the production," Frampton positions the Willis-Faber building against the Venturisque "decorated shed." Elaborating the differences in greater detail in the book's subsequent editions, Frampton consolidates the idea of "the product-form," discussing this, along with numerous examples, in a short pamphlet published in 2007.[13] In retrospect, and in consideration of the British "hi-tech" architecture emerging since and in the aftermath of the Centre Pompidou (1977), Frampton proposition of the "product-form" was timely. It was also a response to Manfredo Tafuri's claim that "the imperative task of the architect today is to master the means of production, not only for the sake of regaining control over the act of building but also, presumably, to be able to participate consciously in the production of meaning."[14] Benefiting from Benjamin's essay "The Author as Producer," Tafuri argued that the architects of the late 1970s should have meaningfully formulated a critical stance *within* (and not against) the production and consumption systems of capitalism. In Chapter 7 of this volume, Frampton's criticism of architects who followed the postmodernist "decorated shed," in addition to the architects discussed in various editions of Critical Regionalism, and the architecture associable with the notion of "product-form" are considered.

The above-noted distinction Frampton makes is convincing. He writes, "The possibility that a reduction in the referential content of built form may be beneficial cannot be peremptorily dismissed, for the policy of 'almost nothing' has already demonstrated its ability to produce a benevolent environment."[15] This statement highlights the critical importance of what is called the "self-referentiality" of Miesian tectonics. It also anticipates the work supporting Frampton's "Six Points for an Architecture of Resistance," a prelude to his theorization of "critical regionalism."[16] For one thing, the last two pages of the book's first edition touch briefly on the work of diverse architects, from Ludwig Hilberseimer to Atelier 5, Josef Kliehuis and John Portman, laying out themes essential for Frampton's critical analysis of architecture then and now. Frampton introduces on the same page new concepts central to the modern and postmodern debate and the formation of modernism in architecture. In addition to the notion of built-form, these include themes such as "settlement;" the importance of differentiating *place* from *Raum* (space), after Heidegger's essay mentioned earlier; and the "urban enclave," if only to extend the scope of Frampton's critical interventions into the public domain. Most important is Frampton's proposed idea of "societal continuity in terms of bounded and articulated form" in the finest work of Aalto, deliberately noted in one of the last statements of Frampton's book that proffers the proposed Mies contra Aalto conundrum. Interestingly enough, as we will see shortly, these last two ideas play an essential role in Frampton's discussion of the Smithsons' Economist building. Two other Framptonian concerns further support the implied epistemic shift: how materiality and the tactile environment tend "to lose [their] concrete responsiveness" as a result of the veil that "photo-lithography draws over architecture."[17] If this statement summarizes the conclusion Frampton offers in the last pages of the first edition of the book, what path should postwar architecture have pursued to stand up to his call for critical praxis?

A clue to this query is Frampton's opening statement in Chapter 4, Part III. Following a quotation from Heidegger's essay, Frampton writes:

> No account of recent developments in architecture can fail to mention the ambivalent role the profession has played over the past decade—uncertain not only in the sense that while professing to act in the public

interest it has sometimes assisted uncritically in furthering the domain of an optimized technology, but also in the sense that many of its more intellectual members have abandoned traditional practice, either to resort to direct social action or to indulge in the projection of architecture as a form of art.[18]

The above is a fair verdict against post-1960s architectural praxis, a state of crisis indexed in two intertwined historical unfoldings: first, the failed project of Modernity and its drastic consequences for Modern Movement architecture. Second, the developmental processes of capitalism, the last nail in the coffin of the Movement theorized and practiced during the 1920s. Hence, the tendency to hand over the culture of the building to *technology* and rethink architecture and the available theoretical discourses, the genesis of which most often related to the strategic divide against the project of Modernity. If Frampton is not explicit about tendencies that merely propagated political solutions, that is, those that "elevated" architecture to the status of art as intellectual and individualistic work, he is clearly targeting practices that had derailed architecture from its public and "traditional practice." These issues are discussed in more detail below, picking up the last chapter of Frampton's book one more time. To plot Frampton's verdict and the historicity of architecture produced during the decade ending with the book's first edition (the 1970s), we should look at the chapters collided in the book's last part.

We can say that the first two chapters of Part III highlight the positive side of the architecture of modernism. Whereas Chapter 1 reviews various tendencies of International Style architecture, Chapter 2 turns to the "new brutalism" of the "welfare state" in England, a promising development considering the developmental process of capitalism before its expansion globally and under the domination of the rising American corporate institutions. The third chapter announces a watershed, the weakening if not the demise of the International Style from inside—Team X challenging the fundamentals of the Congrès internationaux d'architecture moderne (CIAM)! Frampton's dense and helpful discussion of the CIAM in Chapter 3 of the last part of the book ends with Shadrach Woods and Giancarlo de Carlo's critical summation of the organization's life, which lasted almost four decades (1928–68). Their timely criticism brings forth issues internal to the organization's three developmental phases that Frampton outlines, which are beneficial even if one is a contemporary reader. They also highlight the problems intrinsic to the proposed remedies for the emerging megalopolis that the mid-1960s had slowly but surely brought into *visibility* the over-domination of capitalism across the built environment. This development toward the closure of the third phase of CIAM was ideologically similar to the two preceding stages; one informed by the

German ideologues of *Neue Sachlichkeit* and Le Corbusier's vision of the city. As the "father" figure of the movement, Le Corbusier saw most issues in the light of l'spirit *nouveau*.

Nevertheless, Frampton's text establishes a close rapport between the postwar situation in England, the rise of Brutalism and Team X, headed by the British MARS group. It also presents his implicit reservations toward the megastructural approaches evident in the Smithsons' Golden Lane Housing and Berlin-Haupstadt (1958) and Bakema and Van den Broek's project in Tel Aviv (1963).[19] Sympathetic though he might have been to Aldo van Eyck's drive for "place-form," he could not but agree with the verdict announced by Shadrach Woods and de Carlo. Interestingly enough, theirs coincided with the European student uprising of 1968 and the fact that Western society had realized that "urban renewal [was] a euphemism for the dislocation of the poor." Frampton continues:

> In the mid-1960s, this point still largely escaped most Team X members who, except for Van-Eyk, Woods, and De Carlo, seemed to prefer to ignore the destruction of our urban heritage in the name of speculation. The postulated capacities of Team X became paralyzed at this juncture, their creative energies becoming depleted in the face of an impossible situation. Paradoxically, what now endures from their work is not so much their architecture vision as the suggestive power of their cultural criticism.[20]

Here, Frampton comes closest to Tafuri's predicament mapped in *Architecture and Utopia* (1976). Nevertheless, unlike the Italian historian, Frampton felt the need to formulate "critical regionalism" and later "the mega-form," two effective theoretical interventions apropos of the modern and postmodern debates, recalibrating the Arendtian "action," the activity that "goes between men without the intermediary of things."[21] These issues have become politically more tangible today, in the age of global capitalism, than when first pronounced in the early 1980s.

Now, we should ask, to what extent was the International Style architecture international? To respond to this query, we should turn to Frampton's opening statement in Chapter 1 of Part III, a well-tailored epigraph from Henry-Russell Hitchcock and Philip Johnson's 1932 manifesto. Highlighting the style's aesthetics and moving from an extensive masonry construction system to a skeleton frame structure, covered mainly by white-colored planes, Frampton questions its call for homogeneity. His criticism is directed even at Le Corbusier's 1920s villas and the design's dismal failure to engage with issues such as climatic, economic and cultural conditions, not only within the western hemisphere but, more importantly, when the style is exported to non-Western countries. Apropos, the problem of the style's abstract aesthetics paradoxically sheds light on the conflict between modernization and the possibility of a meaningful continuity of regional traditions of the culture of the building. As we will see shortly, the emergence of regional architecture in countries with deep traditional cultures would receive Frampton's support. In turn, it became a springboard for his Critical Regionalism. What Hitchcock and Johnson's manifesto underlined, by contrast, was the possibility of creative engagement with the limits imposed by the masonry construction system despite geographic diversity. In retrospect, and considering that most criticisms of contemporary architecture benefited from theoretical work developed in diverse disciplines, Frampton was quick to highlight themes essential for critical praxis, the scope of which surpassed the debates and practices internal to the CIAM fall.

To make his point, Frampton's first stop on the trail of the International Style's variations was Richard Neutra's design for Dr Philip Lovell's Health House in Los Angeles (1927) (Figure 5.2). The design included several issues encapsulating the gist of "clinical," in association with Los Angeles's climatic conditions, the topography of the building's site and Mr. Lovell's theory of "bio-realism." As the old saying goes, bio-realism would associate one's mental well-being with the well-being of the body. Unproven as this expression is, so was the narrative linking "architectural form to overall health," Frampton writes. Nevertheless, he recognizes that Neutra's biological concern, discussed in a book titled *Survival through Design* (1954), and the design's "extraordinary sensitivity and super-functional attitude" were antithetical to Johnson and Hitchcock's formulation of style's central ethos. These ideas were supportive of Frampton's speculative suggestion that Neutra "may be regarded as the apotheosis of the International Style."[22] What makes this statement plausible has less to do with Neutra's affinity with Frank L. Wright's work than with the architect's friendship with Rudolf Schindler and the influence of Loos on these two migrant architects. More importantly, Alfred Roth compellingly observes that the 20 buildings discussed in *The New Architecture* (1939)[23] come from only a few countries, including Finland, Holland, Switzerland and Sweden. Each of these nations had a small but stable economy and an absence of strong historical traditions of architecture. Roth's observation is relevant to Frampton's position on the subject because the new architecture developed in these countries paradoxically assisted the style's future development in more advanced economies. More specific to Frampton's concern was not Roth's selection criteria for the 20 discussed projects[24] but their architectonic ramifications. Roth wrote, "The ascertainment of a local cachet in examples of the New Architecture points to its consideration of topographical situations, scenic

THE AGENCY OF THE CRITICAL 115

Figure 5.2 Richard Neutra, Dr Philip Lovell's Health House, Los Angeles, 1927, exterior view. Image courtesy of Aren Bogossians.

surroundings, climate, the material dependent on the locality, and living customs." He continues, "Every attachment to rigid formal or constructive principles would be a disregard of these living bases that transformed into vital architectural wealth."[25] In different ways, Roth's observation and Frampton's Critical Regionalism are relevant today. A comprehensive understanding of architecture's contemporaneity cannot avoid the two-way traffic running between architecture produced in non-Western cultures and those designed in advanced capitalist centers. These issues are discussed in the following two chapters.

II

Toward the middle of Chapter 1 of Part III, the reader realizes why Frampton started discussing International Style architecture with Neutra's Lovell's house. For one thing, the building discloses the linguistic modifications enforced by the site's topology, and the climatic condition of Los Angeles. Most importantly, the design was carried out by an émigré of Europe, the style's homeland. Throughout the chapter, Frampton's taxonomical rationale follows the conviction that an immigrant architect of either European or Soviet origin introduced the International Style architecture to other countries. They accomplished this even aside from Le Corbusier's direct or indirect syntactical influence in most Western countries and beyond. Moreover, regardless of their primary education and training with a famous architect enthusiastic about the general categories of the style, these migrant architects soon started modifying the style's syntax according to the recipient country's historical, geographical and regional conditions. These developments are reiterated for their historical significance and the lessons Frampton learned toward Critical Regionalism.

Even though Frampton highlights sociopolitical issues only in passing, he does stress the modifications required when the monumentality of a government center stopped short of responding to its traditional setting; Le Corbusier's Chandigarh is a case in point. Comparing Oscar Niemeyer's design for Brasilia's Capitol (1956–63) with Le Corbusier's project, it seems that, while emulating the French architect's strategies in the distribution of the brief and architectonics of the complex, Niemeyer's design struggled to establish a good rapport between *style* and *scale*. It also showed the incapacity of architecture to "express the technical and social forces predominate in a given epoch" when these forces were out of balance in the design. The resulting conflict, according to Niemeyer, "is prejudicial to the content of the work and the work as a whole."[26] Frampton took Niemeyer's statement as a driving force for contextualizing the International Style's language wherever the suggested balance was impossible to achieve.

Following Frampton's timeline, after the exhibition of 1932, the style's language was modified according to the geopolitical culture of various European nations, and its importation to countries such as South Africa, South America and Japan. Similar to Schindler's and Neutra's work, Antonin Raymond's design of his own house in reinforced concrete (1923), Frampton identifies it as the style's precursor in Japan. Given that several Japanese architects were trained at the Bauhaus, for them as well as for Raymond, the primary issue was "what constitutes a 'Japanese' architect and a modern Japanese architecture"?[27] A Czech-born American architect, Raymond arrived in Tokyo in 1919 and started working as a construction supervisor of Wright's Imperial Hotel. Like Schindler and Neutra, Raymond was formally educated in Europe and trained by Wright and soon abandoned the "constraints of Wright's stylistic influences within a few years of leaving his employ."[28] Likewise, Niemeyer, who interned with Lucio Costa, played a vital role in disseminating modern architecture in Brazil during the late 1930s. We are also reminded of Berthold Lubetkin, a Russian émigré and the principal architect of the Tecton (1932). The firm's work introduced a particular angle on modern architecture to architects working in Britain, the land of the Arts and Crafts movement's forebears. A brief and pointed comparison between Tecton's first two housing projects, Highpoint 1 (1935) and Highpoint 2 (1938), shows the contextualization of the style in association with the architect's shift from an "anarcho-socialist persuasion" to Soviet Social Realism. This unfolding, and Lubetkin's 1950s review of Soviet architecture and the ensuing discussion, speaks for the "ground rules for the ideological struggles of the 1950s: the primacy of the formal concept in architecture and the ultimate significance of the built form." It was as if "a form has been imposed on the rooms (which is an altogether different thing from giving the rooms form),"[29] to recall Anthony Cox's discussion of Highpoint 2 in 1938. For Frampton, however, the differences between these two projects were the starting point for a "conscious attempt to assimilate the rhetorical tradition of the Baroque to the rigors of a cubist syntax," a mannerist neo-Corbusian style evident in Tecton's Finsbury Health Centre, London (1938). Likewise, Baroque was also the driving rhetoric in Niemeyer's Casino Pampulha (1942). Frampton presents a vivid reading of how language and purpose could intermingle with architecture's sociocultural image. According to him, the Casino was a

> narrative building in every respect, from the welcoming double-height foyer to the gleaming ramps rising to the gaming floor; from the elliptical corridors leading towards the restaurant to the ingenious backstage access to the dance area; in short, an explicit promenade which articulated the space of the building as the structure of an elaborated game, a game as intricate as the habits of the society it was intended to serve.[30]

Aesthetic theatricalization and Niemeyer's concern for the lack of a balance between the *logic* internal to the language and the available technique and labor led architecture to subscribe, consciously or unconsciously, to figural and gestural motifs practiced in other artistic forms.

Rather than running the entire course of mannerist strategies, most Japanese architects pursued the country's long tradition of articulated wooden structures. Neither the ever-presence of Corbusian elements nor even Kenzo Tange's optimistic view of the libertine nature of modernization could stop Raymond from detailing the concrete frame of his house according to traditional Japanese wooden construction. Neither strategy was "to become the architectonic touchstone of Japanese architecture after the Second World War." The same can be said about Junzo Sakakura, a member of the same generation and educated at the Bauhaus in the late 1920s. For the Japanese Pavilion at the Paris Exhibition of 1937, Sakakura reinterpreted the borrowed Corbusian elements (open-plan, ramp and a clear articulation of structure), creating a followup to the Japanese traditional tea house. Even Tange's design for the Kagawa Prefectural Office (1955–58) demonstrates an ideal balance between various historical allusions and "elements discretely abstracted from the received vocabulary of the international style," Frampton writes. Such hybridity, part Western and part Japanese, also permeated the Harumi Apartments, Tokyo (1957), designed by Mayekawa, who wrote in 1965 that "human dignity" and a balanced, ethical judgment have failed Western civilization, perhaps hinting at Toynbee. He claimed that one must seek "ethical judgment" in the Orient, if not in Japan.[31] Frampton takes Mayekawa's proclamation as the end of the International Style, not because of the architect's rhetorical vigor but because his design demonstrated subtle references to the culture of wooden structures tightly woven into the Japanese culture at large. But, "despite common roots in the work of Le Corbusier, no two designs of the 1950s could be farther apart than Niemeyer's Three Powers Square in Brasilia, with its simplistic classicism, and Tange's Kagawa Prefecture, with its extraordinary articulate detailing." The difference alludes to the uniqueness of Japanese architects' response whenever Western architecture has been in a state of crisis, especially after World War II.

The diverse work discussed briefly says much about the modifications introduced into the International Style architecture when exported to regions outside Europe. These projects also anticipated Frampton's interest in architecture that neither turns against the traditions deeply rooted in the geographical culture of a region nor relies heavily on the positivistic aspects of modernization. His remarks in this section of the book indict the state of architecture when the global forces of capitalism either totally subsume regional cultures or reduce their architectonic expressions to the spectacle of the commodity form. Frampton's interest in and critical reading of modern architecture produced in non-European centers were consequential to his belief that there should be an unconscious tectonic rapport between form and territory, in the broadest connotation of the term.[32]

III

Since the inception of modernization, the geneses of the crisis of architecture involved the instrumentalization of technology, extending the impact of capitalism on architecture from the technical to the cultural domain, especially after World War II.[33] Traumatic as the war was, it was also a watershed in the short-lived project of Modernity. The war stimulated, among other things, a desire to "return" to ideas that presumably should have prevented such a tragic event in the first place! Thus, for example, during the 1950s, the concept of New Brutalism was introduced into the British architectural scene as a design strategy responding to labor and material scarcity while pumping new blood into outdated issues such as national identity, blended with contradictory ideas reminiscent of the British Arts and Crafts movement in general, and populism, à la William Morris's advocacy for "socialism," in particular. However, specific to the architectonics of Brutalism was an aesthetic shift from the "painterly," initially introduced by the art historian Heinrich Wölfflin, to the sculptural.³⁴ Brutalism, as suggested elsewhere, was the last bastion before blending architecture with the demands of the rising consumer society.³⁵ With these few lines, an introduction to reviewing Frampton's discussion of New Brutalism, presented in Chapter 2, Part III, of the book's first edition, is given.

British by birth, Frampton may have felt at home formulating the argument presented in two chapters of his book, Chapter 1, Part II, and Chapter 2, Part III. One discusses the British Arts and Crafts movement, and the other explores the genesis of New Brutalism in England. There are two reasons for the speculative association: we have already noted Frampton's interest in the critical assessment of *labor*, even expressed by romantic-minded associates of the Arts and Crafts movement. This early discourse on labor attained a critical dimension retrospectively, and after Frampton's exposure to Hannah Arendt's formulation of the differences between work and labor. Frampton underlines at every opportunity Arendt's significance for the formation of his critical discourse on architecture and, to some extent, his approach to architectural history.

Interestingly enough, New Brutalism's rise to *visibility* was more contemporary with the formation of Frampton's own professional and intellectual life. By 1956 he had already finalized his education at the Architectural Association, London. Shortly after, he taught in different academic institutions while working as the technical editor of *Architectural Design* (1962–65). By the time of the completion of James Stirling's Florey Residential Building, Queens College, Oxford, in 1966, Frampton was in a position to agree with Manfredo Tafuri that New Brutalism had metamorphosed into "architecture as an autonomous machine."³⁶ This appraisal coincided with the completion of the Corringham housing project that Frampton had designed while working for Douglas Stephen and Partners (1961–66). The project was reviewed in several British architectural journals, with illustrations, detailed plans and sectional drawings.³⁷ The architectural historian Elain Harwood analyzed the essential aspects of the project associated with Brutalism. She wrote that Frampton

> grouped the entrance, lifts, staircase, heating, and waste-disposal chutes into a distinct unit that, while not entirely detached like that at Balfron Tower, was given a very different architectural treatment. The powerful, vertical emphasis of the lift shaft and boiler flue gave Corringham a reputation as one of the first major buildings in the sculptural, so-called "brutalist" style erected in central London.³⁸

Sympathetic though he was to Reyner Banham's writings, including the historian's later takes on New Brutalism, it is not far-fetched to say that Frampton has not been a die-hard advocate of Brutalist architecture.

However, we should recall his book *British Buildings 1960–1964*, published in 1965 and co-edited with Michael Carapetian and Douglas Stephen. The book included the Corringham building, in addition to several other projects that were considered Brutalist. In a recent interview, Frampton had this to say about the project: "Without any doubt, I designed and detailed the whole thing and supervised the construction, so it was a complete experience," adding that the building is "now a historic monument, Grade II."[39] Frampton was well versed in the genesis of the movement to the point that he wrote the most insightful essays on four projects that were definitive for disseminating New Brutalism. Referenced in the related chapter of the book, each of these four essays says something about Frampton's agile enthusiasm for assessing the homegrown movement. The chapter on New Brutalism is of interest because it focuses on these four essays. In contrast, in the remaining chapters of the book's same edition, Frampton's published articles are referenced only on four occasions: Chapters 13, 17 and 20 from Part II and Chapter 4 from Part III.

To historicize New Brutalism and delve into Frampton's architectural criticism at the time, we should briefly attend to Frampton's four essays, three of which discuss projects from the Brutalist portfolio of the Stirling Gowan firm; the fourth one analyzes Alison and Peter Smithson's Economist building (1959–64). We should then turn to the first projects of the Smithsons, the progenitors of New Brutalism. It is hoped that this retrospective reading will provide clues to postwar British architecture, the rise of New Brutalism and Frampton's strategic approach in analyzing these projects, in particular. Frampton's text on Leicester University Engineering Lab, completed in 1959 (Figure 5.3), is a significant development in postwar British architecture. Frampton's essay is also critical because it offers an alternative reading to Peter Eisenman's formalistic interpretation of the project, referenced in the bibliographic list of Chapter 2, Part III, of the book.[40] Having read the original text published in *Architectural Design* (1964), here we follow Frampton's essay republished in 2002.[41] In the introductory remarks to the section of *Labour, Work and Architecture* entitled "Criticism," Frampton details the rationale behind the content of the collected essays, outlining the criteria for critical analysis of architecture as prescribed in Christian Norberg-Schulz's *Intentions in Architecture* (1965).

In the introduction to his book, Christian Norberg-Schulz is clear about the task he sets himself in opposition to architects' unwillingness to formulate a "satisfactory theory of architecture." One of his goals was to analyze the correlation between a building's task and the final result. The idea was to examine and discuss how design internalizes *architecture* as part of "appearances" that are informative for one's experience of space. Interestingly enough, the implied

Figure 5.3 James Stirling & Gowan, Engineering Building, Leicester University, 1959, exterior view following James Stirling's famous axonometric drawing. Photo courtesy of "Quintin Photography."

idea of "image," as experienced by the spectator, was already introduced in Banham's topology discussion as the fourth element in his redefinition of New Brutalism. For Banham, the Smithsons' departure from the early modernist "elementary geometry" in the Golden Lane Housing Project created a "coherent visual image by non-formal means, emphasizing visible circulation, identifiable units of habitation, and fully validating the presence of human beings as part of the total image—the perspectives had photographs of people posted on to the drawings so that the human presence almost overwhelmed the architecture."[42] The inclusion of the "spectator" in Banham's recognition of topology, especially in the Smithsons' Sheffield University competition entry (1953), was a prelude to the inclusion of the aesthetic of the commodity form in architecture, a turn from the building being "in-itself" to being "for-itself." This was one of the important consequences of the temporalization of art and architecture in the postwar era.[43] Moreover, the Institute of Contemporary Art (ICA), founded in London in 1946, played a significant role in disseminating the importance of the spectator or consumer. In an attempt to weaken the avant-garde's ruptural logic, the group of artists and architects associated with Brutalism (the Independent Group) gathered at the ICA tried to focus on "interactions between the arts, and popular and technologically advanced arts, like cinema, architecture, and advertising in particular."[44] This was an overture to the total submission of architecture to a state of theatricalization (spectacle) that can be taken as "picturesque," an idea espoused by Nikolaus Pevsner. This charge means that after the war and the failure of the project of Modernity, architecture had to adapt itself to the sociopolitical and cultural consequences of that "failure." This unfolding had enormous implications for architecture: on the one hand, architects felt free to theorize architecture as "autonomous," as noted by Tafuri. On the other hand, it attempted to interpret architecture by other means, in particular through tropes formulated in philosophical discourses, the phenomenology popularized by Norberg-Schulz in particular. This unfolding was to open a can of worms if you wish: it facilitated exploring and practicing architecture then and now and regarding the complications that most often have the least to do with the building art.

Without mentioning the phenomenological underpinnings of Norberg-Schulz's framework, Frampton's strategic choice of the suggested modification speaks for itself: in analyzing a building, Frampton takes it upon himself to interrogate the "opposition between the physical *milieu* and the social *milieu*," between "the building task and how it is achieved." His approach is different because he sees himself as an "insider" to the praxis of architecture. In his words: "I write like an architect because I was trained as an architect, therefore, I still approach teaching and writing from an insider's point of view. What makes my teaching and above all, my writing unique is that it's coloured by an awareness of the issues involved in the conception and realization of built form."[45] As we noted, phenomenology was essential for the experiential understanding of architecture launched against the forerunners of a positivistic interpretation of Modern Movement architecture. Phenomenology also disseminated a sentiment of materiality, touch and other sensory experiences, excluded from the early rationalist theorization of architecture. However, it stopped short of contextualizing these issues within the historical impact of modernization, especially the changing parameters informing the formation of modern subjectivities.[46] These issues are revisited in the light of Rudolf Wittkower's *Architectural Principles in the Age of Humanism* (1949). Despite the Smithsons' denial, Banham believed that the Humanist principles significantly impacted a "whole generation of post-war architectural students." Accordingly, "Palladians soon became as thick on the ground as Routine-Functionalists"[47]—as can be seen in the Smithsons' design of a house in Soho (1953), which, in Anthony Vidler's recent account, "inherited the already five-year preoccupation with neo-Palladian geometry: the facades were controlled by regulating lines, the plan was nearly square, and the internal divisions were equally geometricized."[48] The Soho project, designed in brick with concrete lintels and interiors with no cladding, demonstrates the architects' continued allegiance to the mandate of truth to material, tested earlier in the exposed mechanical and structural elements of the Hunstanton School (1949–54). From another perspective, we could say that the empathy for exposed materials and rough surfaces permeating buildings associated with New Brutalism also aimed to reverse Alois Reigl's evolutionary order of artistic experience, from tactile to optical, elevating the latter as the universal vision, at least for some time after the invention of the perspectival regime.[49]

As Jorge Otero-Pailos has discussed, the *turn* to theorizing architecture in other terms was historical.[50] In the wreckage of postwar Europe, phenomenology offered a light at the end of the tunnel through the "return" of many historically suppressed tropes. These included the body, a populist interpretation of the "man in the street" and, most importantly, a way out of the technological determinism that dominated the early modernist theorization of architecture. Ironically, technology was reapproached at this time to structure geometry not only in the purview of proportions highlighted by Wittkower but also according to the attention given to D'Arcy Thompson's book, initially published in 1917 and reprinted in 1942.[51] Considering the actual situation of postwar England, which Frampton outlines in passing, phenomenology seemed a promising narrative for those who were seeking to put together the broken early bourgeois *totality*, Humanism, as such. We are also reminded of the 1951 Festival of Britain, which contained references to the Stockholm Exhibition of 1930, and the Constructivist elements evident in the Asplund's design of the Festival Plaza among other considerations. These unfoldings paved the way for the British rapprochement to Swedish New Empiricism, a significant factor in the emergence of the "Third Generation" of architects, the notable advocates of New Brutalism and Team Ten combined.

Still, in the absence of a reliable Classical tradition operative in postwar Italy, for example, British architects found themselves politically, particularly after Indian independence in 1945, on the same page as William Morris's proclamation of humanized socialism, seen through the lens of the Swedish welfare-state model. Palladian Humanism was recharged with the material culture of redbrick walls associable with British working-class sentiments, if not with "the man in the street." Many architects used the phrase disregarding class division,[52] perhaps in recognition of Henri Lefebvre's formulation of *everydayness* as a "category of capitalism symptomatic of modernity, and post-war consumer capitalism—capitalism as modernity."[53] Interestingly enough, in 1953, the Smithsons declared deep respect for the affinity materials provide "between building and man—which is at the root of the so-called Brutalism."[54] This sentiment recalled bygone images of coherencies associated with peasant societies but was also symptomatic of the colonization of *experience* by the commodity form.[55] Sum total of these "returns" was informative for the best work produced by the British postwar architects. Even though the intellectual developments of postwar Britain were significant for Frampton, he chose to reapproach these issues in light of architecture's ever-increasing subsumption into the technological world and the aesthetics of commodity form.

IV

Before moving to the Smithsons' work, it is clear that one cannot do justice to Brutalism without considering the Engineering Building, Leicester University (1959), the subject of one of Frampton's four mentioned essays. With its prevailing redbrick wall enclosure, in sharp contrast to the soaring glazed tower and mannered exposed concrete columns, Stirling's work raises several issues worthy of attention. The whitewashed modernist aesthetic gave way to colorful, tactile materiality, diverse as steel, glass, concrete and red brick. It was a departure from the clean geometries of silos and surface aesthetics permeating Le Corbusier's Maison Jaoul, decidedly evaded evidence of craft and materiality. In Hamm Common (1958), a similar case to Le Corbusier's work, rough surfaces punctuated with inverted L-shaped window openings are highlighted, recalling the warehouses Stirling had visited and photographed during his tenure at Liverpool.[56] Frampton has this to say about the Hamm Common housing project: "Load-bearing, fair-faced brickwork aspires to a common telluric sensibility: a testament to the existential authenticity of brick,"[57] with particular emphasis on the tectonics of wall enclosure, roofing (vaulting) and covering. Frampton considers this Stirling and Gowan work a case in point, where "the vernacular of the industrial north is returned to its roots."[58] Other scholars have also noted these articulations, a follow-up to the precedents developed in the nineteenth-century industrial structures.[59] Accordingly, using exposed brick and cast concrete and architectural details such as gutter elements were part of the Brutalist attempt to promulgate a poetics of construction and to signal a relentless critique of the priorities prevalent in interwar modernism, which professed a radical departure from such detailing. In retrospect, we could say that the Leicester building was a flash of light in the sky of British postwar architecture before embracing postmodernism.

At this point, and before turning to the Leicester building, we need to recall the Smithsons' Hunstanton School. This work initiated the turn to Brutalism in postwar architecture, which should also be considered a foreword to Frampton's different take on Leicester. This detour is essential considering the tectonic similarities connecting this particular work of the Smithsons to Mies's projects on the IIT campus *ca.* 1942. However, the ethical dimension evident in the Smithsons' handling of materials and "fittings"—exposed plumbing and so on—makes their work different from the aesthetic of abstraction implicit in Mies's American period.[60] For Frampton, the Hunstanton School demonstrates the Smithsons' empathy with "Palladian-cum-Miesian" vocabulary—a British postwar architectonic sentiment that Leicester surmounted.

Now, what Frampton seemingly wanted to highlight in the Leicester building was the design's architectural rationale to achieve an equilibrium between elements rooted in the early nineteenth-century anonymous work of British engineering and the overarching presence of the project's brick podium. He notes, "This engineering building may be seen as a heroic and liberating attempt to reconcile the essential conflict existing between two distinct cultures of the environment." He associates this aspect of the design with the architectonics of two extreme traditions of modern movement architecture: the romantic aestheticization of architecture by L. Kahn and F. L. Wright and the technologically motivated work of early rationalism and Constructivism. Stirling's montage of tectonics in the Leicester building is unique considering other works produced "since the end of the war," which "has been conceived and realized with such authority and precision." Frampton continues, "It is an achievement that is rendered all the more remarkable by the circumstances under which it was designed."[61] On this last point, he is more explicit in *A Critical History*. He writes that it is the "ultimate integration of the British Brutalist aesthetic—the fusion of its 'formalist' and 'populist' aspects into a glass and brick 'vernacular' drawn from the industrial structures of the 19th century" that informs both Leicester and the firm's design of a dormitory project for Selwyn College, Cambridge, also from 1959.[62] Here, Frampton echoes aspects of the Smithsons' manifesto, first published in *Architectural Design* (January 1955). The text claims that "what is new in the New Brutalism among Movements is that it finds its closest affinities, not in a past architectural style, but peasant dwelling forms." This, Banham wrote, has nothing to do with the craft and handling of materials attributed to Wright or the associations made between his work and Japanese architecture. As such, "we see architecture as a direct result of a way of life." In contrast, the Smithsons were thinking of "form" in Japanese architecture as part of a "general conception of life, a sort of reverence for the natural world and, from that, for the materials of the built world."[63] However, the Smithsons' manifesto discloses a sense of realism, empirical or otherwise, that would soon turn its focus on the everyday consumer products of the rising consumer culture in America, from Cadillac to the objects depicted in Richard Hamilton's "collage" of 1956. A similar diversity of references was also evident in the exhibitions curated by the Smithsons and members of "the Independent Group."[64] The consensus prevailing in both the "Parallel of Life and Art" (1953) and the "House of the Future" (1956) exhibitions was that, after the war, high modernism was in crisis and that the rising artistic tendency was tilting toward a national culture based on the amalgamation of craftsmanship, preindustrial cottage dwellings and populism advocated by American mass culture. Frampton sees this unfolding as part of a "split between sympathy for old-fashioned working-class solidarity and the promise of consumerism." He argues that "the Smithsons were ensnared in the intrinsic ambivalence of an assumed populism," and that, by the mid-1950s, "they moved away from their initial sympathy for the life style of the proletariat towards more middle-class ideals that depended for their appeal on both conspicuous consumption and mass ownership of the automobile."[65] Here, and more specifically in the Leicester building, Frampton's contextualization provides an approximation of his search for a *proper* design strategy and the premises for a historical criticism of architecture that had to face architecture's failed early sociopolitical aspirations.

In the second article, published in *Architecture Forum* (1968), Frampton examines Stirling's Cambridge History Faculty building. Presenting a detailed discussion of this project next to Stirling's other work, including the Leicester building, Frampton's text shows the extent to which he had taken into consideration Norberg-Schulz's theorization of how a critique should read a project while having an eye on the building's task, technique and program. To this end, Frampton turns to John Summerson for whom, after the fall of Classical wisdom, "program" had become a major unifying factor for architecture. Without referring to historically defined differences between type and model, Frampton sees in the "initial image" a model (a "shape") modified according to an "empirically determined program." Compared to other competition entries for the Faculty Library building, most of which compartmentalized the library spaces on strictly functional bases, Stirling tried to create a particular building type based on the program and the suggested strategies of distortion. Frampton considers their program primarily informed the Faculty building and the dormitory at St Andrews University: one in its capacity to be perceived as an information hub, and the other in its "naïve expression in the hierarchy of its exfoliated order," the type presented in the nonconventional rapport between the entry-level plan and the volumetric "image" of the complex. Frampton's detailed discussion of the Faculty building concerns if the design complied with the main points that he had extracted from Norberg-Schulz's prescription: whether the building's task was adequately considered in the physical form of the building, and whether the final result was responsive to the site. Frampton's reading, however, moves beyond highlighting the glass and its luminosity. Instead, he tries to demonstrate Stirling's strategic decision to get away from the perception of massing in favor of perceptual lightness. Again, we think of the Leicester, where the building "rose from the solidity of its brick podium into an effervescence of translucent light that diminished ultimately to nothing." The idea of distortion presented a strategy to transform the initial model into a building type that had no precedent but confirmed Stirling's strategic move toward alternative design concepts popularized by the modern and Classical traditions, which seemed almost flushed into the abyss of history. The Leicester building was conceived of as an aggregate of separate volumes, each accommodating a particular task. Novel in Stirling's design for the Faculty building was the "distortion" involved in the transformation of an almost rectangular entry-level plan (the initial model) into an L-shaped massing (an open book?!), with the space between the two arms covered by a sloping glazed roof. This conversion should be considered part of Stirling's retrospective criticism of Le Corbusier's proposed four compositions of 1929. Accordingly, what prevails in both Maison La Roche and Villa Savoye is the correlation between the final form and the original type. There is no erosion involved in Le Corbusier's four villas, where the volume is extruded from the plan. In the final analysis, Stirling's ongoing technical and typological experimentation was carried out with an eye to the Constructivist radical agenda reappearing in the postmodern linguistic mannerism. In this latter field, too, Stirling was to play a significant role.

Before reaching this conclusion and checking its implications for architectural criticism, we should attend to Frampton's discussion of Andrew Melville Hall at St Andrew's University (1964–69), the subject of his third article. Similar to his other two essays, the first paragraph of the essay starts with a two-track analysis: first, it underlines the importance of the site and how the design occupies the given topographic landscape and the coastal line-view in the distance, to the extent that from inland the two wings of the project, housing dormitory rooms, remain out of sight. Frampton's second point focuses on the typological dimension of the design: "the evocation of a baroque palace, the pyramidal concentration towards the center." Having established these points, he moves to demonstrate how the architect's ambitious use of building technique defamiliarized its two classical affinities, evident in dormitory complexes. Stirling and Gowan's move toward "industrialization" represented the closure of their Brutalist period, exemplified in the Melville project. The scale of the newly emerging educational complexes, starting with the architects' Churchill Campus competition entry, forced them to replace the load-bearing brick walls with tile/brick and glass skin enclosures held by a frame or concrete frame structure. Among other projects, the Leicester, the Faculty Library and the Florey Building (under construction at the time of the publication of Frampton's essay) were the forerunners of the idea of industrialization, with architectonic implementations (technical and typological) examined in the design of St Andrew's. In recollection of the importance of liners for Le Corbusier, Frampton makes an analogical comparison between the promenade deck of a ship and the carrier's salons, the former delivering a "communal pledge" to the open sea. At the same time, the latter remains confined "in-itself," as is the case with monasteries and quadrant-type educational buildings. He writes that at "St Andrew's living cells of the dormitory wings aggregate above and below, the essential provision of such a promenade deck, which is detailed to make its maritime connotations inescapable."[66] Frampton extends his critical assessment of Andrew Melville Hall to address the inevitable societal dimension of architecture. He writes that "criticism is only possible through a broader consideration that penetrates beyond the relation of the architect to his product, to include the society and or the client with whom the initial parameters of the work are necessary to be established." This, as we will see below, marked a strategic turn in Frampton's take on architectural criticism.

A case in point is the Smithsons' design for the Economist towers, designed in consultation with the client and the brief but also with a view to the social and architectonic aspects of the site. The subject of Frampton's fourth essay, this project created a unique urban enclave.[67] Frampton reminds us of the allocation of the volume of the bank to the shortest towers. Located along St James Street, the design created a plaza in a rather cramped site. Raised above the street datum, the Plaza opens its interior to the surrounding streets on the three sides. According to Frampton, this design provides a productive alternative to the regular "piecemeal" redevelopment. His assessment benefits from the architects' competition entry for the Hauptstadt in central Berlin (1958), which includes urban elements such as a raised pedestrian deck and the use of architectonic detailing first tested in the Economist's bank building. To examine the Economist building's success in terms of form and space, we refer to the Smithsons' reversal of the Miesian dictum, their belief that it is not the question of "what" but "how." However, starting with "what" as it concerns the Economist building, Frampton was eager to know the importance of asking "how"! To this end, one can read between the lines of Frampton's close-up observation of how the three towers of the Economist complex correspond to each other "theatrically," despite their identical square-shaped geometry. Thus, photographic techniques and tectonics are called upon to critique architecture in modernity. Frampton writes, "In the center of the plaza, the 'photographic' reduction in the scale of the residential block vis-à-vis the main tower has the optical effect of 'zooming' this block away from the observer, with consequent dramatic enlargement in the apparent space of the Plaza." As for the tectonics, we read, "The roach-bed Portland stone cladding which is ingeniously used as a 'skin façade' virtually throughout the site, is unfortunately also open on occasion to a theatrical interpretation particularly in the main entry hall to the offices beneath the tower." Mies, according to Frampton, avoided this strategy, making a clear distinction between "the infill façade, or overall skin and the supporting structure; a distinction which enabled Mies to finish all around the faces of support columns where they stand free at ground level." Mies is recalled again when Frampton demonstrates the conflict between handmade and mass-produced products, one of the many enumerated conflicts permeating the Economist building. The aesthetic implications of these conflicts—that is, the material versus the immaterial, the monumental versus the flexible and the static versus the dynamic—are "largely avoided by Mies through extensive use of appropriate standard sections and extrusions however much they may be welded, and sandblasted finally into a state of virtual, and in this respect superficial, hand-made refinements." These conflicts are further emphasized by the Economist towers' visible theatricality, which for Frampton reconfigures the core crisis of modern architecture, "the legitimate process through which we should create form and enclose space at this time both for the society of the present and the immediate future." Thus the "negative" significance of Mies for Frampton's critical historiography.

In retrospect, the discussed four essays say something essential about the state of criticism in Frampton's intellectual labor. These essays were written when Frampton's reading of architecture primarily focused on the *process* by which an architect would set the task for her/himself and compose a rationale (narrative) relating the brief to space, form and the site. Presumably, both the architect and the critic saw architecture as a craft with inherited historical knowledge, skills, techniques and *solutions*. Industrialization and urbanization created a place for the emergence of new materials, techniques and narratives in the historically accumulated knowledge of architecture. Three of the mentioned articles follow our suggested paradigm, with the difference that the so-to-speak external narrative drew from Norberg-Schulz's phenomenological paradigm formulated during the mid-1960s. In discussing the Economist, Frampton's fourth essay opens the vista of modernist criticism to include the urban setting and how a given site engages with the urban context more often than not. Frampton might have considered Aldo Rossi's discourse in *The Architecture of the City* (1966).[68] Nevertheless, his conclusions drew mostly from the urban impact of the Chicago School architecture, and Henry Sullivan's work in particular. Interestingly enough, in a retrospective account of essays compiled under the subtitle of "criticism" in his significant ontological oeuvre today,[69] Frampton writes that the reviews of buildings he published before 1965 were "appraisal," much of which, to his regret, Tafuri considered "operational criticism." Despite or because of Tafuri's dictum, Frampton decided to test his intellectual work at a pedagogical level in a 1970s seminar entitled "Comparative Critical Analysis of Built Form," later published in a book titled *A Genealogy of Modern Architecture: Comparative Critical Analysis* (2016).[70]

However, the ultimate shift in Frampton's architectural criticism took place when he read Arendt in 1965. In the same preface, he writes, "In one way or another, all my writing from the mid-Sixties onwards has been directly or indirectly influenced by the thought of Hannah Arendt." Frampton realized how Arendt's differentiation of work from labor was "to illuminate the time-honored but invariably confusing distinction between building (process) and architecture (stasis), with architecture having as its primary charge the creation of public realm—within which her third term, namely, 'action,' plays itself out, testifying, as she puts it, to the fact that men, plural, inhabit the world." By publishing *A Critical History*'s first edition (1980), Frampton had also read Walter Benjamin's "Theses on the Philosophy of History," a chapter from the English edition of *Illuminations* with Arendt's introduction published in 1968.[71] One consequence of these turns in Frampton's intellectual life can be detected in the title of the last chapter of his book, "Place, Production, and Architecture: Towards a Critical Theory of Building." Another, as we will see in the last chapter of this volume, was Frampton's formulation of "Critical Regionalism: Modern Architecture and Cultural Identity," included for the first time in the third edition of *A Critical History* (1992).

V

As noted earlier in this chapter, Frampton's discussion in the last chapter of his book begins with a quotation from Heidegger's "Building, Dwelling, and Thinking." In his essay, the German thinker differentiated *Raum* from an abstract and horizonless space. It is interesting to note that "bridge," a purposeful *thing*, emerges in Heidegger's text as a constructed metaphor for a philosophical interpretation of the apartness of two banks of a river, at which point space (*raum*) is localized. Frampton adopts the theoretical implications of the bridge's thingness for a phenomenological discussion of "placemaking." The point is not whether this reading of Heidegger is correct but the tacit conjecture Frampton makes between the metaphor of the bridge and the two illustrations posted on the same page as Heidegger's quotation. One of the images shows a section drawing of Michael Webb's "Sin Centre" project (1962); the other shows Ron Herron's famous "Walking City" project (1964). Both images are presented as a follow-up to Buckminster Fuller's obsessive reduction of architecture to a temporary engineered shelter, culminating in the geodesic dome he proposed to cover part of Manhattan. These images confirm the scope of technology's contribution to the realization of dazzling bridges and other industrial structures conceived and built since the mid-nineteenth century. Having put behind him the failed vision of modernist architects who invested heavily in space and *technique*, it is not surprising to see Frampton critiquing the architects of the 1970s, most of whom had abandoned the traditional practice in favor of designs driven by technological optimization.[72] Frampton continues, "One cannot help regarding it as the return of repressed creativity, as the imposition utopia upon itself," a conclusion that he had already reached in considering the failed project of the historical avant-garde. Nevertheless, according to Frampton, what makes other unsuccessful architectural projects worthy of consideration is that they can be associated with the projects of Ledoux and Le Corbusier, who were both thinkers and builders. As for the neo-avant-garde of the 1970s, Frampton recalls Tafuri's verdict that "the aim of the latter-day avant-garde is to validate itself through the media or to redeem its guilt by executing the rite of creative exorcism in isolation." The reference to Tafuri supports, once again, the point that by the time of wrapping the first edition of the book, Frampton had not yet formulated a definitive critique of architecture in connection with the state of postwar totalization. Heidegger and Norberg-Schulz's prescriptions were good but not enough to critique art and architecture's position within the production system of capitalism, as illuminated by Walter Benjamin in "The Author as Producer."[73]

In the same chapter, Frampton extends his sharp and uncompromising criticism to include Archigram and most of the work associated with the Japanese Metabolist movement. These groups, he writes, "proposed space standards that were well below the *Existenzminimum* established by those prewar functionalists they supposedly despised."[74] An exception to this general verdict was Fumihiko Maki's "additive urban form." He characterizes the Centre Pompidou as an "outstanding popular success—as much for its sensational nature as for anything else" but also because "it is a brilliant tour de force in advanced technique, looking for all the world like oil refinery whose technology it attempts to rival." Interestingly enough, Frampton's critical pen does not exempt his admired British historian, Reyner Banham, who had praised Fuller's technological adventure in the last pages of *Theory and Design in the First Machine Age* (1960). However, we should differentiate the technological euphoria of Archigram and the Futurist groups from Soviet Constructivism. The appropriation of technology by certain affiliates of the

Constructivist movement was dialectical; to deconstruct the native traditional culture of the building effectively, Constructivists had to reimagine the technique in the context of the Soviets' revolutionary everyday life. Heralding the Bolshevik Revolution, their work was "to make possible the envisaging of history in such a way as to foreground the present—the now—in contrast to the past of national narratives that ultimately implied an identity with both past and present."[75] In this regard, it is not far-fetched to say that the historicity of the European avant-garde overshadowed both Frampton's and Tafuri's partial assessment of Constructivism. The difference also says something about Benjamin's "constructive" take on technology compared to Heidegger.

Drawing from the experience of other sectors of modernism, Frampton pursues a critique of the 1960s avant-garde and concludes his observations by calling the prominent members of the Hochschule fur Gestaltung at Ulm, Germany's successors to the Bauhaus. He reiterates that gone in the neo-capitalist society is the Romanticist vision of "community-oriented" art and architecture. We are reminded of Claude Schnaidt, also from Ulm, who concluded his essay "Architecture and Political Commitment" (1967) with the following words: "Modern architecture, which wanted to play its part in the liberation of mankind by creating a new environment to live in, was transformed into a giant enterprise for the degradation of the human habitat."[76] Alternatively, salvation was sought in the work of Superstudio, if not in design methodologies, N. J. Habraken and others advocated, whereas the "Continuous Monument" presented poetry of resistance against the consumer culture that had left its mark on the urban landscape. Habraken instead sought to solve design problems following scientific methods while advocating massive housing projects, a follow-up to the *Neue Sachlichkeit* slum clearance. Habraken's sympathy with the users was the other side of the coin of the "man in the street," a slogan dear to British postwar advocacy groups. In retrospect, remedies proposed during the 1960s were symptoms of a postmodern condition that ran in two parallel lines. Following a Cartesian rationalization, one line of argument saw salvation in science and emerging communication technologies; the other tried to limit the scope of *the common* to the user's access to and consumption of consumer goods.

In the American context, the meta-language of consumer culture was pushed to its extreme in Denise Scott Brown's dictum of "Learning from Pop," an article published in a special issue of *Casabella* (December 1971). Drawing from their design studio teaching at Yale (1968), Scott Brown, Robert Venturi and Steven Izenour developed a narrative of "realism" in tandem with consumer goods' meta-language. Theirs was a "proper" alternative to modern architecture associated with the dictum of "form follows function." By the mid-1970s, and by the publication of *Learning from Las Vegas* (1972) and

Jean-François Lyotard's *The Postmodern Condition* (1979), the crossing point of these two admittedly diverse lines of observation, analysis and argumentation seemed convincing. Apropos Frampton's claims that the "Loosian recognition of the loss of cultural identity" had led to the "impoverishment of the urban environment," Frampton saved his harshest criticism for any analysis and learning from America's commercial and consumerist landscape that had failed to demonstrate the threat these developments posed to "the very notion of place." These words, written in response to Scott Brown and published in the same issue of *Casabella*, unsurprisingly had political consequences. Recalling Arendt, Frampton wrote, "It is ironic that Denise Scott Brown should attempt to bestow upon such a reservoir of process and pseudo points of arrival, like parking lots, those very attributes which previous cultures reserved for 'space of human appearance.'"[77] Frampton further argued that "Levittown could be brought to yield an equally affirmative consensus concerning current American repressive policies, both domestic and foreign." He then turned to Aldo Rossi of *The Architecture of the City* (1966), and Rossi's idea of "analogical architecture," a photomontage of the architectonics of the past and the present. However, the Italian *Tendenza*'s turn to the architecture's disciplinarity, and typological and morphological studies, presented an alternative to learning from Las Vegas. It was also the last-ditch effort to save the city from the exigencies of capitalism. Against the tendency to amalgamate scientific discoveries with postwar new-empiricism, Rossi's *poiesis* offered a critical practice centered on those aspects of architecture that seemed peripheral, if not immune, to the demands of mass culture and the speculative urbanization endemic to historical cities such as Berlin and New York City.[78] Disregarding this dimension of Rossi's praxis, the architect's discourse on "autonomy" was directed toward formalistic ends, especially with regard to the New York Five architects and Peter Eisenman in particular.[79] Furthermore, Frampton could not but associate Rossi's architecture and the drive to the consolidation of the notion of autonomy with the postmodern condition.

This led to the formation of three dominant architectural praxes during the 1970s: formalism, analogical architecture and the simulation of classical languages. In different ways, these three tendencies all stemmed from a shared experience of "closure," where the salvation of architecture was sought in the following strategy: recoding disciplinarity anew while borrowing concepts and ideas developed in the sociocultural and philosophical discourses of the time. Frampton was not an exception to this turn of events, and this in consideration of the quotation he chose to open the concluding chapter of the first edition of *A Critical History*. Choosing Heidegger was an attempt on Frampton's behalf to revisit the culture of the building in the light of the German thinker's critique of the marriage between "instrumental logic" and technology. Heidegger theorized the concept of placemaking with different connotations from the reductive notion of genius loci trumpeted throughout Norberg-Schulz's writings. Frampton's choice had another consequence, especially considering his introductory text to the book, which opens with a quotation from Benjamin's text on "Philosophy of History." The significance of Heidegger, Benjamin and Arendt for Frampton's discourse on the *critical* has been discussed earlier in this volume. Frampton's decision to begin and end the book with epigraphs from Benjamin and Heidegger foreshadows the intellectual direction he would pursue after the book's publication. Arguably, he wrote the last chapter of the book in anticipation of the critical theory of architecture that would come to its full fruition in "Critical Regionalism." His was a fourth alternative theory of praxis to the three theorizations of the architecture of the 1970s mentioned above. In "Place, Production, and Architecture," and following Heidegger, Frampton ties architecture simultaneously to modern technology and the existential dimension of the body experienced through the everyday life of capitalism. Making a tacit distinction between existential and historical time, architecture for Frampton is a semiautonomous practice, the thematic of which is paradoxically defined and redefined by the unpredictable path capitalism pursues to smooth its internal contradictions. For Frampton, however, the homology between the body, place and technique was to open the closure mentioned earlier and the possibility of mapping a critical interpretation of contemporary architectural praxis in the purview of the production and consumption systems of late capitalism. With the addition of Critical Regionalism to the third edition of his book (1992) and the expansion of the book's narrative to include reviews of "world architecture" in the subsequent editions, the book's original purpose and empathy with Benjamin's vision of history is left to the judgment of history.

Notes

1. Searching for clues for the ambiguity of the image led to a review of this project of Foster Associates written by Christopher Woodward in the *Architectural Review*, May 2010.
2. Kenneth Frampton, *The Evolution of 20th Century Architecture: A Synoptic Account* (New York: Springer Wien, 2007), 123–35.
3. For references, see Chapter 7 in this volume.
4. Kenneth Frampton, *Modern Architecture: A Critical History* (New York: Oxford University Press, 1980), 91.
5. Ibid., 42.
6. The epigraph is taken from William Morris, "The Revival of Architecture" (1888).
7. Frampton, *A Critical History*, 95.
8. Kenneth Frampton, "In Spite of the Void: The Otherness of Loos," in *Labour, Work and Architecture: Collected Essays on Architecture and Design*, ed. Kenneth Frampton (London: Phaidon, 2002), 199.

9   Kenneth Frampton, *Labour, Work and Architecture: Collected Essays on Architecture and Design* (New York: Phaidon, 2002), 200.
10 Martin Heidegger, "Building Dwelling and Thinking," in *Poetry, Language, Thought* (New York: Harper & Row, 1971), 143–62.
11 Frampton, *A Critical History*, 295.
12 Ibid., 294.
13 Kenneth Frampton, "The Ascendency of the Product-Form," in Frampton, *The Evolution of 20th Century Architecture*, 123–36.
14 Frampton, *A Critical History*, 295.
15 Ibid., 296.
16 Kenneth Frampton, "Towards a Critical Regionalism: Six Points for an Architecture of Resistance," in *The Anti-Aesthetic*, ed. Hal Foster (Washington, DC: Bay, 1983), 16–30.
17 Frampton, *A Critical History*, 297.
18 Ibid., 280.
19 This project was later included in Frampton's text on mega-form.
20 Ibid., 279.
21 Hannah Arendt, *The Human Condition* (Chicago: University of Chicago Press, 1958), 7.
22 Frampton, *A Critical History*, 248–49.
23 Here the *Les Editions d' Architecture* (Erlenbach-Zurich, 1946) has been used.
24 These are: spatial planning, technical considerations, economic factors and aesthetic aspects. Alfred Roth, *The New Architecture* (1946), 7.
25 Ibid., 8. This association in consideration to Kenneth Frampton's *A Genealogy of Modern Architecture* (New York: Lars Muller, 2016).
26 Frampton, *A Critical History*, 256–57.
27 In addition to A. Raymond, Yamada Mamoru and Horiguchi Sutemi also played a significant role in introducing modern architecture during the interwar period in Japan. See Ken Tadashi Oshima, *International Architecture in Interwar Japan: Constructing Kokusai Kenchiku* (Seattle: University of Washington Press, 2009). See also Harry Harootunian, *Overcome by Modernity: History, Culture, and Community in Interwar Japan* (Princeton, NJ: Princeton University Press, 2002); and Arata Izosaki, *Japan-ness in Architecture* (Cambridge: MIT Press, 2011).
28 Frampton, *A Critical History*, 257–58.
29 Ibid., 252.
30 Ibid., 255.
31 Ibid., 261.
32 On this subject, see Vittorio Gregotti, "The Form of Landscape," *OASE* 80 (2007): 7–22. The essay was first published in *l'Architecture d'Aujourd'hui* (218 (1981)).
33 This is the present author's position. See Gevork Hartoonian, *Architecture and Spectacle: A Critique* (London: Routledge, [2012] 2017).
34 Heinrich Wölfflin, *The Principles of Art History* (New York: Dover, 1950).
35 Gevork Hartoonian, *Time, History, and Architecture: Essays on Critical Historiography* (London: Routledge, 2017), 130–50.
36 The reference is from Manfredo Tafuri, "L' Architecture dans le Boudoir," *Oppositions* 3 (May 1974): 37–62. For Frampton's account of Manfredo Tafuri's assessment of postwar architecture, see Frampton, *A Critical History*, 268.
37 See, for example, Dick van Gameren, "Efficiency through Complexity," *Delft Architectural Studies on Housing (DASH)* 4 (2010): 107–12. Also *Architectural Design* (September 1964): 442–48.

38 Elain Harwood, May 1996, http://www.corringham.eu/Documents/ChamRecommendation.pdf (accessed March 27, 2019).
39 Cynthia Davidson, "On the Record with Kenneth Frampton," *Log* (Fall 2018): 29.
40 Peter Eisenman, "Real and English: The Destruction of the Box. 1" *Oppositions* 4 (October 1974): 5–34.
41 Frampton, *Labour, Work and Architecture*, 258–63.
42 Reyner Banham, "The New Brutalism," *Architectural Review* 118 (December 1955). Here quoted from Anthony Vidler, "Another Brick in the Wall," *October* 136 (Spring 2011): 125.
43 Wrapping up the final draft of this chapter, a similar discussion was found in Susan Laxton, "*Psicofotografía*: Grete Stern and the Administration of the Unconscious," *October* 172 (Spring 2020): 35–67.
44 Peter Osborne, "Temporalization as Transcendental Aesthetics," *Nordic Journal of Aesthetics* 44–45 (2012–13): 40. On the Independent Group, see a special issue edited by Hal Foster and Benjamin H. D. Buchloh, *October* 94 (Fall 2000).
45 Kenneth Frampton, "Kenneth Frampton with Carlos Brillembourg," *Brooklyn Rail* (December 7, 2010), 16.
46 On this, see Bryan E. Norwood, "Disorienting Phenomenology," *Log* (Winter/Spring 2018): 11–22. Most entries in this issue of the magazine present critical reflections on architectural phenomenology.
47 Banham, "The New Brutalism," 13.
48 Vidler, "Another Brick in the Wall," 110.
49 See M. Iversen, *Alois Riegl: Art History and Theory* (Cambridge: MIT Press, 2003); and Alberto Perez-Gomez, *Architecture and the Crisis of the Modern Science* (Cambridge: MIT Press, 1983).
50 Jorge Otero-Pailos, *Architecture's Historical Turn: Phenomenology and the Rise of the Postmodern* (Minneapolis: University of Minnesota Press, 2010).
51 D'Arcy Thompson, *On Growth and Form* (Cambridge: Cambridge University Press, 1961).
52 On the subject of brick and New Brutalism, see Vidler, "Another Brick in the Wall," 105–32.
53 Peter Osborne, *The Politics of Time: Modernity and Avant-Garde* (London: Verso, 1995), 192–93. Henri Lefebvre pioneered the "critique of everyday life" in the 1930s.
54 From the Smithsons' manifesto, first published in January 1955. Here taken from Reyner Banham, *The New Brutalism: Ethic or Aesthetic?* (London: Reinhold, 1966), 46.
55 Osborne, *The Politics of Time*, 192–93. We should also consider the "do it yourself" an offshoot of the same processes.
56 Mark Crinson, *Stirling and Gowan: Architecture from Austerity to Affluence* (New Haven, CT: Yale University Press, 2012), 48–49.
57 Kenneth Frampton, *Studies in Tectonic Culture* (Cambridge: MIT Press, 1996), 360.
58 Kenneth Frampton, "Transformations in Style: The Work of James Stirling," *A+U* 50 (1975): 135.
59 Amanda Reeser Lawrence, *James Stirling: Revisionary Modernist* (New Haven, CT: Yale University Press, 2012), 41.
60 On this subject, see Lauren Stalder, "'New Brutalism,' 'Topology,' and 'Image': Some Remarks on Architectural Debates in London around 1950," *Journal of Architecture* (June 2008): 263–81.
61 Frampton, *Labour, Work, and Architecture*, 262.

62 Frampton, *A Critical History*, 266.
63 Banham, *The New Brutalism*, 134.
64 The group comprised artists and architects such as Alison and Peter Smithson, Reyner Banham, Nigel Henderson and Richard Hamilton.
65 Frampton, *A Critical History*, 265.
66 Kenneth Frampton, "Andrew Melville Hall, St Andrew's University, Scotland," *Architectural Design* 9 (1970): 460–62.
67 Kenneth Frampton, "The Economist and the Hauptstadt," *Architectural Design* (February 1965): 61–62.
68 In a conversation with this author, Frampton expressed his preference for G. Grassi's discourse on *type* over Aldo Rossi's.
69 Kenneth Frampton, "Preface," in Frampton, *Labour, Work, and Architecture*, 7.
70 For a review of Kenneth Frampton's book, see Gevork Hartoonian, *Domus* (February 2017): 18–21.
71 Walter Benjamin, *Illuminations*, edited, with an introduction by Hannah Arendt (New York: Schocken, 1969), 1–58.
72 Frampton, *A Critical History*, 280.
73 See Walter Benjamin, *Reflections* (New York: Harvest/HBJ, 1978), 220–38.
74 Frampton, *A Critical History*, 282.
75 Harry Harootunian, *Uneven Moments: Reflections on Japan's Modern History* (New York: Columbia University Press, 2019), 179.
76 Frampton, *A Critical History*, 286.
77 Kenneth Frampton, "America 1960–1970," *Casabella* 359–60 (1971): 30.
78 See Diane Y. F. Ghirardo, *Aldo Rossi, and the Spirit of Architecture* (New Haven, CT: Yale University Press, 2019), 47.
79 See Pier Vittorio Aureli, *The Project of Autonomy: Politics and Architecture within and against Capitalism* (New York: Princeton Architectural Press, 2008).

Chapter 6

AALTO CONTRA MIES: A CONUNDRUM?

Overture

Following the genealogical investigation of architects mapped in the previous two chapters, and, more specifically, Mies van der Rohe's work, several questions related to the Finnish architect Alvar Aalto are raised in this chapter. For example, what is the genealogical index of his architecture? How does it amount to the "humanism" Kenneth Frampton has frequently attributed to Aalto? Furthermore, this also concerns the "humanism" that the organizers of the 2018 Venice Biennale associated with Frampton's vision of architecture.[1] Whether Aalto's take on Humanism intersects with Frampton's is a subject that will be addressed later in this chapter. However, what concerns us in the first place is the possibility of reconstructing Aalto's later work in analogy to Frampton's reconstruction of late Mies in terms of the "monumentalization of technique," and of Le Corbusier in terms of "monumentalization of vernacular," discussed in Chapter 5 of this volume. Still, if we can contextualize Mies's late work after he migrated to America and Le Corbusier's after failing to establish the linguistics of civic architecture in modernity, how should we contextualize Aalto's architecture? This inquiry will shed light on the problematic notion of "humanization," and the subject concerning Aalto's work as discussed in the following pages.[2]

The postwar situation opened a vista for rethinking and challenging many modernist assumptions formulated during the late 1920s. However, this general observation should be indexed regarding the particularities of Aalto's work. For one, he subscribed to the idea of the "organic" which was also dear to Frank L. Wright. This line of theorization was dismissed by those involved in the institutionalization of International Style architecture (*ca.* the 1930s). However, after the war, Bruno Zevi took the idea to a different level.[3] Aalto also gave ample attention to the notion of regionalism,[4] another vital theme for immediately postwar architecture in the aftermath of Le Corbusier's early villas and his work in India. Regarding Le Corbusier's "monumentalization of vernacular," it is helpful to differentiate the historicity of regionalism from that of vernacular. During the 1950s, emerging capitalism in America exported consumer and cultural goods and construction techniques, especially those instrumental for disseminating the modern language of architecture, to most countries then tagged as "Third World." Congenial to this development was the dissemination of industrialization in several European countries, although this remained marginal compared to earlier in England, Germany and France. This so-called unequal development within European nations, discussed in the next chapter, is central to Frampton's formulation of Critical Regionalism and Aalto's work, a late modernist forerunner. A third factor unique to Aalto's architecture is the eclecticism permeating his work, which differs from the postmodernist simulation of historical languages. This phenomenon relates to the suggested marginal position of Finland, particularly the delay in the country's total appropriation of the fruits of modernization. A detailed discussion of the outline so far demands a start with the genealogies of Aalto's work before attending to the architect's grasp of Humanism and the possibility of reformulating Frampton's assessment of Aalto in conjunction with Mies.

Aalto's perceptive analysis of a Karelian vernacular work (located in eastern Finland) might be a key to understanding what Frampton calls the "creative contact" between Mies and Aalto. His interest in vernacular included, among other things, the uniformity between material and a construction system, the tectonics of which derived from the "inner" open organizational structure revolving around a single modest cell. This observation recalls the authenticity of the vernacular buildings that Adolf Loos noted in his famous 1910 essay "Architecture." However, the uniformity Aalto pursued was different from typical vernacular work. Central to his later architecture are tactile sensibilities of telluric materials such as brick, marble and wood. Surprisingly enough, the Miesian architecture of steel and glass comes closest to the material uniformity implied in Aalto's comparison between a Karelian vernacular house and the ruins of Greek temples. The marginality of material diversity, stone in the former and steel and glass in the latter, stands out in Greek temples and Mies's later work.

On the other hand, Aalto pursued an organizational system comparable to an organism with the possibility of continuing growth. Like a Greek temple, Mies's later work centered on a geometric cell (a square), resisting any organic expansion except repeating the square-shaped plan in different sizes ranging from a house to a gallery and an office building. Arguably, through repetition of a particular syntax, Mies distanced his work from subjective expressionism and the dictates of the new tendencies that framed early modernism in architecture. And yet, if we follow the Sigfried Giedion of *Mechanization Takes Command* (1948), we should see in the Miesian repetition Giedion's own two-tier ramifications: first, that repetition of objects led to a "devaluation of symbols." In Hal Foster's words, "Craft became deskilled and ornament became rote." Second, by the early twentieth century, mechanization had "penetrated the subconscious." Accordingly, "the psyche came to be understood as a mechanism, even an automatism, in its own right."[5] Mies's planimetric organization devalues functional and symbolic attributes turning it into a constructed *cell* if you wish. Aalto, by contrast, drew from the biological analogy of growth, from a room to a heterotopic ordering of several rooms. Moreover, whereas the tectonic was for Mies's architectural through and through, the tectonic in Aalto's architecture is allegorical. His work reveals multiple meanings and a drive to modify the *meaning* attributed to the International Style architecture.[6] Herein lies the nucleus of Frampton's proposed possibility of a "creative contact" between the tectonics of Mies and the regionalism of Aalto. This subject is addressed later in these pages, specifically, in the next chapter where Frampton's Critical Regionalism is discussed.

Rhetoric!

Discussing the work of the architects known as the "third generation,"[7] Philip Drew claimed that "Aalto closed his attacks on the Miesian cube with the purposeful use of natural materials and uninhibited disposition of forms which enjoin the primitive darkness of the enclosing woods." Drew's statement opens a Pandora's box of Aaltoesque mystifications stemming from the early 1970s' misreading of Martin Heidegger and Existentialism. Frampton presents an alternative view of the same subject, highlighting Mies's significance for Jørn Utzon, a prominent member of the third generation of architects listed in Drew's book and influenced by Aalto. In a chapter discussing the tectonics of Utzon's architecture, Frampton enumerates three Miesian traces in the work of architects included in Drew's list. These are susceptibility to the intrinsic qualities of the material, a Miesian concern for "precision of detailing, combined with rational, modular assembly" and a Mies-like "application of standard rolled steel that demonstrated the productive logic Utzon would apply to the creation of three-dimensional, curved form." Frampton goes further, reiterating what Mies had told Utzon: that "once the design was established and finalized, he made every effort to ensure emphasized this in the design's secondary elements, such as doors, windows, non-load bearing walls and so on."[8] Implied in this statement is the uniformity Aalto tried to achieve, albeit in analogy to organic group-forms. In retrospect, it is not far-fetched to posit that the umbilical cord connecting these three architects is tectonic detailing.

To shed further light on the historicity of Aalto's architecture, we should turn to Frampton's reading of Aalto's discussion of "Architecture in Karelia," in the geopolitics of Finland, a country twice colonized, once by Sweden and then by Russia. This historical background was a significant reason for the *delay* in disseminating various tendencies of modern movement architecture in Finland, a country where, until the mid-1920s, civic buildings were dressed up with the garments of Romantic Classicism and National Romanticism. Frampton provides a detailed and dense account of these two mid-nineteenth-century architectural tendencies in Nordic countries. Nevertheless, he suggests that Aalto's work stopped short of alluding to the architectonics of either language explicitly. According to Frampton, a detailed examination of the origins and aims of National Romanticism would lead us to an in-depth understanding of Aalto's architecture.[9] He also mentions the tactility evident in the architectonics of National Romanticism and the "astringencies of the Doricist form," the elements of which were neither classical nor vernacular. In retrospect, Aalto's domestic work was imbued with the lyricism of diverse materials and tectonics. In contrast, his large-scale and civic work borrowed from the two styles mentioned above. For instance, in the Agricultural Cooperative building Turku (1928), the architect blends Neo-Classicism with the building's unadorned and punctuated white cladding, an aesthetic valorization much in the spirit of Loos.

There is no single reference to Frampton's published essays on Aalto in the "Selected Bibliography" of Chapter 22 of *A Critical History*, 1980. It is reasonable to assume that Frampton's preliminary reflections on Aalto benefited from his review of Paul David Pearson's book *Aalto and the International Style* (1978). Frampton's review was published in *Oppositions* (1997),[10] a journal for which he was one of the three founding editors[11] and the most productive.[12] In any event, Frampton's review of Pearson's book is vital for several reasons: it acknowledges Pearson's in-depth knowledge of Aalto and that Pearson had read most of the literature written on Aalto's architecture. Considering Frampton's later writings on the subject, and his part-time editorial tenure at *Architectural Design* (*AD*) magazine (London), what draws attention is the inclusion of a section drawing of Aalto's Town Hall, Saynatsalo (1952) (Figure 6.1) on the first page of the text. He postponed the building's discussion to page 6, the last page of a short review text illustrated with 18 figures! This technical and ideological curatorship demonstrates the significance Frampton gives to drawings and photographic images for a successful analytical review of a building. It also hints at Frampton's later writings on Aalto's work, taken up in this chapter. For now, we should underline the theme of the concluding paragraph of Frampton's review text: praising Pearson's pioneering work on Aalto. Frampton nevertheless expresses regret that the author had not provided a vantage point "from which to assess Aalto's overall achievement."[13] The required Archimedean position, a prerequisite for *historical criticism* of architecture, can indeed be

Figure 6.1 Alvar Aalto, Saynatsalo Town Hall, Saynatsalo, 1949–52. Photograph courtesy of Andrew Metcalf.

traced in almost every chapter of Frampton's book, with varying degrees of success.

In addition to the previously mentioned concept of delay, Frampton's background reconstruction of Aalto's architecture within the Nordic region suggests that, before the realization of his late career, the Finnish architect was exposed to a host of eclectic languages, including Romanesque syntaxes of the kind prevalent in H. H. Richardson's work. More often than not, Frampton's preliminary remarks focus on the specificity of Finland, both historically and regionally. He associates the presence of Richardsonian elements with the abundance of local granite. In contrast, he contextualizes the neo-classical elements evident in the Finnish Parliament House, Helsinki (1931), in the broader scope of European architectural traditions. Opinion varies, however, as to whether Aalto's choice of this or that element from the palette of past linguistic syntaxes was an attempt to formulate a national-regional style architecture or an exercise to consolidate his take on modern architecture. Most of the recent writings on Aalto highlight both directions. Eeva-Liisa Pelkonen writes, "The idea of international influence developed in the late 1920s, specifically through an interest in international modernism as Aalto became more and more aware that Finland needed to establish reciprocal relationships with other countries." For Pelkonen, the transformation taking place in Aalto's postwar work, such as "universalist and humanist," was in tandem with the country's strategic politics designed to avoid geopolitical conflicts.[14]

Before attending to Frampton's discussion of Aalto's work, and the numerous essays published after the first edition of *A Critical History*, it is useful to turn the focus of the argument once again to the origins and various interpretations of the historicity of Aalto's architecture. To this end, we should consult with two major historiographies, the publication of which preceded Frampton's book, and a third study published in 1982. This detour is necessary because Aalto's architecture occupies a significant place in Frampton's critical discourse. In his most recent (at the time of writing these lines) interview with Cynthia Davidson, Frampton reiterated what he considers to be "humanistic" in Aalto's architecture:

> I recently thought that if there is one architect whose work could be developed by society in the future, with a level of complexity and the way the architecture is thought about vis-à-vis societal need and desire, it is Aalto. His legacy still has that powerful dimension to it.[15]

In an earlier interview with Pelkonen, Frampton highlights the complexity of Aalto's architecture, mainly how his "inner sense" of form and rhythm comes across in handling the "space of arrival, the moment of transition before you enter the building."[16] This turn to other historians' discussions of Aalto intends to unlock the "complexity" Frampton attributes to Aalto, which, interestingly enough, founded a postmodernist vocation in Robert Venturi's *Complexity and Contradiction in Architecture* (1966). Comparing Aalto's notion of "valid order" to Le Corbusier's architecture, Venturi wrote that "Aalto, in contrast to Le Corbusier, seems almost to create the order out of the inconsistencies, as can be seen in the Cultural Center at Wolfsburg." He goes further suggesting that "although Aalto's order is hard to grasp easily at first glance, it involves similar relationships of order and the circumstances."[17] Venturi used the complexity detected in Aalto's work to frame a particular interpretation of architecture's rapport with the given circumstances. Frampton's reading instead unpacks the complexities involved in reapproaching the culture of the building within the prevailing technical and cultural apparatuses of late capitalism. There is a sense of autonomy involved in Venturi's discourse that Frampton deconstructs Critical Regionalism, in which Aalto plays a vital role.

A precedent to Frampton's attribution of Humanism to Aalto is implied in Sigfried Giedion's historiography. Introducing a section on Aalto in the third edition of *Space, Time, and Architecture* (1954), Giedion associated the origins of Aalto's architecture with the characteristics of the Finnish landscape, the horizontality of the country's coastal lines and the verticality of its dense forests in particular.[18] To consolidate this notion, Giedion presented the idea of the organic advocated by both Wright and Aalto as a third way to cleanse the architecture of classical elements. The other two ways, Giedion continues, are (1) to bring forth the bare steel and concrete skeleton (Mies?), and (2) to do away with the pseudo-individualism inherited from the old regime. According to Giedion, the proposed third way was part of a more significant movement that unfolded toward "the middle of the twentieth century," when Western culture was entering decentralization processes. Many countries once considered "fringe," such as Finland, energized modern movement architecture in new ways. Aalto's work, Giedion writes, is regional but also imbued with the spirit of the age. In this regard, his work is similar to the Brazilian architects who contributed to "a universal conception of architecture."[19] Still, in "The Human Side," Giedion likens the regionalism of Aalto's architecture to the architect's personality, writing that Aalto had empathy for human beings to the point that "he approached people directly and without inhibitions, in the same way, that he approaches the organic material wood."[20] Should this statement be taken in analogy to Giedion's choice of title for the newly added section on Aalto, which reads, "Alvar Aalto: Irrationality and Standardization," under which Giedion tries to map the complexity involved in the architect's work? Or was it his intention to elaborate on organic regionalism, the union between life and architecture? The differences between Giedion's and Frampton's discourses on regionalism are discussed in the next chapter. In any event, Giedion provided a detailed account of Aalto's Humanism while discussing the architect's most praised work, Tuberculosis Sanatorium, Paimo (1929). We read that to humanize architecture, Aalto separated the balconies from patient rooms, putting the rest area above the patient wing. According to Giedion, this design strategy, discussed in his text under the rubric of humanizing architecture, provides patients with the opportunity to look into "the tops of the nearby fir trees and see the forest beyond them."[21] Interestingly enough, Giedion considered this project the third most crucial institutional work linked to the rise of modern architecture. The other two mentioned projects are the Bauhaus School building (1926), designed by Walter Gropius, and the League of Nations Palace (1927), designed by Le Corbusier and Hannes Meyer.[22] Giedion's observation underlines the differences between his and Frampton's historiography and suggests that Aalto's Humanism offered Frampton a concept for sharpening his critical discourse. Disregarding all evident confusions, Giedion saw in Aalto's work a promise for "unity, a secret synthesis, in our present," the unearthing of which he considered to be a significant purpose for his vision of modern movement architecture.

To examine a different theorization of Aalto's early architecture, we should turn to Manfredo Tafuri. In his co-authored book with Francesco Dal Co, they dedicated no chapter or section to the work of the Finnish architect. Instead, they discussed Aalto in connection with Hugo Haring's understanding of organicism that Frampton employs in his later essays on Aalto. However, the confrontation between a quest for temporal significances and psychological intimacies became "the central aspect of Aalto's work," the two Italian historians argued.[23] Held up against the "cruelty of the Avant-Garde," their reading introduced a concept of periodization that is closer to Frampton's. Of further interest is the distinction Tafuri makes between the pre- and postwar architecture of Aalto. This much is evident from Tafuri's totalization of the linguistic sources of most architects of the 1930s, Aalto included. In *Theories and History of Architecture* (1980), the Italian edition published in 1968, he mentions Aalto three times, none connected with the architect's work. Drawing from Walter Benjamin's discourse on the loss of aura, Tafuri expands on the historical consequences of the symbolic loss of art and architecture. He then underlines the concept of a structural *crisis* relevant to the mechanical reproducibility of the object, a deterministic consequence for artwork in circumstances when the reproductive process inflects the meaning and reception of the object. Giving special attention to the regime of mass media that was enforced at the dawn of the 1930s, Tafuri concludes:

> The organicism of Haring and of what we can call the Berlin school (from Taut to Erwin Gutkind), the entire work by Le Corbusier from 1919–1938, Asplund after the Stockholm Library and Pre-war Aalto, all worked on a complex and multi-valent structuration of architectural images, with the many possible planes of reading and use in mind.[24]

The architects excluded from the above quotation are presumably those whose work did not require "concentration," to be comprehended in rapt attention, to rephrase Walter Benjamin. Interestingly enough, and in place of emphasizing the significance of Benjamin's theorization of historiography, Tafuri and Frampton both highlight the late work of Mies and Le Corbusier, though for two different reasons. For Tafuri, the late architecture of Mies and Le Corbusier demands the spectator's attention, first because of the reduction of the *image* to pure and repetitive constructive elements, and second because the work presented "itself as permanent *Total Theatre*."[25] Seemingly, this observation aligns with Giedion's proposed two strategies for cleansing the symbolic orders, a remnant of the auratic state of art and architecture. It all goes well with Frampton's characterization of Mies and Le Corbusier's late work, the monumentalization of technique and vernacular, respectively. If these associations do have merit, are these three historians not then mapping, among other things, the state of postwar architecture, the end of modernity and the rise of the postmodernist indulgence in a pseudo-communicative dimension of architecture that leaves the spectator with the illusion of having comprehended the work as such? And, if this is the case, is Frampton not then correct in considering Aalto's mature work unique compared to the postwar architects associated with the neo-avant-garde and postmodern linguistic tendencies?

One year after the publication of Frampton's book, Demetri Porphyrios edited *Architectural Design*, entitled *On the Methodology of Architectural History* (1981). Several historians, including Frampton and Tafuri, were invited to reflect on a relevant historical text of their choice. The aim was, Porphyrios wrote, "to raise the level of consciousness of the epistemological foundation of the various architectural histories."[26] Titled "Notes on a Method," his entry championed a structuralist approach to the historical understanding of architecture drawing on Michel Foucault's notion of discursive formation, *episteme*. Porphyrios's argument was convincing as it concerned formulating a critical response against the prevailing linguistic theories of the late 1970s. A year after the *AD*'s publication, Porphyrios published his PhD dissertation (Princeton University) under the title *Sources of Modern Eclecticism*,[27] promoting a genealogical analysis of Aalto's architecture. His methodology centered on the notion of *difference*, based on which he highlighted the specificity of Aalto's architecture despite the predominant generalities and uniform interpretations of modern architecture. He wrote, "The similarity between Aalto and Modernism is much less than has been supposed; or rather if it exists, it lies in areas where it was not thought to lie."[28] Page after page, Porphyrios examines the "sensuously loaded materiality" of this or that architectonic element in Aalto's work. Was his intention in part to recount Aalto's historical knowledge of the communicative dimension of architecture, including vernacular and other architectural formations discussed along with the nineteenth-century debates on style? Be that as it may, the reader is left with no specific clues as to whether the sensuously charged architectonics were expected or intended to be registered by the spectator as part of the shared ethos of Humanism, the common implied in the word "culture," which, according to Aalto, refers to "the balanced mentality which emerges from […] straightforward everyday life."[29] Seemingly, the strategies Aalto pursued in delivering such a sense of commonness were centered on the conviction that "the passage from representation to signification had to be harnessed and kept within the realm of a continuity of discourse established by history."[30] Without going further into a detailed examination of the examples Porphyrios provides, it is not far-fetched to say that "humanism" for Aalto meant, on the one hand, historically charged architectural elements, including the material and compositional rules that had governed architecture before its turn to modernity. On the other hand, it alluded to Aalto's unconscious attempt to establish elective associations between nature, craft and technique, a higher state of uniformity evident in vernacular buildings.

The intention here was to cite summary reviews to underline the commonality in the mentioned authors' assessments of Aalto and their thematics and Frampton's reading of the same subject. However, the most frequently discussed issues were the centrality of Humanism, regionalism and organicism for Aalto's theorization of architecture; the general account of the historicity of Nordic countries; and the significance of the work of three architects, Le Corbusier, Mies and Aalto, for the state of Western architecture in the decade following the war. In highlighting these commonalities, the idea was to avoid plotting Aalto according to regional and national issues. It is vital to contextualize Aalto in the broader situation of what, in retrospect, was the beginning of the end of the project of Modernity. This strategic revisionism provides a different understanding of Frampton's interpretation of Aalto's work, particularly if reviewed next to the late work of Le Corbusier and Mies. It will also allow us to historicize Frampton's critical discourse beyond the limited scope of the available, rather too close, reading of his valuable essays on Aalto, significant aspects of which are examined below.

Humanism Humanized!

Admittedly, architecture comprises cultural artifacts intimately engaged with users' daily experience, especially when it comes to building types and interior spaces organized accordingly. These assumptions are somewhat consistent with the stance of Adolf Loos, for whom the task of architecture was to raise particular feelings in the populace using telluric materials with tactile qualities deposited in the generational memory of a region. If we do not read Loos's words dogmatically, there is no reason why non-telluric materials would not be experienced the same way, given due time. Accordingly, to humanize architecture means to conceive and build architecture not as an *object* but as a purposeful, durable and sustainable cultural artifact. It also means to produce architecture without an eye on the discipline of Humanism, which has had a long-lasting influence on Western architecture. However, modern architecture did try to humanize architecture and the machine under the auspices of the project of Modernity. We can think of Le Corbusier's association between a Delage sports car and the Parthenon in *Towards a New Architecture* (1923). Modern architecture partially succeeded in modifying traditional sensibilities while investing in materials and techniques that necessarily had to break with the traditions of building culture. However, it failed to deliver on its clear, complete mission, "the integration of art and life," when the project hit the hard wall of ideology operative internally and externally. At the time, there was an ongoing confrontation between the disciplinary history of architecture and what Louis Althusser eloquently coined the state apparatus; its many sociopolitical and economic manifestations had (and still have) a massive impact on architecture.

In contrast to most of his modernist colleagues, Aalto attempted to humanize architecture in more ways than one. Porphyrios has elaborated on this dimension of the Finnish architect's work, as noted earlier. Aalto skillfully studied the palette of available materials according to their tactile sensibilities and tectonic suitability. He set out to conceive diverse building types, from residential to civic to factory buildings.[31] However, in Frampton's account, Aalto turned to the humanization of architecture after walking away from his constructivist period evident in the Turun-Sanomat Newspaper Building (1928). Frampton associates the unadorned street elevation of this building, with window openings flush with its white surface cladding and a sizeable street-level display window (agitprop!), with the A. Vesnin's Pravda Building (1923).[32] This association also says something about the disjunctive geometrical composition of the Paimo Sanatorium (1929). Constructivist trademarks are also evident in the two-part elementary composition of Paimo, with the floor-to-ceiling glass entry door positioned next to a glass wall similar to that which separates the glazed main stairway of the final version of the Viipuri Library, Turku (1935). If Johannes Duiker, the Dutch Constructivist architect, energized Aalto's constructivist phase, his preference for timber over concrete was formed after meeting a patron who ran the Finnish timber industry (*ca.* 1929).

Starting with the stripes of the undulating redwood ceiling of the hall of Viipuri Library, Frampton detects a further valorization of Humanism as Aalto began separating the conceptual scheme "into two distinct elements and the space in between is articulated as the space of human appearance," a reminder of Hannah Arendt. Examining the planimetric organization, "the space in between" separates the two volumes of the same building, accommodating the main circulatory vein. Aalto's design strategy is essential compared to Le Corbusier's obsession with circulation, which is evident in every project, and disregards scale to the point that each plan component is seemingly dictated

Figure 6.2 Alvar Aalto, Muuratsalo Experimental House, Jyvaskayla, Finland, 1952–54. Photograph courtesy of the author.

by the space allocated to circulation. This is in contrast to the planimetric organization of the late Mies, where the geometric cell of the plan is the actual space of human interaction. The frozen space in Mies's architecture, neither a circulatory vein nor a comforting ambiance, provides a *room* for the contemplation of the impossible: humanity's solitude in modern times. Nihilism had no room in Aalto's architectonic vocabulary! In addition to the Finnish Pavilion designed for the World Exhibition, Paris (1937), there is a similar work where Aalto tried to "create an intimate relationship between Man and Architecture."[33] Frampton's list includes Saynatsalo Town Hall (1952) and the Muuratsalo Experimental House (1952) (Figure 6.2). As for the first building, the human experience prevails as the visitor passes the entrance to the council chamber, encountering a sequence of material tactilities.[34] This phenomenological dimension of Aaltoesque tectonics demands further investigation into the nature of the additional design elements, the excess, that Aalto employed to humanize architectural space, otherwise a constructed form.

Interestingly enough, and relating to Aalto's interest in two-part composition, is the L-shaped configuration of the Villa Mairea (1939), a work that allegorically (excess?) "represents a conceptual link between the rational-constructivist tradition of the 20th century and the evocative heritage of the National Romantic movement."[35] Frampton's detailed analysis of this house aims to highlight the notion of Humanism, presenting it as a mosaic of whatever might relate Aalto to the Finnish landscape: the lakes, the forests and the materiality of wood and brick, primarily associated with the dormant vernacular experience, and the Finnish culture of the building at large. Frampton indexes Aalto's strategies to humanize his work beyond materiality. He includes "modification of the site," attention to "the intrinsic nature of the site" and, most importantly, the Finnish architect's conscious modification of the ethos of Functionalism to create a friendly ambience in response to both the physical and psychological needs of occupants.[36] Frampton's observation suggests that "complexity" in Aalto's architecture is centered on the concept of modification, a strategic move to conceive of architecture beyond a single deterministic reference point. And, in consideration of the prevailing technological determinism during the early formation of Modern Movement architecture, Aalto sought to revisit this tendency. He wrote, "Nature is the most remarkable standardization institute of all [...] Every blossom is made of innumerable, apparently uniform proto-cells, but these cells have a quality that permits the most extraordinary variety in the linkage of cells."[37] This was a plea to rethink the mechanical understanding of social and architectural issues in the light of biological models, hinting at another dimension of Aalto's take on humanizing architecture.

There are other layers in Aalto's drive to "humanize architecture," not reducing a simplistic interpretation of the "organic" attributed to his work. Aalto's Muuratsalo Experimental House (1952) is exemplary in many ways. For example, the architect's valorization of the tactility of the brickwork covering the walls and floor of the courtyard next to the fireplace offers a perfect atmosphere for "human appearance," relatively public space of gathering. However, if the fireplace can be associated with the "heart" in Gottfried Semper's theorization of architecture, patches of brickwork soldiered in different directions on the same exterior face of the entry wall recall Semper's notion of material animation, the transformation of material to materiality. As such, the same wall looks like a quilt made of different patches, turning its cladding into *fabrication* in its literal sense. This surface articulation was not the only instance where Aalto used brick disregarding its load-bearing and material *nature*. Discussing the brick mullions in the Helsinki House of Culture (1952–58), Pelkonen writes that this decontextualization "stretches the limits of the material, not set into a priori ideas about what is an appropriate formal language for brick." She continues, "Architecture is here made to transcend actual conditions and contingencies, and it is exactly the ambiguity of meaning so created that reflects Finland's political goals; to transcend Russia's political influence and become, at least in people's imagination, a politically ambiguous neutral zone with no ideological influence."[38] Similarly, Aalto claimed that "architecture is about turning a worthless brick to gold,"[39] a statement that recalls Mies, who made an art form out of cuts of steel products in the columns of the Barcelona Pavilion. These observations underline the usefulness of introducing Semper essential for Frampton's juxtaposition of the architecture of Utzon and Mies with Aalto, as noted earlier.

Akos Moravanszky establishes a direct connection between Aalto and Semper. In addition to Van de Velde's notion of the "animation of material," Semper's writings also influenced Aalto.[40] The idea of animating material is suggested in Semper's notion of *Stoffwechsel*,[41] meaning the modification needed to transform figural experiments produced in one material industry to another, particularly from textiles to architecture. Interestingly enough, in a 1952 text, Aalto emphasized Van de Velde's contribution "to architecture's becoming a creative factor in shaping our modern forms of society." He presented Van de Velde as the precursor to transforming the ornamental form into "an organic impulse which continues to stir us like some embryonic motif."[42] This understanding of ornament is Semperian if interpreted along with the German architect's formulation of tectonics, wherein the ornament is neither an additive nor directly derived from the construction process.[43] Reading Aalto's architecture in the light of Semper's *Stoffwechsel* allows us to see the folding profile of the hall's ceiling in the Viipuri Library in analogy to hanging fabric, rather than as being merely about organic forms. The concept of modification noted by Frampton does indeed play a central role in Aalto's creative design process. According to Pelkonen, it involves historical transformations: a classical column, she writes, "contains a memory of its wooden tectonic origins, while evolving through time." In Aalto's words, "The transformation depends on the investment of 'human qualities which can be interpreted as the ability to turn a purely material condition into a cultural symbol."[44] Apropos, "humanization," for Aalto, was a design strategy to overcome all kinds of fixations on a reductionist understanding of architecture, be it technical, functional or organic. Aalto tried to expand the agency of architecture to include modified genres of a wide range of aspects of the culture of the building, the scope of which in his later work is not limited to those canonized in Finnish architectural history.

Aalto's Experimental House is essential for another reason: it was built when he had the "expressive problems" that continued until 1949, when the mature phase of his work began blossoming. Like the Villa Mairea, both the Experimental House and Saynatsalo Town Hall (1952) were designed according to a conceptual scheme dividing the building's mass into two halves, an L-shape in Villa Mairea and a U-shape in the other two designs. The genealogy of this *parti*, which is identified in Aalto's National Pensions Institute (1956), derived from the architect's study of "the traditional Karelian farm and village complexes that he had first written about in 1941."⁴⁵ What stands out in these projects is creating a public forum, a constructivist social condenser, the purpose of which varied depending on the scale of the project, from a sauna and pool in Villa Mairea, to a courtyard in the other two projects. In Saynatsalo Town Hall, the courtyard is a Semperian earthwork, accommodating the spatial needs allocated in the lower level. It also creates a plateau, a terrace for public engagement in a setting surrounded chiefly by trees. Aalto highlights this aspect of the design further through the positioning of the two stairs by which the spectator reaches the courtyard, and the double-height courtroom adjacent to the arrival corner, another reminder of the civic character of the complex. Still, to "humanize" the courtyard and to further highlight the civic look of the complex, the slanting roofs are directed toward the courtyard, creating a distinctive experience of the space surrounded by the building's U-shaped volume and leaving the exterior walls to the eyes of the absent public. Here the architectonic elements lending Frampton to praise this complex are at work in Mies's National Gallery though emulated from a cosmopolitan perspective.

The human factor and the treatment of the site, transforming the ground into a terrace, captivated Frampton. Reminding his reader of Mario Botta's slogan "building the site," Frampton writes, "All of Aalto's sites were built in this topographical sense, and his achievements as an architect cannot be separated at any stage of his career from his capacity as a designer of the landscape."⁴⁶ This statement demands recalling the section drawing of the Town Hall that Frampton used for the first page of his review of Pearson's book, discussed earlier. The section cuts through the courtroom, a small square-shaped room approached and at the same time separated from the main corridor by ascending brick stairs, the materiality of which resonates in the cladding of the interior walls of the courtroom. Without discussing the many complexities involved in its realization, the chosen section does indeed speak to Frampton's interest in materiality, tectonics and natural light. Of these, he wrote, "the high mono-pitched roof (comparable to the studio in the Villa Mairea) announces the honorific status of the council chamber, a differentiation that is reinforced by the introduction of a boarded timber floor in the chamber itself and by exposed elaborate timber trusses supporting the roof above." The comparison with Villa Mairea leads us to see a bigger picture of Aalto's career. In the same review article, Frampton wrote, "The line of development that links his Munkkiniemi house of 1936 to his MIT dormitory of 1947 marks the progressive evolution of Aalto's updated National Romantic manner and leads eventually to its resolution in Saynatsalo." He praised this relatively small-scale project because it "breaks with the collages and textured structuralism of the Villa Mairea and the national pavilions for Paris and

New York." He continues, "As with Sunila pulp mill and the MIT dormitory, the power and rhythm of its form stem from the sculptural impact of its brick profile and the fact that it is largely executed in a single material, brick."[47] This appraisal is taken up again in what has become Frampton's signature text today, "Towards a Critical Regionalism,"[48] which will be examined in the next chapter. However, it is crucial to stay focused on Frampton's reflections on Aalto for the present discussion. Again, the starting point should be the image accompanying the text subtitled "The Visual versus the Tactile." The photographic image, also used in the book's chapter on Aalto, shows the main entry stairs leading to the Town Hall's courtyard. The image is framed by the adjacent volumes next to the stair, on the one hand, and the soaring volume of the council chamber in front, on the other. In rapt attention, the composition highlights the "visual." Upon entering the courtyard, this visual effect is compromised by the excessive tactile presence of brick. It not only covers the walls but, in analogy to the vernacular, is also used for the treads and the risers of both the external entry stairs and those leading to the council chamber. To modify the image under consideration, pretending as if a spectator observed in a still position. Frampton uses cinematic analogy, supported by his self-reflective experience of the circulatory system leading to the chamber council, the interior of which remains invisible. I want to continue this discussion and claim that the implied filmic experience disposes of Frampton's simultaneous interest in the work of Russian Constructivism and the idea of humanizing architecture, to recall the title of Aalto's text, initially published in 1940.[49] This rather aporetic narrative provides a clue to the abyss of Frampton's critical historiography and to how Aalto's multifarious strategies of humanizing architecture are considered a plausible alternative to the Miesian "almost nothing."

To support the filmic analogy here, the cropped entry image of the Town Hall should be juxtaposed next to the image of the Parthenon that Sergei Eisenstein used to support the proposition that filmic montage had its roots in architectural techniques dating back to the realization of the Acropolis and detectable in Christian (Catholic) cathedrals.[50] A vertical volume highlights the visual in both images, which is transformed as the spectator moves through the field. Eisenstein assesses how the moving spectator's scope of visual field changes while passing each, in a way that is similar to Frampton's experience of Aalto's Town Hall. Likewise, and again following in Frampton's footsteps, the dominant visual experience of the chamber of the council is modified by the tactile experience of the walls hugging the courtyard of the Town Hall. The intention here is to differentiate Frampton's uncompromising criticism of the technologies used to accelerate the process of global modernization (read global capitalism) from the "critical" he associates with the tactile and the tectonic-joint that, interestingly enough, was in the first place attributed to photographic and montage techniques used by some circles of Russian Constructivists.[51] Should we claim that Mies and Aalto represent the two plausible significant *readings* of Russian Constructivist traditions as the other modern movement architecture institutionalized in Europe and America?

Addendum

As for Frampton's interest in the work of Russian Constructivism, an essay published in 1976,[52] in which he reflects on a body of work generally associated with "constructivism," comes to mind. In Anthony Vidler's introductory remarks to the essay, he tries to explain his intentions in publishing Frampton's text, originally presented at the Guggenheim Museum, New York City, in December 1972. In retrospect, the essay reads like a palimpsest for a chapter of *A Critical History* titled "The New Collectivity: Art and Architecture in the Soviet Union 1918–1932."[53] Frampton's essay outlines and discusses Constructivism's various tendencies for an English-speaking audience, especially the young architects of the late 1960s who had to adjust their practice according to the emerging American mass culture. The essay is also relevant to our foregoing discussion and the proposed Mies contra Aalto paradigm. For several reasons, including Aalto's short-term interest in Constructivism and the role he played in establishing the avant-garde "Projecto" film club in Helsinki (1931), harnessed by the authorities[54]; and Frampton's interest in the architectonic appropriation of techniques of photomontage and filmic montage, the basic precepts of Productivism. As for Dziga Vertov in film, we read that montage "was to be as much the imperative of constructive creation as it was for Aleksandr Rodchenko in his graphics and Konstantin Melnikov in his architecture," in particular the Melnikov's early timber constructions. Still, in his British tenure as a practicing architect and the technical editor of *AD*, Frampton was exposed to the work and aspirations of Russian Constructivism not only as part of the lesser-known history of modern movement architecture but, more importantly, through the work of Berthold Lubetkin, a Soviet émigré who studied architecture at Vkhutems. In addition to his practice, *Tecton*, Lubetkin published an essay on Russian Constructivism in the May 1956 issue of *Architectural Association Journal (AAJ)*.[55] Lubetkin's critical position in this piece was in sharp contrast to his approving tone in another essay written in 1932, "about Soviet utopian planning." Lubetkin had argued that "urban quarters are simply the obsolete survivals of capitalist principles of planning."[56] Frampton borrows an excerpt from Lubetkin's 1956 essay for the epigraph to the previously mentioned chapter of his book and the concluding remarks of the essay published in *Oppositions*. The critical tone of Lubetkin, placed alongside the negative quotation from Le Corbusier that crowns the opening of Frampton's essay, begs the question: What is the significance of this essay's two negative moments for Frampton's oeuvre generally? His reservations about formalism, constructivist or otherwise, are well-known and need no emphasis here. We should instead give attention to the untold story of what the future held in store for not only Frampton but also Rem Koolhass and Bernard Tschumi, three unlikely amigos who were facing the 1970s enthusiasm for colorful historical returns. They turned instead to exploring the experience of Russian Constructivism, each toward a different end. This turn of events has been significant for each of these three architects, and more so for Frampton's interest in the political agency of architecture and public space, which yields to the central agency of his critical positions after reading Hannah Arendt's *The Human Condition* in 1965, and after the publication of his text on Arendt's book in 1979.[57]

To formulate an answer to the question raised earlier, what we should note in the first place is the prefix critical in Frampton's reformulation of regionalism and historiography of modern movement architecture: the fact that at the time of the publication of the first edition of *A Critical History* (1980), he had not yet attended to regionalism in critical terms. Thus, it is vital to briefly examine the genealogy of "critical,"[58] which will help to explain why Frampton has given particular attention to Aalto's work. Obviously, and similar to the rest of his generation of architects and critics, Frampton was aware of the revisionism launched by Team X and other groups, targeting the deterministic ethos of modern architecture. Their theories and practices aimed at retooling architecture through concepts and ideas borrowed from Humanism and/or advanced by existentialism and phenomenology. On the other hand, Frampton was also familiar to a certain extent with postwar Marxism and Frankfurt School critical theory. As mentioned before, Arendt was a primary referent for Frampton's criticism of architecture, especially after he published a reading of her work in 1979.[59] However, in the book's first edition, there are no references to critical thinkers, phenomenologists or Marxists, even Arendt, except Walter Benjamin's three essays cited in previous chapters. Concerning Frampton's essay and other writings on the subject, what stands out in the Productivist project was how architecture, among other progressive arts, was theorized and conceived of as a "comrade," propagating and sustaining the revolutionary milieu unique to the Soviets of the 1920s. Despite criticism launched against the movement's total rejection of the past, and their scant regard for the country's weak building industry,[60] this *rejection*, elusive as it may have been for Productivism, arose out of a desire not to search for the *new* but to open a space for rethinking the collective anew and beyond both classical and bourgeois reappropriations of Humanism. Here, the aim is to establish the claim that both the Revolution and the work produced by Russian Constructivism are inevitably part of the unconscious of our very modernity, and this is in contradistinction to Manfredo Tafuri, who presented Piranesi's work as the "crime scene" of the avant-garde.[61] Following the orthodoxies of a Marxian agenda, Tafuri's enormous contribution remains in the vicissitudes of deconstructing the Classical traditions of European architecture. In contrast, an alignment between revolution, collectivity and architecture is what the "critical" evokes in Frampton's theorization of the history of modern architecture. As pedantic as this might sound, it is one of the reasons why he has occasionally been at pains to convince his audience that his vision of history is critical. To put this in Benjaminian terms, it is aspects of the rubble of the unconscious of modernity that Frampton has tried to save in his best critical moments. This does not mean that Frampton was not sympathetic to the architects and buildings discussed in each chapter of his book. Moreover, Frampton's work demonstrates a vision of totality in historiography that could not but remain *invisible*. Its protagonists attain visibility in the two figures of Aalto and Mies. In different ways, each contributed to forming the concept of the critical permeating Frampton's historiography of modern architecture.

Another critical point to note, related to the first, is that Frampton appropriated modified versions of three major conceptual frameworks of Productivism to launch his critical theorization of the past and present contemporary architecture. Of these, mention should be made of Productivists' tendency toward (1) faktura, the "organic" transformation of material to materiality in rapport with its intrinsic nature; (2) tecktonica, the exploitation of industrial techniques; and, finally, (3) fabrication, the art of construction, and this in distinction to both modernist and traditionalist understandings of composition. In addition to Frampton's long-standing aspiration for tectonics, what we should recognize in Frampton's examination of materiality in Aalto's handling of wood, brick and other telluric materials is Vladimir Tatlin's appropriation of materiality and detailing in its most primitive possible sense. Intellectual prejudice aside, the probable analogy here goes well with Aalto's insistence that "to examine how human beings react to forms and constructions," rationalization should be expanded to physical, perceptual and psychological domains.[62] On the other hand, Tatlin's percept of steel and glass, and his impulse "to reduce and purify both language and form," but more importantly, his transformation of ordinary materials to "three-dimensional intellectual abstractions," evident in the artist's corner relief constructions, can be detected in Mies's architecture of steel and glass. There are conflicting primitive impulses in both Mies and Aalto. Mies's tectonics was to disband formal excess attributed to an architect's subjective choices. Similar to the work of Dadaists, the display of constructiveness in Mies's tectonics was a rebellion against organic architecture and the classical notion of composition. The classical idea that, after its completion, nothing could be added or taken away from work comes to mind. Still, a sense of primitiveness and how things are put together (*assemblage*) prevails in Mies's tectonics and photomontage work, wherein a "dialectal montage of real facts" rather than a "subjective combination of invented facts" prevails.[63] Aalto, by contrast, imbricated architectonic elements, not necessarily toward any interpretative tectonics but to be both modern and traditional in elusive ways. This dimension of his praxis welcomes diverse readings, from comparison to Porphyrios's structuralism to Venturi's postmodernism, too, in between, a host of ahistorical and anti-modern returns to the ethos of the Arts and Crafts movement. In this vista, Frampton has tried his best to present an Aalto who embraces landscape and "placemaking" among other ethos that could be part of a broader Aaltoesque drive toward humanizing architecture.

Now, where do these observations leave us with the Mies contra Aalto, a conundrum? From a historian's viewpoint, a plausible response to this query should start from the present state of architecture. In various editions of *A Critical History*, and since the book's first edition in 1980, Frampton has tried to address the contemporaneity of architecture without revising the content and positions expressed in each chapter since their original print. The book's later editions attempt to expand the scope of architects' work examined in "Part III" of the book's first edition, with criticism drawing, especially after 1983, from Hannah Arendt and Frampton's text, "Towards a Critical Regionalism: Six Points for an Architecture of Resistance." This unfolding had enough substance that, during his tenure as chairman of the Architecture Division at Columbia University (1986–87), five similar points, in addition to "type" and "tectonic form," were introduced into the school's pedagogical vision.[64] These last two tropes are also central to any critical assessment of the two courses of future action that Frampton outlines in the introduction to the book's first edition and have remained intact even in the latest available edition of the book. The difference between Mies's and Aalto's take on the type/tectonic, however, comes down to two main approaches to tectonics: the frame and infill system, and that which takes the form of masonry enclosure; one modern and the other premodern in essence, as it concerns the culture of the building.

Frampton presents these two alternatives in the context of 1980s postmodernist linguistic and formal theorizations of architecture. With the eclipse of postmodern eclecticism, Frampton's prognostics, shown in the book's introduction, is still a plausible scenario. Yet, its one-dimensional tone needs to be edited in the context of the prevailing parametric design against which Miesian tectonics validates a strategy of "resistance" evident in the best work of Renzo Piano and others.[65] Central to the suggested resistance is the work's capacity to transform the junkyard of the building industry into a three-dimensional intellectual abstraction, wherein a "primitive" sense of making prevails without allegorical references to humanization as is the case with the best architecture of Aalto.[66] Still, embracing the architectonic possibilities of industrialization, Mies's later work injects a sense of order into the urban chaos of capitalism,[67] an interventionist agenda missing in Alto's portfolio. Furthermore, the tectonics in the Berlin National Gallery deconstructs the Classical column and wall rapport. Since Leon Battista Alberti's presumption that the column is an ornament, the masonry wall is considered the primary constructive and enveloping element of architecture. Since then, the architectonics of an enclosing and supportive wall topped with the Greek trabeated system consolidated Alberti's dictum of civic architecture. A deconstructivist recoding of this Classical tradition in Mies's later work is worthy of attention. In Mies's architecture, what used to be *ornament* is turned into the load-bearing element. The envelope approximates the Semperian clothing with no load-bearing task. On the other hand, an Aaltosque concern for placemaking, materiality and local tectonic traditions are detectable today in the best work produced in countries where architects have chosen to resist the dissemination of globalization beyond the technical and in the local culture of the building. Moreover, the mature work of Mies and Aalto represented a "minor language"[68] critical to the institutionalized pre- and postwar architectural tendencies that intended to internalize the thematic of the spirit of the time (technical and formal) of late capitalism.

Notes

1 Kenneth Frampton received the Golden Lion for Lifetime Achievement at the May 26, 2018, opening of the 16th International Architecture Exhibition of the Venice Biennale.
2 As for Mies, the reader should consider Gevork Hartoonian, *Time, History, and Architecture: Essays on Critical Historiography* (London: Routledge, 2018), Chapter 5.
3 Bruno Zevi, *Towards an Organic Architecture* (London: Faber and Faber, 1950). The Italian edition was published in 1945.
4 On this subject, for specific references, see the next chapter in this volume.
5 Here, we benefit from Hal Foster's rewording of Sigfried Giedion's take on the ramifications of the mechanization. Hal Foster, *Brutal Aesthetics* (Princeton, NJ: Princeton Architectural Press, 2020), 163–64. On this author's take on repetition and demystification of construction in Mies's architecture, see Gevork Hartoonian, *Ontology of Construction* (New York: Cambridge University Press, 1993). For the latest edition of the chapter on Mies, see Hartoonian, "On Mies," in Hartoonian, *Time, History, and Architecture*, 91–114.
6 See Fredric Jameson, *Allegory, and Ideology* (London: Verso, 2019), 10.
7 Philip Drew, *The Third Generation: The Changing Meaning of Architecture* (New York: Praeger, 1972), 41.
8 Kenneth Frampton, *Studies in Tectonic Culture* (Cambridge: MIT Press, 1995), 253–54.
9 Kenneth Frampton, *Modern Architecture: A Critical History* (New York: Oxford University Press, 1980), 193.

10. Kenneth Frampton, "Alvar Aalto and the Origins of His Style," *Oppositions* 11 (Winter 1997): 124–29.
11. The other two editors were Peter Eisenman and Mario Gandelsonas. See Michael K. Hays, *Oppositions Reader* (New York: Princeton Architectural Press, 1998), ix.
12. Cynthia Davidson, "On the Record with Kenneth Frampton," *Log* 44 (Fall 2018): 31.
13. Kenneth Frampton, *Oppositions* 11 (Winter 1977): 129.
14. Eeva-Liisa Pelkonen, *Alvar Aalto: Architecture, Modernity, and Geopolitics* (New Haven, CT: Yale University Press, 2009), 5–6.
15. Cynthia Davidson, "On the Record with Kenneth Frampton," *Log* 44 (Fall 2018): 29.
16. Eeva-Liisa Pelkonen, "In Conversation with Kenneth Frampton," in *Alvar Aalto—Second Nature*, ed. Mateo Kries and Jochen Eisenbrand (Vitra Design Museum, 2015), 206.
17. Robert Venturi, *Complexity and Contradiction in Architecture* (New York: Museum of Modern Arts, 1966), 47. Alvar Aalto is mentioned 19 times in the main text of Venturi's book.
18. Sigfried Giedion, *Space, Time and Architecture: A New Tradition* (Cambridge: Harvard University Press, 1954), 618–67.
19. Ibid., 549.
20. Ibid., 665.
21. Ibid., 629.
22. Ibid.
23. Manfredo Tafuri and Francesco Dal Co, *Modern Architecture* (New York: Harry N. Abrams, 1979).
24. Manfredo Tafuri, *Theories and History of Architecture* (New York: Harper & Row, 1980), 88.
25. Ibid., 91.
26. Demetri Porphyrios, "Introduction," *Architectural Design* 51.6/7 (1981): 2. For more on this valuable manuscript, see Gevork Hartoonian, "Introduction," *The Mental Life of the Architectural Historian* (Newcastle: Cambridge Scholars, 2013), 1-14.
27. Demetri Porphyrios, *Sources of Modern Eclecticism* (London: Martin's, 1982).
28. Ibid., 14.
29. Ibid., 38.
30. Ibid., 44.
31. On the industrial work of Alvar Aalto, see Andrew Metcalf, "Four Cardinalities: Alvar Aalto's Industrial Architecture, 1929–1925," unpublished PhD dissertation, University of Canberra, 2019.
32. Frampton, *A Critical History*, 197. See also Paul David Pearson, *Alvar Aalto, and the International Style* (New York: Whitney Library of Design, 1978), 80.
33. Frampton, *A Critical History*, 197.
34. Frampton, *Studies in Tectonic Culture*, 12.
35. Frampton, *A Critical History*, 199.
36. Ibid., 198.
37. Alvar Aalto is edited and annotated by Goran Schildt, *Alvar Aalto in His Own Words* (New York: Rizzoli International, 1998), 154.
38. Pelkonen, *Alvar Aalto*, 195–96.
39. Alvar Aalto, "Between Humanism and Materialism," in Schildt, *Alvar Aalto in His Own Words*, 179.
40. Akos Moravanszky, "In the Alchemist's Laboratory: Aalto and the Materials of Architecture," in Kries and Eisenbrand, *Alvar Aalto*, 210.

41 See Gevork Hartoonian, *Ontology of Construction: On Nihilism of Technology in Theories of Modern Architecture* (Cambridge: Cambridge University Press, 1994), 85.
42 Alvar Aalto, "Henry Van de Velde," in Schildt, *Alvar Aalto in His Words*, 246–47.
43 On this subject, see Hartoonian, *Ontology of Construction*.
44 Eeva-Liisa Pelkonen, "Symbolic Imageries: Alvar Aalto's Encounter with Modern Art," in Kries and Eisenbrand, *Alvar Aalto*, 143.
45 Frampton, *A Critical History*, 200.
46 Kenneth Frampton, "The Legacy of Alvar Aalto," in *Labour, Work and Architecture*, ed. Kenneth Frampton (New York: Phaidon, 2002), 238. The essay was originally published in Peter Reed (ed.), *Alvar Aalto: Between Humanism and Materialism*, exh. cat. (New York: Museum of Modern Art, 1988).
47 Kenneth Frampton, "Alvar Aalto and the International Style," *Oppositions* 11 (Winter 1977): 129.
48 Kenneth Frampton, "Towards a Critical Regionalism," in *Anti-aesthetic: Essays on Postmodern Culture*, ed. Hal Foster (Washington: Bay, 1983), 16–30.
49 Schildt, *Alvar Aalto in His Own Words*, 102–7.
50 Sergei M. Eisenstein, "Montage and Architecture," *Assemblage* 10 (December 1989): 110–31.
51 For a classic text on this subject, see Christina Lodder, *Russian Constructivism* (New Haven, CT: Yale University Press, 1983). Also Maria Gough, *The Artist as Producer: Russian Constructivism in Revolution* (Berkeley: University of California Press, 2005). Both authors discuss the differences between "composition" and "construction," among other issues.
52 Kenneth Frampton, "Constructivism: The Pursuit of an Elusive Sensibility," *Oppositions* 6 (Fall 1976): 26–44, reprinted in Kenneth Frampton, *Labour, Work and Architecture* (New York: Phaidon, 2002), 150–67.
53 Frampton, *A Critical History*, Chapter 19, 167–77.
54 Thank are due to Andrew Metcalf for bringing up this point.
55 Berthold Lubetkin, "Soviet Architecture: Notes on Its Development, 1917–1932," *Architectural Association Journal* (May 1965): 260–61.
56 Owen Hatherley, *Landscapes of Communism* (London: Penguin, 2016), 97.
57 Kenneth Frampton, "The Status of Man and the Status of His Object: A Reading of 'The Human Condition,'" in *Hannah Arendt: The Recovery of the Public World*, ed. Melvyn A. Hill (New York: St. Martin's, 1979).
58 Kenneth Frampton's available records show that, aside from the first edition of the book, the first time that the concept of critical appeared, as far as it relates to his discourse, was in "Towards a Critical Regionalism," *Perspecta* 20 (1983): 147–62.
59 See note 47 above.
60 Berthold Lubetkin, for one, has written, "Disarming itself by rejecting the whole past architectural tradition, the profession gradually lost confidence in itself and its social purpose." Lubetkin, "Soviet Architecture: Notes on Development from 1917 to 1932," *Architectural Association Journal* (1956).
61 Manfredo Tafuri, *The Sphere and the Labyrinth: Avant-Gardes and Architecture from Piranesi to the 1970s* (Cambridge: MIT Press, 1987).
62 Alvar Aalto, "The Humanizing of Architecture," in Schildt, *Alvar Aalto in His Own Words*, 103.
63 Martino Stierli, *Montage and the Metropolis: Architecture, Modernity, and the Representation of Space* (New Haven, CT: Yale University Press, 2018), 13.

64 The other three points were "topography," understood with the type and tectonic form; "public" and "private" aspects of built form; and, finally, architecture's "close" connection with technology. See Kenneth Frampton, "Introduction," in *ABSTRACT 87–88* (New York: Graduate School of Architecture, Planning, and Preservation of Columbia University, 1988), 5.
65 Hal Foster, "Light Modernity," in *The Art-Architecture Complex* (London: Verso, 2011), 52–67.
66 Rephrasing Kenneth Frampton's assessment of Vladimir Tatlin's corner relief constructions in Frampton, "Constructivism: The Pursuit of an Elusive Sensibility," 31.
67 Stierli, *Montage and the Metropolis*, 140.
68 See Gevork Hartoonian, *Ontology of Construction: On Nihilism of Technology in Theories of Modern Architecture* (Cambridge: Cambridge University Press, 1994), Chapter 5.

Chapter 7
FROM THE CRITICAL TO RESISTANCE

Opening

The title of this chapter sums up, in a nutshell, Kenneth Frampton's project of critical historiography of Modern Movement architecture and beyond. Frampton has remained sympathetic to the humanistic and sociopolitical aspirations of modernity's project, which had significant repercussions for the intellectual labor of architecture produced between the two wars. Frampton penned most of the manuscript of *Modern Architecture: A Critical History* during the 1970s when he could not but share aspects of various criticisms launched against the International Style architecture. The language of this unique architectural tendency evolved during the first two decades of the past century in Europe, and the Museum of Modern Art (MoMA) institutionalized it in the famous exhibition of 1932. Following this exhibition, Philip Johnson and Henry-Russell Hitchcock co-authored a book celebrating the event. As stated in previous chapters, the scope of Frampton's intellectual work during the writing of his book was informed by many sources, including the English reformist concern for the social condition of the working class.[1] However, unlike their German counterparts, the English reformers showed less interest in matters concerning theory and history. At another level of consideration, and as discussed in previous chapters, Frampton celebrated Walter Benjamin's philosophy of history, Martin Heidegger's take on technology and "placemaking." Equally important was Hannah Arendt's distinction between labor and work and her advocacy for the "space of human appearance," the *res publica*. In contemporary circumstances, ushered in by global capitalism, the virtual network of communication has almost invalidated Arendt's idea, at least for now. What Frampton has taken away from the work of these three thinkers and their associates is a discourse of the critical, the scope of which includes the state of architecture in contemporary fully-fledged commodity form. If Benjamin is central to Frampton's historiography, the other two thinkers have assisted him in formulating a discourse of resistance detectable in Critical Regionalism.

In the preface to the book's second edition (1985), he dedicated a chapter to the subject. Frampton wrote:

> Critical regionalism is a critical category rather than an identifiable artistic movement in the avant-garde sense. In writing about it, I wish to draw attention to the fact that a regionally inflected but critical and "revisionist" form of modern architecture has been in existence for the past forty years or more.[2]

Accordingly, the concept of the critical intended to challenge the universal aspirations of modern architecture, which most often ignored the culture of the building accumulated and practiced in different geographies, even more pointedly, when architects in non-Western regions of the world used its syntax. The term "the culture of the building" designates both typological and morphological dimensions of the built-form of a region and its corresponding labor, skills, materials and construction techniques. Together, these contribute to disseminating the visual and tactile correspondences between built-form and a particular appreciation and comprehension of materiality and tectonics, evoking a sense of "belonging" to avoid using the problematic notion of "rootedness." As such, the culture of the building is not an ossified entity. Instead, both internal and external forces modify its scope of operation. We could claim that, in modern capitalism, regional architecture could not have been realized in a strict sense of the term if vernacular elements were not transgressed and modified according to the subjective and objective demands of modernization. Following Paul Ricoeur's 1961 essay "Universal Civilization and National Cultures," Frampton subtitled the last chapter of the third edition of his book "Critical Regionalism: Modern Architecture and Cultural Identity," making phenomenological associations between the culture of the building and the ethos of national identity. Frampton's reading and inclusion of Ricoeur's essay in Critical Regionalism raise several concerns that this chapter intends to attend to, among other related issues.

In one of his recent returns to Critical Regionalism, Frampton addresses the dichotomy between center and periphery. It is not the implied territorial divide that interests him. The issue is how architecture could or should define the periphery in contrast to the hegemonic architecture produced in the center. The divide between center and periphery stems from Western European epistemology, slashing the world into two major camps of modern and traditional based on technology's ascendency in the centers. Frampton's position hinges on how technological apparatuses, under the auspices of capitalism, transform the built-environment one-dimensionally. From China to any place where capital today finds room to disseminate the commodity form, we witness "the mediagenic impact of spectacular form which is as much due to the capacity of 'superstar architects' to come up with incredible, novel images as to their organizational competence and technical abilities."[3] The notion of center and periphery and the concept of resistance will be dealt with below. However, what we should note first is the shift in Frampton's choice of title, from resistance to "agnostic." Frampton seemingly moved away, without being explicit about it, from the duality of civilization versus national culture, rather turning the focus of his criticism on global capitalism. This is convincing considering Fredric Jameson's writings on late capitalism and his reading of Frampton's Critical Regionalism, published in 1994.[4] Discussing the postwar disintegration of the sociopolitical structures of the nation-state, Jameson writes that the looming global capitalism slowly but surely undermined national differences, disseminating a sense of "identity" implicit in standard products, both material and intellectual, to the point that alternatives such as "local culture" and "alternative modernities," including "critical regionalism," could not offer effective scenarios outside of the invisible networks of multinational capitalism.[5] Accordingly, despite regional differences, everyday life in capitalism lacks a full picture of the totality's presence. Jameson's observation warrants attention because he tacitly distinguishes between global capitalism and capitalism permeating the 1960s. The distinction helps to contextualize Ricoeur and Frampton's Critical Regionalism and the notion of "world architecture" elaborated below.

These preliminary remarks allow proceeding in the remainder of this chapter with the following two sets of correlated discussions. First, a comprehensive understanding of Frampton's position on Critical Regionalism should necessarily run through three cardinal points: (1) regionalism versus critical regionalism; (2) Paul Ricoeur's "Universal Civilization and National Culture"; and (3) capitalism and uneven development. Second, a close reading of Critical Regionalism must take apart Frampton's proposed six points of resistance, first introduced in an essay entitled "Towards a Critical Regionalism: Six Points for an Architecture of Resistance."[6] This edition of Frampton's text presents the most concise formulation of the subject today. Other editions, published in *Perspecta* (1983) under the title of "Prospects for a Critical Regionalism" and in the second edition of *A Critical History* (1985), each elaborate the subject extensively with ample examples of buildings selected from architecture produced in different countries. To this end, the three proposed cardinal points will be discussed first, and then Frampton's six points will be revisited in the remaining pages of this chapter.

I

There are many ways to proceed with the proposed three cardinal points. We could start by decontextualizing these points in the light of a temporality concept that is not locked in the modernist space-time coordinates. Binaries such as regionalism and critical regionalism and universalization, and national culture collocate Ernst Bloch's notion of uneven temporalities.[7] Bloch's formulation of "non-contemporaneity" responded to the early twentieth century's voluntary association between architecture and the Zeitgeist and National Socialism's successful orchestration of a coalition composed of different classes and strata of German society. To accept the Blochian dictum that "not all people exist in the same Now" means highlighting the nonsynchronicity of temporality experienced in technologically advanced and less advanced countries. However, at the dawn of the modern bourgeoisie, the concept of nation-state was nothing more than an allegorical ploy propagating a homogeneous national culture despite class conflicts and ethnic diversity. In contemporary geopolitics, ethnic wars are frequent across underdeveloped, developing but also developed countries in different ways. This commonality raises questions concerning "identity" and "placemaking," two pillars of Critical Regionalism. Even in the best examples, Frampton has presented a case for *regional* specificities, Catalan and Ticino architecture. For example, these regions belong to broader geography, Spain and Switzerland, respectively. We should associate the identity Frampton pursues with the phenomenological residues of a definitive everyday life that was not yet necessarily totalized and synchronized with the exigencies of the nation-state. Today, "everydayness constitutes a cultural form that shares with modernity the experience of capitalism, and is thus coeval with it," writes Harry Harootunian.[8] Frampton is not nostalgic about cultural residues of once upon a time that admittedly has left lasting architectonic expressions on the culture of the building of most regions. Following Benjamin, Frampton wanted to seize the past in recognizable now-time and under the hegemonic presence of late capitalism than in its historical context.[9] Frampton's fidelity to the past, if you wish, injects *history* into Critical Regionalism, an essential dimension of his discourse that most critiques dismiss.[10] Ironically, this is also the moment when Frampton comes closest to the complex rapport Bloch establishes between "heritage" and temporality.

Reviewing regional architecture in different countries, Frampton felt obliged in the *Perspecta* essay to elaborate on the differences between "regional" and "critical regional" architecture. In the essay, he registers the interaction between climate, culture, myth and craft for spontaneous realization in vernacular forms. He associates regional architecture with "those recent regional 'schools' whose aim has been to represent and serve, in a critical sense, the limited constituencies in which they are grounded." Accordingly, regionalism "depends, by definition, on a connection between the political consciousness of a society and the profession." While regional expression(s) are necessary, essential to critical practice is "a strong sense of identity." Frampton writes, "One of the mainsprings of regionalist culture is an anti-centrist sentiment—an aspiration for some cultural, economic and political independence."[11] If we avoid a reductive association between "identity" and genius loci, it would be more productive to read Frampton along with what for Japanese intellectuals of the interwar period was to "overcome the modern," a collective and politically motivated action against Japan's "slavish reliance on Westernization."[12] Harry Harootunian's observation illuminates Ricoeur's call for "National Cultures," first published in 1951, which looked retrospectively at the situation in Japan, and a prelude to the emerging postwar discourses on "unequal development." Another side to the Japanese drive for nation-building became attractive to most nations compartmentalized under the Third World's rainbow umbrella. Most of these countries pursued political and cultural diversity. They sought independence from old colonialist powers and the imperialistic agenda of rising capitalism in the United States.[13] Disregarding the postwar United States' Marshal Plan for Europe and aid programs tailored for Japan, the Japanese experience stood tall during the 1973 oil crisis. This formed the background for the symbolic dimension of Expo 70 that Kenzo Tange and his army of Metabolist architects championed. Taking no notice of historical and political differences, Expo 70 was a success on many levels, including in offering design and architecture that were representative of nation-building in non-Western nations and a zeal for a different engagement with modernization. Beyond the publications addressing Tange's urbanistic projects in the Middle East,[14] much historical investigation demonstrates how modernization failed in several Middle Eastern countries for various reasons, including political tumults taking place in the late 1970s. Simultaneously, large groups of architects and urban designers from the Eastern European block made inroads into many Middle Eastern and African countries. The idea was to help these nations expand the urbanization process and design schools and other collective amenities "celebrated as monuments to decolonization and national independence."[15] By the end of the Cold War, however, "democratic capitalism suddenly became synonymous with modernity. To be modern meant to adopt Western values, attitudes, and institutions. The imitation of the West was almost universally judged to be the fastest route to freedom and prosperity."[16] This brief digression to the height of the symbolic side of Japanese modernization, which faced stagnation by the late 1980s and the rise of American corporate capitalism, is an appropriate prelude to measuring the success and failure of Critical Regionalism.

II

In any event, the uneven encounter between modern capitalism and national identity connoted, on the one hand, the political awareness in non-Western countries of the stakes involved in entering the processes of modernization at different stages of the historical development of capitalism. Highlighting the dialectics between internationalization and historicization unfolding from 1966 to 1974, John Roberts writes, "The experience of cultural 'simultaneity' (of collective intellect) for this generation is also shaped and qualified by the need for the recovery and reinterpretation of a workable artistic history which is not modernism-as usual, not national*ist* in color and destiny."[17] And yet, the inevitable *desire* to internalize modernity's everyday life grafted into the fabric of traditional cultures through the importation of various products, including mediatic cultures (Hollywood movies and pop culture, particularly after the war), was a hot issue regardless of its political consequences. The analogical basis of Robert's observation is the belatedness of the 1960s avant-garde. In particular, there were no documents available at the time of the work of Russian Constructivism. Accordingly, the postwar avant-garde in the centers "had to be reconstructed in the process of recovering its critical horizon." In this line of consideration, we should reintroduce and contextualize the political dimension of Frampton's Critical Regionalism along with the state of the European avant-garde, and the rise of political consciousness in non-Western nations. Related to the dialogue between the center and the periphery, Roberts introduces another dimension of belatedness in the periphery. Since its inception, the aforementioned dialogue excluded an effective role for peripheries to recover traditions of the historical avant-garde on their own terms. One consequence of this exclusion was that these places had limited or no appropriate opportunity to produce art and architecture in association with national identity and amalgamate modernist and traditionalist architectonic elements. Furthermore, and in the image of the historical avant-garde, architects working in non-Western countries could not, speaking historically, uphold an indigenous culture against anti-imperialist imperatives. Neither scenario succeeded in its mission because history was not serving as a "template for those societies which had not yet achieved the status of modernity."[18] Reading "Critical Regionalism" along with Harootunian and Roberts, we can empower Frampton's discourse on the critical beyond Heidegger's ethos of "dwelling." Interestingly enough, and considering the present state of global modernization, Frampton's scenario has recently received the due currency denied in the 1980s.

Apropos, it is not far-fetched to say that Frampton's Critical Regionalism had an eye on the belatedness experienced in both the center and the periphery and toward two different ends. Ricoeur's argument was appealing due to the prevailing postwar American culture and the beginning of its political hegemony throughout most of the world, but more specifically in non-Western countries, where the intrusion of American consumerist culture introduced a soft alternative to colonial regimes. It was a dreamwork aspiring to political "independence," even though the consumer *culture* was, deep down, internal to capitalism's political economy. Despite this, the suggested shift in the political and cultural hegemony of capitalism unfolding after World War II was promising to regions that had achieved independence from Britain and other colonial empires, founding themselves in alliance with countries tagged "Third World."[19] In light of this dichotomous encounter, we can argue that disregarding its claim for homogeneous progress, capitalism is structured by uneven development. At a theoretical level, we should also credit Frampton with highlighting the essentiality of the "political consciousness of a society and the profession" for the actualization of Critical Regionalism, a viable radical and politically correct project, according to Jameson's two-tier reading of the Third-World notion.[20] Noting the problematic divide between literature produced in Third-World countries and the canon, the "world literature" developed in Europe, Jameson suggests that, from a cultural perspective, the "Third World" denoted countries that, in the 1980s, were considered less "developed" than America and Russia (the First World), and Europe (the Second World). From this geopolitical perspective, the term "Third World" attained peculiar ideological inclusiveness. It embraced nations that, in one way or another, were aligned either with America or Russia (the First World) and conditionally claimed independence from both superpowers. However, the recent dissemination of global capitalism has diminished the old tiers of compartmentalization based on the notion of hierarchical development. The absence of this porosity, and a proper architectural canon, has, it can be argued, undermined the relevance of national identity to architecture in most regions of the world. This proposition puts Frampton's "Critical Regionalism" in the interesting position of having been written from the viewpoint of a critic and architect/historian once considered the Other. Frampton is seemingly the historian who captures the world of architecture from a peripheral position. That is why his stance conflicts with that of Jameson who seeks to take apart the diverse manifestations of global capitalism within the prevailing totality, denying any viable alternative or independent scenario.

III

To get to the bottom of the above observations, we should turn to Frampton's reflections on the work of diverse architects, from Alvar Aalto to Tadao Ando, inked in the *Perspecta* essay of 1983. Each of the discussed architects was conscious of the political dimension of architecture in one form or another. However, essential for Frampton is the architect's capacity to reveal the architectonics that directly or through memory will recollect aspects of specific cultural experiences, despite architecture's inevitable encounter with modernization. We have noted in the previous chapter Frampton's esteem for Aalto's work, and will return to it shortly. For now, we should focus on Ando and Mario Botta, two architects whose work Frampton has discussed on several occasions. After the *Perspecta* essay, Frampton has not missed the opportunity to disseminate Critical Regionalism in various publications. In 1984, he edited and wrote an introductory essay on Ando's architecture[21] while publishing an article on Botta's early work in *Progressive Architecture*.[22] In the latter article, focused on the architect's four houses built during the early 1980s, Frampton explains why he has given up pursuing the architect's later work, which most often repeats earlier motifs and tactile sensibilities, a signature language. In a finely articulated residential work, Botta departed from his initial agrarian metaphor, "the linear asymmetrical structure" of the Cadenazzo residence, Switzerland (1970). These projects also revealed the architect's tendency to twist Classical formalism, à la Louis I. Kahn, into pristine geometric games. His was a station between the abstract formalism of the New York Five and the postmodernist simulation of historical motifs, a phenomenon explicitly in line with the developmental process of James Stirling's architecture, noted in Chapter 5. While underlining the attention Botta gave to the site, surface opening, the element of the enclosure and the densification of the surrounding environment, nevertheless, there seems to be "an affinity in these works for the Neoclassical procedure of deriving the 'figurative' image of a work from the arbitrary assembly of Platonic solids."[23] As for Ando, knowing the pervasiveness of the "modern predicament," this Japanese architect avoids any fictitious "homecoming" or simulation of traditional Japanese timber construction. More importantly, and because of the presence and practice of traditional elements of Japanese culture even to this day, Ando "has stoically refused to nostalgic ethos which such vernacular elements imply."[24] As for the political dimension of Ando's design, the architect shows a "critical understanding by remaking on the comparable devaluations suffered by the post and the colonnade as a consequence of the invention of the reinforced concrete frame." Ando uses the wall, one of the oldest tectonic elements, to make a contained enclosure where nature, light and materiality are experienced differently and away from the "instrumentality of the megalopolitan dimension" prevailing in cosmopolitan cities such as Tokyo. Drawing on Frampton's similar assessment of other architects associated with Critical Regionalism, we could say that regional architecture in the age of capitalism must engage modernization politically. In terms of negative dialectics, it is convincing to say that there has been no genuine "regionalism" since capitalism hijacked modernity's project, except for the possibility of poetic articulation of the impact of modernization on the culture of the building. Here, Frampton tacitly considers the strategy of defamiliarization that Liane Lefaivre and Alexander Tzonis borrowed from Russian formalists in recollecting the cultural experience of *difference*.[25] However, instead of rendering the work familiar and strange at once, Frampton pursues a Heideggerian regressive strategy desiring unity between work and the world. A bygone unity that given the circumstances its "memory" might lead us to a future unknown to the civilization. In Herbert Marcuse's words, "Modifications no longer sustained by external forces would collapse" and "regression assumes a progressive function" and "the forbidden images and impulses of childhood begin to tell the truth that reason denies."[26] Herein lies Frampton's sympathy with the Ruskinian yearning for labor, light, materiality and tectonics of Gothic architecture, an unbaked state of resistance against the capitalistic drive for rationalization.

The complexity involved in Frampton's take on cultural identity is rooted in the postwar westernization of cultural and political consequences, which attained full visibility during the 1960s. Frampton reads this historical opening in conjunction with Adolf Loos's critical reflection on the state of culture in early modernity, stating that, after "the disjunctive cultural approach practiced by Adolf Loos, Critical Regionalism recognizes that no living tradition remains available to a modern man other than the subtle procedure of syntactic contradiction."[27] Thus, to have an appropriate *use*, the culture of the building must of necessity pass through the process of modernization and accommodate its tectonic potentialities to the broader aspects of the aesthetic culture of modernism. Furthermore, Frampton presents Aalto's "collage approach" in conjunction with Alvaro Siza's architecture (Figure 7.1) and normative typologies drawn from the work of Italian neo-rationalists. Meanwhile, writing these lines at a time when the populist appeal of postmodern eclecticism had not yet passed into the dust of history, Frampton was seemingly self-conscious of the fact that one might take the dichotomy between modernity and tradition for the Venturiesque idea of both-and. To differentiate the architecture of Critical Regionalism, which might simultaneously look both "familiar" and "different," from the metanarratives of postmodernism, Frampton correctly associated the latter with rhetorical culture and "techniques and imagery of advertising" billboards.[28] Central to this association is the issue of culture,

Figure 7.1 Alvaro Siza Viera, Leca Swimming Pool, the Tea House, Matosinhos, Portugal, 1966. Photograph courtesy of the author.

which is expected to communicate with both experts and nonexperts. If we agree with Frampton that architecture is semiautonomous, how then, out of theoretical necessity, would the architectonics of Critical Regionalism differ from both the local and the universal aspirations of modernism (modern Regionalism and *Neue Sachlickeit*) and the historicist languages of postmodernism and formal autonomy? Nevertheless, with a dialectical approach to the culture of building, Critical Regionalism presented a viable alternative against the two prevailing praxes of the late 1970s.

If in one instance it was the Catalonian brick tradition that would secure *identity* in Barcelona's architecture, in another Frampton turned to the vernacular elements in the old houses of Botta as well as Ando's esteem for a "trans-optical architecture." For Ando, detail is the most important element for expressing identity. The centrality of the architectonic expressions of materiality, light and tectonics in Frampton's discussion of regional identity is a collective phenomenon. On the other hand, the idealization of the "opposition between universal civilization and autochthonous culture" attains political connotations in Greece, where "historicist regionalism in its neo-classical version had already met with opposition before the arrival of Welfare State and modern architecture."[29] Interestingly enough, the American architect Harwell Harris wrote in 1954 that, to be effective politically, critical regionalism should attain a dimension of many architects sharing its intentions while establishing a case for its collective reception and appropriation. This much is also evident in the distinction Harris draws between two opposing regionalisms. In contrast to what he called the "Regionalism of Restriction, the Regionalism of Liberation is the manifestation of a region that is specifically in tune with the thought of the time." For him, architecture is regional "only because it has not yet emerged elsewhere." The architectural expression of this Regionalism, Harris continues, necessitates its dissemination within a host of buildings, so its power and merits will be sufficient "to capture people's imagination and provide a friendly climate for long enough for a new school of design to develop."[30] Frampton will take up Harris's position again in a 1987 article where he maps the thematic discourse of regionalism in ten points.[31] Juxtaposing oppositional dualities in each point, Frampton grafts the idea of regionalism onto the predicament of architecture as capitalistic organization conquers the socio-cultural, technological, and economic realms. Even though aspects of Frampton's points are still relevant for promoting a sustainable architecture, however, we should ask how Harris's position is different from Lewis Mumford's Regionalism, mapped in "The Bay Region Style," an essay published in 1947. This comparison is vital on two accounts: first, both authors underline the importance of "expression" for regionalism; and, second, they both see the importance of Los Angeles regionalism as a way of resisting the modern European architecture that New England architects embraced because their own "regionalism had been reduced to a collection of restrictions," as Harris claimed. Mumford had raised similar concerns against major advocates of modernism who had gathered at a 1942 symposium held at the MoMA, with the telling title of "What Is Happening to Modern Architecture?"[32] Drawing from the work of Californian architects John Galen Howard and Bernard Maybeck in particular, Mumford characterized the "Bay Region Style" in the following words: "free yet unobtrusive expression of the terrain, the climate, and the way of life on the coast." He continued, "Style is truly universal since it permits regional adaptations and modifications."[33] The missing point in Harris's and Mumford's analyses is capitalism's transformation and its infusion into American geopolitics and everyday life. If at one point America was seen as an aggregate of separate regions, each with its own local culture, after World War II, regional differences, at least at the cultural level, slowly but surely were obliterated. Today's Los Angeles is nothing but a spread-out megalopolis with no collective social structure except its highways![34]

In introducing Mumford into this discussion, the idea was to ask: Why in various editions of "Critical Regionalism" does Frampton mention neither Mumford's article nor the 1942 MoMA event? Maybe Frampton wanted to differentiate his take on regionalism from a "restrictive regionalism" that is not receptive to the "emerging thought of the time," and from the restrictive ways Mumford related regionalism to "place," wishing to foreground a biological relationship between the "human-artist and the environment." In this context, the prefix "critical" in Critical Regionalism confirms the earlier assessment of the problem of cultural identity in modernity. Francesco Dal Co's claim that the tradition Mumford sought to weave into American architecture "is a rooted anti-capitalist ideology which if exalting the epic era of commerce, does so because it finds in the age of laissez-faire the survival of that individualism that industrial capitalism wipes out by photographing its silent face in the indifference of the masses and the apparent chaos of the metropolis." For Dal Co "the contradiction in Mumford's discourse consists in the impossibility of finding a correct synthesis between the consequences of technical and scientific conquest and the values of tradition."[35] Nothing short of Dal Co's criticism assesses the problem of the oppositional nature of Mumford's discourse. Seemingly, Frampton wanted to highlight the impact of capitalism on architecture and to differentiate Critical Regionalism from the Romanticist discourse on regional semantics. This observation assists us in seeing the early modernists' problematic image of modernity as a uniform entity devoid of internal contradictions, the ideological cornerstone of the first modern bourgeois world. Therein lies the centrality of the *critical* for Frampton's historical criticism.

Back to *Perspecta* essay, Frampton expands his argument to include Emilio Ambasz, Luis Barragan, Jørn Utzon and Botta as architects who, each in a different way, engage with the dichotomy between the regional and the universal. At times, his extensive investigation relies primarily on the architects' statements concerning tropes such as site, light and climate. We may also consider the late Carlo Scarpa "to be a regionally oriented architect," so was Kahn's commitment to Philadelphia "both as myth and reality, throughout his life."[36] The implied disjunction extended to include Botta's preoccupation with "building the site" and his "deep conviction that the loss of the historical city can only now be compensated on a fragmentary basis." No wonder Frampton's essay ends with Heidegger's differentiation between place and space and the Arendtian call for the *space of public appearance*. Frampton writes, "The universal Megalopolis is patently antipathetic to a dense differentiation of culture. It intends, in fact, the reduction of the environment to nothing but a commodity." However, his discussion in "Prospect for a Critical Regionalism" did not draw the attention it deserved for several reasons, including the attractiveness of formalism as theorized by Colin Rowe and practiced by some members of the New York Five architects.[37] Furthermore, Frampton presented the case for Critical Regionalism along with a reading of Heidegger which was already radicalized by post-structuralist thinkers, the Italian Gianni Vattimo in particular.[38] More recently, Jameson has detected a deconstructionist agenda in Heidegger's "enlargement" of the existing gap between what he calls World and Earth, or History and Nature. Against any attempt toward "naturalization or humanization" of the gap between history (art and objects produced by humanity) and nature (meaningless organic life), Jameson sees Heidegger's aesthetic as "allegorical." He writes:

> Heidegger's deployment of his opposition at the moment in which he touches on art object as such point a way out of this dilemma: it is the materiality of the object, he tells us, the sonority of the language, the smoothness of marble, or the slick density of the oil, which marks the part of Earth in it: while it is the semiotic features of the work, the meanings and meaningfulness—what is paraphrasable in the verse, the function of the building, the object imitated by the painting—which is the share in it of World as such.[39]

We could say that the Heideggerian refusal and, at the same time, acceptance of the persistence of subject-object dualism was the attraction to critics and historians disenchanted with the postmodernist "both-and" agenda, Frampton included.

At any rate, overstating Ricoeur's paradoxical juxtaposition of *culture* and *civilization*, Frampton was also tuned by the historico-theoretical import of Jürgen Habermas's position in "Modernity—an Incomplete Project."[40] In the introduction to his classical take on postmodernism, Hal Foster writes, "True, the word may have 'lost a fixed historical reference' [...], but the ideology has not: modernism is a cultural construct based on specific conditions; it *has* a historical limit."[41] Paradoxically, Aalto, Siza and other architects, including a few working in Australia and the Catalan and Ticino regions, reinvented building's local culture because of the "distance" these regions happened to secure, for historical reasons, from the velocity of modernization unleashed in central Europe and America. Obviously, in late capitalism, and with the globalization of information and commodity forms, geographic distance is virtually conquered by the over-presence of consumerist culture. The same goes for the adaptation of regional architecture, with uniform images disseminated in parametric design.

Finally, if in the *Perspecta* essay Frampton attempted to expand the scope of regional diversity, in "Critical Regionalism: Modern Architecture and Cultural Identity," the title of Chapter 5 of the third edition of his book (1985), Frampton reiterated almost his entire argument selectively with one significant exception. Even though in this later edition of the text Frampton again starts with the long quotation from Ricoeur, in this case, the conclusion presents a summary of the issues formulated in his famous "Six Point for an Architecture of Resistance" (1983). These points will be revisited in the remaining pages of this chapter.

1. *Culture and Civilization*

Ricoeur's text was a timely response to the changes taking place in the economics and geopolitics of postwar capitalism. In addition to expanding the scope of civilization, it also had to deconstruct the state of subjectivity nurtured by the old system of beliefs and relationships that were cracking apart. Given the velocity of modernization, technical innovations and urbanization inevitably transformed the cultural beliefs and habits inherited from auratic moments. Innovations in each technical realm introduce particular skills and tools and subjectivity suitable for an urbanized everyday life experience. Consider the extensive transformations inaugurated by photography and film, in general, and brought about by teaching curricula at the Bauhaus school, in particular. Presenting a convincing story of civilization, Ricoeur's viewpoint nevertheless tended to totalize "humankind" as a uniform phenomenon and at times narrowed the scope of critical practice to the performance of a committed individual artist. What was lost between these two poles was the class interests and the formation of subjectivities essential for delineating one's position within the production and consumption systems of capitalism. However, what was *new* in the late 1950s was the intensification of the rapport between the triad of civilization, technology and the phenomenon of consumer culture. Concomitant with this development was importing aspects of civilization to underdeveloped countries with different languages, myths and political and religious beliefs.[42] Most of the recipient nations had one thing in common: they did not follow the historical path to realizing a national bourgeoisie that had established its institutions in Europe. Accordingly, the historical confrontation between the technical and the cultural remains central to Frampton's historiography and takes the driver's seat in Critical Regionalism.

For Frampton, the 1960s was a turning point, not only for the Western countries but for a concrete understanding of the historicity of history. Equally important was America's worldwide dissemination of "the culture industry."[43] The otherness of Western lifestyle images, American-made automobiles and Hollywood moving pictures extended to marketing technologies and economic planning worldwide. In Reinhart Koselleck's words, "What was new was the expansions that reached out for the future became detached from all that previous experiences had to offer."[44] Interestingly enough, the two-tier competitive development of culture and civilization is indeed evident in the content of Parts I and II of the first edition of *A Critical History*. Each of these parts maps various architects' strategies for confronting the dilemma of civilization without dismissing the transformations the culture of the building had to go through to stand up to the radical manifestoes of the time. As demonstrated in the previous chapter, Part III of the same edition of the book discloses Frampton's critical assessment of civilization's negative impact on the design and production of architecture, including the cityscape. By the 1970s, various government agencies synchronized the emergence of megapolitan centers with economic and political planning.[45] Whereas the "high-tech" approach inevitably remained central to the production of buildings, what concerned Frampton the most had tectonic ramifications: the fact that the postmodernist simulation of historical languages hijacked the Corbusian coordinates of the Dom-Ino frame and the free-facade. In Frampton's words, the "compensatory façade" exemplified in Michael Graves's design of the Portland City Annex, Oregon, was an attempt to dress-up the "harsh realities of this universal system"[46] with outdated garments. Reminding the reader of the factors that transformed the fabric of the nineteenth-century city, Frampton exonerates this turn of events, presenting the free-standing high-rise building and the serpentine freeway as the two universal components of the megalopolis exported to and superimposed on the landscape of developing countries.

Apropos, during the late 1950s, the space-time experience of everyday life in Western cosmopolitan centers slowly but surely challenged local traditions, no matter how deeply they were rooted in regional and cultural practices. This was also one reason why the Third World aspirations for an "autonomous form of regionalism" did not last long.[47] Even though "there is a culture of consumption of a worldwide dimension, displaying a way of living which has a universal character,"[48] Ricoeur saw the solution in a dialectical understanding of "absorption" and "creativity," a task he assigned to individual artists of developing countries.[49] Following Ricoeur, Frampton claimed that a hybrid "world culture will only come into being through cross-fertilization between rooted *culture*, on the one hand, and universal *civilization*, on the other."[50] This is where the formation of subjectivity in capitalism becomes the core problem of the predicament Ricoeur posed: "How to become modern and return to sources." By the 1960s, the notion of the "modern" lost its early-century meaning when commodity form had not yet taken over all cultural sectors. However, recalling Hannah Arendt, Frampton remained committed to the idea that "specifics of expression" and "*collective* psycho-social reality" are not artistic graffiti. To this end, he tried to establish the diachronic passage of auratic elements of history from Adolf Loos to Alvar Aalto and Alvaro Siza. This creative rappel a l'ordre, he conceded elsewhere, was to "reconcile the tradition of the Arts and Crafts with the *Neue Bauen* movement."[51]

Nevertheless, the drama of civilization continues as we move to the era of digital reproductivity, with unexpected consequences for Frampton's proposed reconciliation.

2. *The Rise and Fall of the Avant-Garde*

The historicism implied in this subtitle has shadowed left-inclined thinkers like a cloud since Marx considers that the second time occurrence of a phenomenon is nothing but a farce. Frampton is not an exception to this generalization. The following two points speak for it: that the inception of the avant-garde was integral to modernization and aimed at nurturing the formation of various artistic and political strategies. That art and architecture could play a decisive role in the advancement of modern industrialized society. The artistic and political project of the avant-garde, however, took a negative attitude toward the established bourgeois regime. Instead of looking backward, as was the case with "the Gothic Revival and the Arts-and-Crafts movements," the avant-garde looked forward to the realization of a *new* society heralded in the 1909 Manifesto of Futurism. The "negative" became the core position of the avant-garde after the advent of World War I. Still in the absence of a "collective subjectivity" of the Bolshevik Revolution, the "negative" soon collided with the nihilism of technology. One major consequence of this implied missed encounter was the impossibility of envisaging "history in such a way as to foreground the present—the now—in contrast to the past national narratives."[52] Another is suggested in Frampton's following observation:

> In the 1930s, however, the prevailing backwardness and chronic insecurity of the newly urbanized masses, including the upheavals caused by war, revolution and economic depression, followed by a sudden and crucial need for psycho-social stability in the face of global politics and economic crises, all induced a state of affairs in which the interest of both monopoly and state capitalism are, for the first time in modern History, divorced from the liberative drives of cultural modernization. Universal civilization and world culture cannot be drawn upon to sustain "the myth of the State," and one reaction-formation succeeds another as the historical avant-garde founders on the rocks of the Spanish Civil War.[53]

For Frampton, the consequence of the Spanish Civil War ending with the domination of Franco's Fascist regime was the "watershed" for the possibility of radical and progressive alternative architectural projects. Here, Frampton tacitly sides with what he calls the "limits of any particular historical moment,"[54] an attitude shared by Walter Benjamin. Writing in 1930s,

Benjamin "felt that he was living in a time in which everything valuable was the last of its kind. He thought Surrealism was the last intelligent moment of the European intelligentsia, an appropriately destructive, nihilistic kind of intelligence."[55] Frampton was simultaneously thinking of the conditions of postmodernism that reinvigorated "Neo-Kantian aesthetics as a substitute for the culturally liberative modern project." Without calling out specific architects or groups, Frampton criticized that stream of the Frankfurt School which followed Theodor Adorno's concept of *hibernation* and "recommended a strategic withdrawal from the project of totally transforming the existing reality." He wrote these lines when Clement Greenberg was one of the available left-wing authorities on matters concerning the historical avant-garde in art and architecture.

In addition to looking at Greenberg's 1939 essay "Avant-Grade and Kitsch," Frampton also quotes from "Modernist Painting" (1965), criticizing the author's advocacy for autonomy. For Greenberg, "The arts could save themselves [...] by demonstrating that the kind of experience they provide was valuable in its own right and not to obtained from any other kind of activity."[56] Dismissed in Frampton's text was Renato Poggioli's *The Theory of the Avant-Garde* (1968) and the distinction he makes between "two Avant-Gardes," useful categories for understanding the sociopolitical roots of the avant-garde in the twentieth century. Poggioli associates the early avant-garde with the left-wing politics of the mid-1800s, which led to activities culminating in the revolutionary events of 1848 and the Paris Commune. Starting with the late nineteenth century, he continues, the avant-garde's focus shifted from politics to aesthetics. Interestingly enough, Frampton's essay "Continuity and Avant-Garde," an entry for a special issue of *Architectural Design* on the occasion of the publication of the first edition of *A Critical History* (1980) begins with Poggioli. The art historian claims that avant-gardism was "initially predicated on a revolutionary culture that sought to combine in a single spontaneous movement to create new forms of art but also the orientation of this art towards the transformation of society."[57] In the same essay, Frampton underlines the semiautonomous nature of architecture. He writes that, compared to other arts, architecture is "restrained by power and material production." Recalling Poggioli's proposition of two avant-gardes, Frampton associates the loss of the political dimension of the first avant-garde with the mid-1870s, arguing that the "split into two avant-gardes coincided with the rise of monopoly capitalism." However, since the 1960s, significant architectural theorizations have highlighted the concept of autonomy and Greenberg's later position on Neo-Kantian aesthetics. Energized by theories of semiotics, structuralism and post-structuralism, neo-avant-garde formalism challenged both postmodern historicism and the "Realism" of mainstream commercial urbanizations.

To contextualize Frampton's criticism of the neo-avant-garde architecture of the 1970s, we should turn to the English translation of Peter Burger's *Theory of Avant-Garde* (1984). Initially published in Germany in 1965, Burger historicized the failure of Dadaism and Constructivism to reintegrate art with life, thus relegating the historical project of the avant-garde to the abyss of history. Of further interest and related to Frampton's position is Burger's critique of *autonomy*. Burger wrote, "The relative dissociation of the work of art from the praxis of life in bourgeois society thus becomes transformed into the (erroneous) idea that the work of art is independent of society."[58] While the Italian Futurists and the Dutch Neoplasticists founded their ideas on the physical and perceptual horizons offered by technology, the Productivists, Frampton writes, "sought to develop a new rooted culture based on the everyday production of the people themselves and the fulfillment of their immediate informational needs."[59] Given the conditions of the 1980s, marked by postmodernism and the neo-avant-garde's search for the *new*, Frampton contested this "closure," the proclamation of the end of history. Insisting on the importance of historically grounded tropes, Frampton believed that aspects of modernism's attempt to recode tradition had sowed the seeds for a critical formulation of the stakes involved in architecture's rapport with capitalism. The historicity overshadowing Frampton's position was due to the inscription of early European and Soviet avant-garde practices, anticipating the "emerging post-abstract art models of practice in the US."[60] Interestingly enough, John Roberts reminds us of two publications attesting to Frampton's detailed knowledge of both constructivist sculpture and architecture.[61] As discussed in the previous chapter, facing the failure of the historical avant-garde, Frampton's Critical Regionalism suggests the modifications needed to reiterate architecture's political project as seen from the geopolitics of the periphery.

3. Critical Regionalism and World Culture

The main ideas that Frampton plots in the third point of his architecture of resistance are discussed in his *Perspecta* essay. Critical Regionalism is against neither "world culture" nor technology, the two pillars of the Enlightenment vision of progress that Frampton revisited from an arrière-garde standpoint. We have already noted in previous pages that Frampton associates the genealogies of the arrière-garde with Loos. This architect believed that modernity had already accomplished its project and thus emphasized the importance of recoding tradition accordingly. Alternately, one could reapproach the pillars of the Enlightenment from the standpoint of the peripheries of the Occidental world. This view is suggested in Ricoeur's strategic announcement, "No one can say what will become of our civilization when it has met different civilization."⁶² Leaving aside bygone images of "civilization encountering the savage," any such exchange in the contemporary situation cannot avoid the fact that the mentalities of both sides are already contaminated, to various degrees, with the culture of the commodity form. For Frampton, and speaking in terms of architecture, in modern times, one should avoid "a reactionary, unrealistic impulse to return to the architectonic forms of the preindustrial past." Accordingly, "it is necessary to qualify the term arrière-garde to diminish its critical scope from such conservative policies as Populism or sentimental Regionalism with which it has often been associated."⁶³ This statement implicitly refers to critics and scholars who, in the high days of Theory, considered his position conservative, if not out of sync with neo-avant-garde aspirations for autonomy. Their stance was a dismissal of Loos, who had already made a sound and historical distinction between art and architecture. For this Viennese architect, architecture belongs to everyone, and "culture" should pursue critical strategies to resist the provision of an optimized technology. In the 1980s, however, the odds were against Frampton, to the point that neither Ricoeur nor Hannah Arendt was much help.

To further explore the particulars of Frampton's position on Critical Regionalism, we should turn to Lefaivre and Tzonis, the progenitors of the idea.⁶⁴ In *Critical Regionalism: Architecture and Identity in a Globalized World* (2003), Lefaivre and Tzonis redefined this concept for a third time according to the state of contemporary architectural praxis. At the outset, we should note the dialogical rapport the authors wished to establish between contemporary architecture and the word "critical." In their 1981 essay, critical regionalism designated architects who formulated an alternative architecture against the postmodernist simulation of historical forms. They insisted that regionalism could be either associated with "movements of reform and liberation" or "a powerful tool of repression and chauvinism." They saw the limits of Critical Regionalism in the light of " an upheaval of the populist movement—a more developed form of regionalism." Whereas the first statement recalls the Californian architect Harwell Hamilton Harris, also mentioned in Frampton's *Perspecta* essay, their second statement speaks to the state of postmodernism. The authors' intellectual comfort with the Realism advocated by more advanced circles of postmodernism is evident in the following statement: "No new architecture can emerge without a new kind of relations between designer and user, without new kind of programs […] Despite these limitations, critical regionalism is a bridge over which any humanistic architecture of the future must pass."⁶⁵ In the same book, the word "critical" is not used in opposition to or resistance against anything internal or external to architecture. For them, the architecture of critical regionalism "recognizes the value of the singular, [and] circumscribes projects within the physical, social, and cultural constraints of the particular, aiming at sustaining diversity while benefiting from universality."[66] Given this, we could say that Lefaivre and Tzonis's rapprochement to critical regionalism intended to "design" identity for a given context despite the prevailing order of globalization. If Critical Regionalism was once sought in confrontation with hegemonic architectural discourses—the international style architecture of the 1930s and postmodernism of the late 1970s—the word "critical" was now subdued by Realism. One reason for this shift might have been to avoid the problem of national identity. In a postmodern paradigm, Realism meets the universal dimension of technology outside of history, leaving no room for the issue of identity, national or otherwise.

If the turn to Realism defined Critical Regionalism according to a paradigm centered on differentiating modernity from capitalism, a distinction essential to Fredric Jameson's reading of Frampton's discourse on the same subject,[67] then we could claim that Lefaivre and Tzonis's text failed to meet this criterion. Furthermore, the same differentiation allows us to see the relationship between regional and late capitalism as parallax, meaning that, in late capitalism, forms or tropes that define the identity of a region are paradoxically by-products of commodity form culture. The experience of identity image is thus not *rooted* in a place anymore. In this line of consideration, critical practice designates the capacity of architecture to direct one's attention to a larger entity, that is, the globalization of capitalism. This implied totalization is also central to differentiating Critical Regionalism from both regionalism and the vernacular.[68] Once this is established, the raison d'etre of the argument supporting various buildings accompanying Lefaivre and Tzonis's text collapses.

From this rather dense reading of Lefaivre and Tzonis's discourse on the subject, we can approach Frampton's Critical Regionalism differently. Those aspects of Frampton's argument that are useful for critiquing contemporary architecture as it intertwines with commodity form's world culture need to be underscored. To this end, two imperatives are suggested: first, we should not underestimate the importance of technology and the architectonic adventures of postmodernism for any critical understanding of the complexities of architecture's confrontation with late capitalism; and, second, the importance of tectonics for a semiautonomous architecture paradoxically presents the disciplinary history of architecture as the subject matter of what Hal Foster once referred to as "strategic autonomy." His argument alluded to the historicity of 1920s modernism. Against the fetishism of past styles, the early modernists leaned toward autonomy and embraced the machinery of progress unreservedly.[69] Thus the double processes of mediation internal to Critical Regionalism: in the first place, "it has to 'deconstruct' the overall spectrum of world culture which is inevitably inherited; in the second place, it has to

Figure 7.2 Jørn Utzon, Bagsværd Church, Bagsværd Sogn, Sokkelund Herred, København Amt, Denmark, 1976, exterior view. Image courtesy of Wikimidia Commons.

achieve, through synthetic contradiction, a manifest critique of universal civilization."[70] The architectonic implications of this double-edged strategy in Jørn Utzon's Bagsværd Church (1976) (Figure 7.2) and Alvar Aalto's Saynatsalo Town Hall (1952) (Figure 6.1) are demonstrated below.

4. The Resistance of the Place-Form

The central ideas in this section of Frampton's entry are some of the most controversial he has written today. In the 1980s, there was a turn toward using philosophical concepts to support a particular brand of architectural theory, and Frampton's recourse to Martin Heidegger and Hannah Arendt was no exception to this intellectual ambiance.[71] If it was easy for an architect to follow linguistic theorists and work toward a formalistic recoding of architecture, it was a daunting task for critics and historians to take on board, for example, Heidegger's notion of dwelling. Equally daunting was the task of critiquing architecture without becoming trapped in the phenomenological assumption that a *common* subjectivity underpins the beings (Being) evident in Heidegger's writings on "dwelling." As we have seen in previous pages, this was not the first time that Frampton addressed "Building, Dwelling, Thinking," a 1954 Heidegger essay. In Frampton's text under consideration here, he also recalls

Arendt's reflections on "the space of human appearance." There is nothing new in saying that Heidegger and Arendt have deeply influenced Frampton's discourse, to the point that their positions have overshadowed his affiliation with the Frankfurt School of critical theory.

Throughout this volume, attention has been drawn to Frampton's editorial text on Heidegger published in *Opposition* 4 (1975), and his seminal lecture/ essay on Arendt's *The Human Condition*, published in *Architectural Design Profile* (1982). Frampton presents Arendt's call for "the space of human appearance" as a state of resistance against the featureless density of the megalopolis. On the other hand, Heidegger's Raum, a bounded place, allows "being" to dwell, presenting an alternative to the universal placelessness unfolding since the 1960s. These unverifiable expectations from the discourses of these two thinkers are problematic. There is no room here to engage with philosophical issues; nevertheless, Frampton also notes in passing that we cannot but remain cautious about the agrarian roots of expressions such as "*being, cultivating* and *dwelling.*" Whereas the second part of the quotation Frampton chose from Arendt's text was relevant to the politics involved in the contemporary state of urban life, the assignment of "power" to people who "live so close together" cannot be taken at face value, especially after the rise of Fascism in the 1930s, the tendency toward state-sponsored terror experienced and the contemporary surge of populism. Against this historical backdrop, Ernst Bloch's formulation of *Erbschat dieser Zeit* (1935) was alarming; he contested the uncritical acceptance of inheritance and the habits of people living close together as a "community" with shared ideals defined by nation-state politics.

However, Frampton is convincing when he turns to the history of modern architecture and the city. Benefiting from relevant chapters of *A Critical History*, he demonstrates the slow but definitive process of degeneration of "urban forms," the nucleus of old European cities and their conversion to Megalopolis as part of a two-track development. On the one hand, there have been ongoing failures reducing the scope of urban design to "a theoretical subject" independent of city-state politics. On the other is the urban planning authorities' mismanagement of "land-use and logistics of distribution," a phenomenon that attained full visibility after the war. In Chapter 15 of his book, Frampton notes the efforts of Ernst May and Martin Wagner during the Weimar years. These architects attempted to reconcile a socialist administration of land-use with a notion of planning that had been overdetermined by the speculative value of private property ownership.[72] More specifically, Frampton reminds us of "the fate of the plan" practiced during the rebuilding of Rotterdam after World War II, the ultimate instance of planning being reduced to "little more than the allocation of land use and the logistics of distribution."[73] In the same chapter, he refers to the transformation taking place in May's work, from an early tendency toward planning for "the creation of self-contained urban space, after the model of the traditional Prussian Anger village," into a "more generalized approach," evident in his 1926 master-plan for Neue Frankfurt. As an award-winning architect and historian, Frampton demonstrates an awareness of capitalism's political economy, regarding issues such as urban design and social housing. Frampton's intellectual engagement with Heidegger and Arendt aimed at proposing a strategic resistance, providing a *concrete* solution for the crisis of architecture and the city. It is reasonable to say that, in the face of capitalism, no space/place of urban life has remained aloof from the instrumental logic of technology and the prevailing culture of the commodity form.

In light of the developments outlined above, it is not surprising to witness the inevitable separation of architecture from the city since the 1970s. Aldo Rossi's revisitation of the subject could not resuscitate the neo-rationalist concept of architecture, even though Rossi's idea of architecture as an urban artifact was a plausible alternative to the Venturiesque reduction of memorability to simulated classical languages. The postmodernist venture into the past was nothing more than recoding the walls of architecture along with advertising billboards! Frampton correctly considered Robert Venturi's proposition that "Americans do not need piazzas since they should be at home watching television" a reactionary attitude. As we will see under the next two headings, Critical Regionalism was an attempt, on the one hand, to resist both the autonomous and the aestheticized *object*. On the other, it foresees the possibility of an experience of the *collective* and place-form in architecture's engagement with the landscape while emulating typologies, historical and modern. To this end, we are reminded of "the perimeter block, and introspective types such as the gallery, the atrium, the forecourt, and the labyrinth." To these, we should add "social condensers," a historical type associable with "the space of public appearance" Russian Constructivists delivered. However, we should note in passing that most of these building types were originally designed to house commodities, facilitating social encounters. During the 1980s, commodities had already lost their *purpose*, and buildings *housing* these commodities had embraced the postmodernist simulacra and the exhibitionist value of commodities. These developments subdued the type/tectonic essential for a creative reactualization of place-form.

5. *Culture versus Nature: Topography, Context, Climate, Light and Tectonic Form*

Frampton delivered the conceptual pair of type/tectonic as a pedagogical vision during his short chairmanship of the Division of Architecture, GSAPP,

Columbia University (1986–87). Putting aside the formalistic interpretation of type, the topics listed in the above second heading have been, in one way or another, the basis of most building types. Theoretically, these tropes could also provide the basis of construction, even though most materials today are manufactured in different places and delivered to construction sites anywhere, thanks to the global circulation of commodities. However, it is essential to note that the above title was inked when Frampton had not yet published his magnum opus research on tectonics. To address this subject, toward the end of his fifth point, he recalled the architectural historian Stanford Anderson's remarks on tectonics. To paraphrase Frampton, the constructed form is appropriated in cultural terms when its architectonics reveals "the presentation of a structural poetics rather than the re-presentation of a facade."[74] For Frampton, the Semperian urge to elevate the core-form (construction) into the art form (poetics) was a double-edged sword: on the one hand, it plots an alternative architectural praxis against both the postmodern simulation of historical languages and the abstract formalist traditions of the avant-garde; on the other, Frampton makes a case for positioning Critical Regionalism against alternative theories of architecture. More importantly, the conceptual coupling of type/tectonics was symptomatic of the ongoing opposition between universal civilization and regional culture.

Particular to Critical Regionalism is Frampton's claim that "the primary principle of architectural autonomy is tectonic." As such, autonomy is "embedded in the revealed filaments of the construction and in the way in which the synthetical form of the structure explicitly resists the action of gravity."[75] Not only that, but tectonics should not be equated with the exhibition of building's support system. Essential to the poetics of type/tectonic is the Semperian notion of earth-work, the act of terrace making. Most critics dismissed the vitality of tectonics for Critical Regionalism. Still, against the self-referentiality of object-form, architecture attains signification when the tectonic is grafted into the act of terrace making and wall fenestration. And these in consideration of light and climatic conditions. Again, we are reminded of Mario Botta's idea of "building the site" to receive the work that is also positioned according to light, wind and surrounding views. In doing so, "the idiosyncrasies of place find their expression without falling into sentimentalism." The "critical," for Frampton, is validated not only by tectonics but also by the discrete articulations of the joinery of a building's engagement with the landscape, to the point that its rapport with the final work neither evokes the vernacular nor the picturesque. The work rather recodes traditions of modern architecture in the postmodern condition.

Most building examples accompanying various editions of "Critical Regionalism" are limited to the residential type. However, Frampton has not dismissed the need to extend aspects of tectonics into the urban fabric. His enthusiasm for articulating the outer membrane of a building taking into account orientation, climate and the size of the surface fenestration is paramount. The street facade of tall office buildings, on the other hand, can hardly resist "the optimum use of the universal technique." This building type has failed to extend surface articulation into the depth, "to express the place in which the work is situated." Among other alternative building types, Frampton discusses artificial light in most art galleries and offers two critical points. Highlighting the importance of natural light for painting, he sees contemporary art curators' insistence on having the work of art displayed in a box-like artificially lit space as reducing the displayed art to the exigencies of the commodity form. He writes, "The loss of aura, attributed by Walter Benjamin to the processes of mechanical reproduction, also arises from a relatively static application of universal technology." Interestingly enough, and related to the loss of aura, one cannot but note, in between the lines of Frampton's urgings for regional sustainability, his antipathy toward three types of machinery that have diminished the urban fabric—the bulldozer, the artificial light and the air conditioner. These three elements, along with the serpentine highway and the free-standing high-rise building, do indeed structure contemporary built-form, as various agencies of capitalism extend their presence further into the city's everyday life.

6. The Visual versus the Tactile

By the advent of electronic technologies in the 1980s, it was clear that vision and visuality were conquering domains of culture beyond what photography and film had done. Martin Heidegger's essay "The Question Concerning Technology,"[76] presented an alarming account of these unfoldings, and he presented the recollection of the Greek notion of *techne* as an alternative to the mechanical laws of divisions enforced by the machine. Thus, he avoids the Benjaminian "loss of aura" in favor of the essence of technology, the "standing reserve." His critique of technology coupled with allusive references to the poesies of making was taken as an alternative to a historical interpretation of modernity. Here we should agree with Jameson's position that "Heidegger's anti-modernism (by no means as original as the phenomenological explorations of *Sein* und *Zeit*) cannot imagine a solution to technological alienation except by way of regression."[77] In any event, Heidegger seemed appealing and "critical" during the rise of phenomenology and a postmodernist anti-modern sentiment of the 1980s. Heidegger's shadow was felt here and there. In search of a meaningful departure from prewar modernism, the Smithsons, a member of the British Independent Group, wrote: "We were concerned with seeing of materials for what they were: the woodness of wood, the sandiness of sand. With this came a distaste of the simulated."[78] We are tempted to think of Heidegger's "thingness of the thing" most often taken for a materialist realism.

Frampton's affiliation with phenomenology is also evident in the opening statement of the sixth point. Pitting the tactile against the visual, Frampton reminds the reader of "the capacity of the body to read the environment in terms of other than those of sight alone."[79] No one can deny the essentiality of the body for tactile, visual and other sensory experiences. Nor can anyone deny that, throughout the history of humanity, technological developments have opened different perceptual horizons, enriching the body's engagement with the surrounding physical and emotional environments, including those central to the formation of different social subjectivities. We might think of the opening scene of Stanley Kubrick's 1968 film *2001: A Space Odyssey*, where a simple tool encapsulates the future technological domination of Earth and sky. Frampton is not a stranger to class issues either. He has directed the sharp edge of his criticism toward architects and critics who stop short of resisting the domination of universal technology. Frampton's exposure to phenomenology set his early career as a writer, and as a practicing architect with hands-on experience of the material conditions of production, squarely against post-modern architecture, which had the least patience for "intensity of light and darkness, heat and cold." More importantly, and perhaps in recollection of the work of Loos, Aalto and Siza, he wrote of "the almost palpable presence of masonry as the body senses its confinement." To highlight his point further, Frampton shared his enthusiasm for film and architecture, recalling Luchino Visconti's *The Damned* and the director's insistence that the actor should walk on a real wooden parquet. In light of these observations, Frampton turns one more time to Aalto's Saynatsalo Town Hall (1952), highlighting the importance of materiality for the "kinetic impetus of the body in climbing the stairs. Thus, it is checked by the friction of the steps, which are 'read' soon after, in contrast to the timber floor of the council chamber itself." What is involved here is the transformation experienced in the moving body from one materiality to another, resonating in the spectator's auditory system.

In the previous chapter the critical importance of Aalto for Frampton's formulation of critical praxis has already been discussed. In conjunction with Critical Regionalism, Saynatsalo Town Hall, along with Utzon's Bagsværd Church, is discussed in brief here. These two works are significant for several reasons, including that their illustrations are the only ones that accompany the 1983 edition of "Critical Regionalism" and that both are civic buildings, one designed for a religious purpose, and the other for the judiciary. Also, Frampton illustrates his discussion of these buildings with a careful choice of photographs shot from a particular view, in addition to each building's representational drawings. As for Aalto, the Town Hall exemplifies the architect's profound juxtaposition of civic expectations with elements borrowed from domestic architecture.

In the Town Hall, the courtyard resonates with Aalto's design strategies in the "experimental house" discussed in the previous chapter. Whereas in the latter work, topography was modified in analogy to terrace making, in the Town Hall, the earthwork is a *fabrication*; it comes across as a mound with delicate articulations, to the point that the ascending visitor notices the so-to-speak underground floor in a retrospective experience of the courtyard. The other dimension of the same juxtaposition is the architect's extensive use of brick, covering both floors and walls. Critical in the Town Hall is the council room, which plays a significant role in transforming the courtyard, surrounded by brick walls, into a public work. The most vertically articulated volume of the complex, the council room, is cleverly placed next to the main entry stair. This might be one reason why the council room's external presence is photographed from the stairs located on the opposite side. The implied filmic experience intertwines *place* with civics, a strategy that de facto undermines the fact that the complex is located almost in the middle of nowhere, amid surrounding lush trees.

A similar strategy of juxtaposition operates in Bagsværd Church. Utzon's architectonics works toward turning an agrarian industrial-looking building into a religious one without simulating historical typologies. Following Kahn's idea of served/service spaces, this church's planimetric organization comprises sequences of rooms leading to the main public gathering hall. These geometrically organized rooms are surrounded on almost all sides by substantial volumes of housing-related service spaces. The sequential volumetric stepping up of these rooms attains its highest point toward the middle of the gathering space. Neither its complex planimetric organization nor its honorific external views of the church assist the spectator's expectation of the building's sectional organization. As is the case with Aalto's Town Hall, the sectional profile of Bagasvaerd draws attention to the earth-work, first "by building it out of precast concrete planks set on top of the reinforced concrete basement and second by assembling the dais and pulpit out of precast hollow concrete slabs similar to the planking used for the floor."[80] Equally important tectonically is the technique of poche, a device traditionally used in plans enclosed by masonry wall construction systems. In this particular work, Utzon converts the poche into the cladding of the section, a cloth-like membrane hovering above the believers like a cloud, with a profile that echoes the external stepping up of the building. It is to Frampton's credit to demonstrate the relevance of Critical Regionalism for civic architecture. However, in these two projects, it is the coupling of type/tectonics that makes the suggested *relevance* comprehensible. In this permutation, the metaphysics of *genius loci* evaporate, and Frampton's concept of placemaking becomes primarily congenial to tectonic articulation, "distilling play between material, craftwork, and gravity, to yield a component which is, in fact, a condensation of the entire structure," and also topography. Kindred to the claim here is that what stands out in the public buildings of these two architects is the element of roofing which is tectonically grafted into the earth-work, to recall Gottfried Semper.

IV

What should we make of the title of this chapter? In the first place, the suggested move from the "critical" to resistance speaks for Frampton's aspiration toward a rear-guard position, as noted in the second entry point above. As for the question of the avant-garde, Frampton is seemingly in agreement with Peter Burger that the historical project of the avant-garde is history. In the present state of global capitalism, it is hard, if not impossible, to pursue the movement's artistic and political agenda further, at least in architecture. The intellectual work produced during the early years of the 1980s came short of appreciating Frampton's Critical Regionalism. At the time, in the tradition of modernism, the political was most often associated with the avant-garde. The shift from the critical to resistance also meant abandoning the suggested association wherein the critical in postmodernity was among many other possibilities associable with the diverse avant-garde attitudes of the time. Accordingly, the operative domain of "critical," we should say, is confined and validated within Western Humanism, whereas resistance is a stern refusal of any status quo, center and periphery. Frampton used *resistance* in its most common political connotation: the act of standing against overwhelming power, political, economic and/or cultural. In a conversation, Frampton recalls Bent Flyjvberg's *Rationality and Power: Democracy in Action*, stating that "Critical Regionalism is a rearguard position, a holding operation. It is committed to sustaining a dialectic between the local and the global, to cultivating an environmentally sensitive architecture, and to a discourse between the architect and the client, which aspires to be 'democratic.'"[81] This general understanding of resistance, Howard Caygill writes, "is rooted in practice and articulated in tactical statements and justifications addressing specific historical contexts."[82] Under the title of "Anti-Fascist Theories of Resistance," Caygill recalls Antonio Gramsci's and Walter Benjamin's contributions to our understanding of resistance when "total domination" attains *visibility* in almost every dimension of the lifeworld. As a philosophy of defiance, however, resistance has historico-theoretical connotations that could map the Framptonian six points of resistance, along with Walter Benjamin's vision of history, as discussed in Chapter 2 of this volume.

Interestingly enough, on various occasions, Frampton recalls Gramsci's speculation that "the crisis consists precisely in the fact that the old is dying and the new cannot be born; in this interregnum, a great variety of morbid symptoms appear." However, by opening his book with Walter Benjamin's "Thesis on the Philosophy of History," Frampton had already grafted *resistance* into his historiography as the unconscious of the "critical" formulated in conjunction with the historicity of Fascism in Europe. According to Caygill, this distinction is important because of the urgency felt in resisting the overwhelming experience of Fascism in 1930s Europe. A major preoccupation of a Marxist theory of resistance was to distance itself from "the problem of consciousness that dominated" various innate tendencies, from the messianic to the "expression of the new."[83] There are moments in Benjamin's text where resistance is intertwined with the unconscious dimension of history if the historian abandons the Enlightenment vision of linear progress and its twin concept, technological determinism. In conjunction with the global presence and experience of capitalism in many geographies today, this concept of resistance is indispensable to Frampton's Critical Regionalism. Similar to the provocation implied in Benjamin's reading of the "angel of history," Critical Regionalism provokes a temporality, debunking the linear flow of time and revealing the architectonics suggested in Frampton's six points as the future-now of which our modernist forebearers dreamed. In conformity with Benjamin's angel of history, Frampton agrees that the present "is as much the future for the past as it is the past for the future."[84] In Fredric Jameson's words, "Critical Regionalism continues to seek a certain deeper historical logic in the past of this system, if not its future: a rearguard retains overtones of a collective resistance."[85] Critical Regionalism thus offers a strategic resistance to reducing architecture to the positivistic exigencies of technology, foregrounding temporality as a site of war against the pressure globalization that exerts on the art of building. It thus offers historical criticism and conjugates temporal changes (history) with type/tectonic forms with roots in different geographies and temporalities. However, these are invisible in the present overwhelming obsession with the *new* instigated by the latest technological inventions.

Another dimension of the aforementioned shift relates to Frampton's particular comprehension of "region" in the age of global capitalism. This much is clear from his insistence that Critical Regionalism should not be reduced to localized sentimentalism, a phenomenon popularized by capitalism today. During the past two decades, we have witnessed "the appearance and expansion of industrial capitalism and its propensity to install similar conditions everywhere it is established."[86] The once-upon-a-time notion of regional identity is today merged with the universal vocation for commodity consumerism, not only in the public realm but also in domestic spaces. For Frampton, Critical Regionalism is a strategy for resisting total absorption into the commodity form culture produced and distributed by late capitalism, without denying the positive fruits of modernization. In this sense, the preface "critical" suggests the *impossibility* of "translating" one language into another[87] and the futility of seeking to reproduce regionalism as such today.[88] Allegorically, we are speaking of grafting two disjointed elements: intertwined as they are, each remains tectonically distinct, and this rather complicated rapport between region and center is key to understanding Frampton's move from critical to resistance. The architecture of Critical Regionalism does not represent regional style; instead, it demonstrates the totality of the region's dialectical engagement with modernity. This issue is the least discussed dimension of Critical Regionalism, as Fredric Jameson noted, along with two additional insightful observations. For Jameson, "Critical Regionalism can be opposed both to modernism and to postmodernism alike" and it alludes to "a distinctive regional culture as a whole, for which the distinctive individual building becomes a metonym."[89] This was music to Frampton's ears! In a 2005 essay and his 2018 "Plenary Talk" to the Society of Architectural Historians (SAH), he quotes Jameson extensively. In the former text, Frampton recalls Jameson's appraisal comparing Tadao Ando's "self-enclosed modernity" with Jørn Utzon's Bagsværd Church, where both architects utilize a reinforced concrete construction system, though toward two different interpretations of tectonics.[90] As for the second interview, Frampton stated that "no one has understood what I intended by Critical Regionalism more sensitively than the Marxist critic Frederick Jameson."[91] Critically addressing alternative architectural praxes that were available throughout the postmodern condition, which pursued certain "traits of high modernism," Jameson writes that Critical Regionalism

> distinguishes itself by attempting at the same time, to negate a whole series of postmodern negations of modernism as well [...] seeks to resist. Yet, it is positing of an arrière-garde would seem to be incompatible with a postmodern end of History [...] The current slogans of marginality and resistance, as Frampton evokes them, would also appear to carry somewhat different connotations than those deployed in, say, current evocations of multi-culturalism.[92]

In Frampton's turn to "resistance," we are cautioned about the extent to which the production of architecture has been dependent on technological innovations and aesthetics that have the least to do with the métier of architecture.

In conclusion, two observations need attention: the first concerns periodization, the historicity of modernity's project; the second concerns how the specific thematic of the Enlightenment had to adjust itself—if these themes have not lost their sociopolitical and cultural relevance—as late capitalism took over what retrospectively we can call the period of early modernism. Frampton is seemingly aware of the essentiality of the notion of identity for the formation of bourgeois society. Even though national identity has lost its traditional currency, particular to architecture is the *identity* it evokes. Therefore, Frampton's interest is in architects whose work focuses on the projection of identity as such, rather than mirroring the zeitgeist, technically or aesthetically. This brings us to the second issue, the certainty of architecture's rapport with capitalism's production and consumption systems. What differentiates architecture from other art forms is its capacity to be both temporal and historical. The longevity of architecture is the result of it being a constructed *object*, the use and appropriation of which are inseparable from the modalities of everyday life. Architecture is both *history* and historical. Critical Regionalism is an attempt to demonstrate the historicity of this encounter.

Should Critical Regionalism still be taken seriously today?[93] Although the seeds of its time have inevitably touched Critical Regionalism, nevertheless, we should recognize and extrapolate its potentialities for transforming and humanizing the ongoing one-dimensional technological progression. How should architecture respond to the ecological crisis, the inflation of migration and Jameson's suggestion that "aestheticization can only be energizing if it becomes an allegory of productivity and radical constructivism"[94]—and this at a time when globalization redefines the scope of national identity once characterized by the nation-state phenomenon. Considering the expansion of the marvel of world architecture, the work once theorized within the nation-state boundary is today broken into two categories, the local and the national. Whereas the former refers to what used to be discussed in terms of regionalism, as distinct from the vernacular, at least throughout early modern times, the latter is gauged against the background of world architecture and trademarks made up of digitally reproduced work, parametric. In this line of consideration and as a project, Critical Regionalism tends to recode regionalism within world architecture. It can also be suggested that overshadowed by world architecture, Frampton's Critical Regionalism offers a sustainable alternative to both the straitjacket modern colonial naturalization of the vernacular and the nation-state regionalism.

Notes

1. This discussion looks at the changes taking place in William Morris's positions on labor, work and architecture. See Chapter 1 in Kenneth Frampton, *Modern Architecture: A Critical History* (London: Thames & Hudson, 1980), 42–50.
2. Kenneth Frampton, "Preface to the Second Edition," in *A Critical History* (London: Thames & Hudson, 1985), 7.
3. Kenneth Frampton, "Towards an Agonistic Architecture," *Domus* 972 (September 2013).
4. This claim is made following Fredric Jameson's essay "Third-World Literature in the Era of Multinational Capitalism," *Social Text* 15 (Autumn 1986): 65–88. And Fredric Jameson, *The Seeds of Time* (New York: Columbia University Press, 1994), 185–205.
5. Fredric Jameson, *Allegory and Ideology* (London: Verso, 2019), 25–26.
6. Hal Foster, *The Anti-aesthetic: Essays on Postmodern Culture* (Washington, DC: Bay, 1983).
7. Ernst Bloch, *The Heritage of Our Times* (Los Angeles: University of California Press, 1990), initially published in Frankfurt am Main, 1962.
8. Harry Harootunian, *Uneven Moments: Reflections on Japan's Modern History* (New York: Columbia University Press, 2019), 44.
9. Walter Benjamin's reflections on history are useful here. See his "Thesis on the Philosophy of History," in *Illuminations* (New York: Harcourt, Brace & World, 1969), 261.
10. See "Critical Regionalism Revisited," the entire issue of *Journal of Architecture, OASE* 103 (2019).
11. Kenneth Frampton, "Prospects for a Critical Regionalism," *Perspecta* 20 (1983): 147–62.
12. Harootunian, *Uneven Moments*, 199.
13. On the rise and fall of the Non-Aligned Movement, see Vijay Prashad, *The Darker Nations: A People's History of the Third World* (New York: New Press, 2007).
14. See Rem Koolhaas and Hans Ulrich Obrist, *Project Japan: Metabolism Talks* (Koln: Taschen, 2011), the section titled "Expansion/Exile," in particular.
15. Lukasz Stanek, *Architecture in Global Socialism: Eastern Europe, West Africa, and the Middle East in the Cold War* (Princeton, NJ: Princeton University Press, 2020), 2.
16. Ivan Krastev and Stephen Holmes, "Of Course They Gave Up on Democracy," *New York Times*, Monday, March 9, 2020.
17. John Roberts, "Belatedness, Internationalism and the Global Avant-Garde," in *Revolutionary Time and the Avant-Garde* (London: Verso, 2015), 131.
18. Harry Harootunian, "'Modernity' and the Claim of Untimeliness," *Postdoctoral Studies* 13.4 (2010): 367–82.
19. Here, we benefit from Harootunian, *Uneven Moments*, 49.
20. Jameson, "Third-World Literature," 65–88.
21. Kenneth Frampton (ed.), *Tadao Ando: Buildings, Projects, Writings* (New York: Rizzoli International, 1984), 6–10.
22. Kenneth Frampton, "Botta's Paradigm: Houses in Origlio and Morbio Superiore, Switzerland," *Progressive Architecture* (December 12, 1984): 82–90.
23. Ibid., 85.
24. Frampton, *Tadao Ando*.
25. Liane Lefaivre and Alexander Tzonis, "Why Critical Regionalism Today?" *Architecture and Urbanism* 236 (May 1990): 23–33.
26. Herbert Marcuse, *Eros and Civilization* (New York: Vintage, 1955), 18–19. A Freudo-Marxist, Marcuse is quoted in the first edition of Kenneth Frampton's book in the context of Superstudio's "anti-futuristic" utopia. Frampton had borrowed the book from

Allen Colquhoun. See Cynthia Davidson, "On the Record with Kenneth Frampton," *Log* (Fall 2018): 32.
27 Frampton, "Prospects for a Critical Regionalism," 149.
28 Ibid.
29 Frampton quoting Alexander Tzonis and Liane Le Faivre, "The Grid and the Pathway: An Introduction to the Work of Dimitris and Susana Antonakakis," *Architecture in Greece* 15 (1981): 164–78.
30 The quotation is from Harwell Hamilton Harris's speech at the Northwest regional committee meeting of the AIA in Eugene, 1954. Kenneth Frampton recall Harris's speech in, "Prospects for a Critical Regionalism," *Perspecta* 20 (1983): 154–55.
31 Kenneth Frampton, "Ten Points on an Architecture of Regionalism: A Provisional Polemic," *Center 3: New Regionalism* (1987): 20-27. The article was reprinted in Vincint B. Canizaro, ed. *Architectural Regionalism* (New York: Princeton Architectural Press, 2007), 375-385.
32 For a summary of the delivered lectures, see *Museum of Modern Art Bulletin* (Spring 1948): 4–21.
33 Quoted in Joan Ockman (ed.), *Architecture Culture 1943–1968* (New York: Rizzoli International, 1993), 109. The article was first published in the *New Yorker*, October 11, 1947.
34 Following Fredric Jameson, *Raymond Chandler: The Detections of Totality* (London: Verso, 2016), 6.
35 Francesco Dal Co, "Winners and Losers, Interpreting the Mumford of the Brown Decades," in *Autonomy and Ideology: Positioning an Avant-Garde in America*, ed. R. E. Somol (New York: Monachelli, 1997), 198–211.
36 Frampton, "Prospects for a Critical Regionalism," 156.
37 The Five's timely departure from the language of late modern architecture was seen, at the time, as a radical alternative to the postmodern simulation of historical forms.
38 For Kenneth Frampton's reading of Martin Heidegger, see "On Reading Heidegger," *Oppositions* 2 (1976): 1–4. See Gianni Vattimo, *The End of Modernity* (Minneapolis: University of Minneapolis Press, 1985). This Italian thinker presents a fresh departure from the phenomenological reading of Martin Heidegger. His discourse was significant for my approach to the tectonic. See Gevork Hartoonian, *Ontology of Construction* (Cambridge: Cambridge University Press, 1994).
39 Jameson, *Raymond Chandler*, 76–81.
40 Hal Foster (ed.), *The Anti-aesthetic: Essays on Postmodern Culture* (Washington, DC: Bay, 1983).
41 Hal Foster, "Postmodernism: A Preface," in ibid., x; original emphasis.
42 The center/periphery was symptomatic of a more complex rapport between countries in the Middle East, West Africa and the two powers dominating the Cold War, namely the United States and the Soviet Union. However, the ground players in most of the countries emerging out of the yoke of colonialism were many. In addition to the political, educational and economic agendas delivered by President Truman's Point Four Program, mention should be made not only of the Socialist Bloc but also of the members of the Non-Aligned Movement, OPEC and pan-Islamic World Muslim League. See "Introduction," in Stanek, *Architecture in Global Socialism*.

43 This might sound a bit of generalization; however, the Capitalist importation of American goods and lifestyle initially focused on countries with oil resources. It seems not much changed in this regard!
44 Reinhart Koselleck, *Future Past: On the Semantics of Historical Time* (New York: Columbia University Press, 2003), 266–67.
45 The idea of the Megalopolis is extensively discussed in Jean Gottman, *Megalopolis* (Cambridge: MIT Press, 1961).
46 Michael Graves is mentioned in a footnote to Kenneth Frampton's "1. Culture and Civilization," in Foster, *The Anti-aesthetic*, 30.
47 See Harootunian, *Uneven Moments*, 49.
48 Paul Ricoeur, "Universal Civilization and National Cultures," in *History and Truth* (Evanston, IL: Northwestern University Press, 1965), 274.
49 Ibid., 281.
50 Frampton, "Prospects for a Critical Regionalism," 148; original emphases.
51 From an interview with this author, January 2001, New York City. For the full text of the interview, see Gevork Hartoonian, *Global Perspectives on Critical Architecture* (London: Routledge, 2015), 43–48.
52 Harootunian, *Uneven Moments*, 179.
53 Kenneth Frampton's "The Rise and Fall of the Avant-Garde," in Foster, *The Anti-aesthetic*, 18.
54 Kenneth Frampton, "In Conversation with Kenneth Frampton," *October* 106 (Autumn 2003): 57.
55 Susan Sontag, "Introduction," in *One-Way Street*, ed. Walter Benjamin (London: Verso, 1997), 24.
56 Frampton's "The Rise and Fall of the Avant-Garde," 19.
57 Kenneth Frampton, "Avant-Garde and Continuity," *Architectural Design* 7–8 (1982): 21.
58 Peter Burger, *Theory of the Avant-Garde* (Minneapolis: University of Minnesota, 1984), 46. See also Gevork Hartoonian, "Avant-Garde: Re-thinking Architecture," in *Modernity and Its Other: A Post-Script to Contemporary Architecture* (College Station: Texas A & M University Press, 1977), 103–20. For pros and cons of Burger's book see footnote 1 of the same chapter.
59 Kenneth Frampton, *Architectural Design* 7–8 (1982): 23.
60 John Roberts, "Belatedness, Internationalism and the Global Avant-Garde," in *Revolutionary Time and the Avant-Garde* (London: Verso, 2015), 123–25.
61 Kenneth Frampton, "A Lost Avant-Garde" (1968), reprinted in *Art in Revolution*, an exhibition catalogue of Hayward Gallery, London, 1971. See Roberts, "Belatedness, Internationalism and the Global Avant-Garde."
62 Quoted in Kenneth Frampton, "Towards a Critical Regionalism," in Foster, *The Anti-aesthetic*, 21.
63 Frampton, *The Anti-aesthetic*, 20.
64 A. Tzonis and L. Lefaivre, "The Grid and the Pathway: An Introduction to the Work of Dimitris and Susana Antonakakis," *Architecture in Greece* 15 (1981): 121–34.
65 Ibid. Also quoted in Frampton, *The Anti-aesthetic*, 21.
66 Alexander Tzonis, "Introducing an Architecture of the Present: Critical Regionalism and the Design of Identity," in *Critical Regionalism: Architecture and Identity in a Globalized World*, ed. Liane Lefaivre and Alexander Tzonis (New York: Prestel, 2003), 20.
67 Jameson, *The Seeds of Time*.
68 Hartoonian, "Avant-Garde: Re-thinking Architecture," 1997.

69 Hal Foster, *Design and Crime* (London: Verso, 2003), 100–103.
70 Frampton, *The Anti-aesthetic*, 21.
71 Jorge Otero-Pailos, *Architecture's Historical Turn: Phenomenology and the Rise of the Postmodern* (Minneapolis: University of Minnesota Press, 2010).
72 Frampton, *A Critical History*, 137.
73 Frampton, *The Anti-aesthetic*, 24.
74 Ibid., 28.
75 Ibid., 27.
76 Martin Heidegger, "The Question Concerning Technology," in *Basic Writings*, ed. D. F. Krell (New York: Harper and Row, 1977), 287–322.
77 Fredric Jameson, *Representing Capital: A Reading of Volume One* (London: Verso, 2011), 101–3.
78 Hal Foster, *Brutal Aesthetics* (Princeton, NJ: Princeton University Press, 2020), 139.
79 Frampton, *The Anti-aesthetic*, 28.
80 Kenneth Frampton, *Studies in Tectonic Culture* (Cambridge: MIT Press, 1995).
81 Gevork Hartoonian, "Kenneth Frampton Interviewed by Gevork Hartoonian," in *Global Perspectives on Critical Architecture: Praxis Reloaded*, ed. Gevork Hartoonian (London: Routledge, 2017), 44.
82 Howard Caygill, *On Resistance: A Philosophy of Defiance* (London: Bloomsbury, 2013), 6.
83 Ibid., 139.
84 Paraphrasing ibid., 144.
85 Jameson, *The Seeds of Time*, 191.
86 Harootunian, *Uneven Moments*, 43.
87 See Walter Benjamin, "The Task of the Translator," in *Selected Writings Vol. 1, 1913–1926*, ed. Walter Benjamin (Cambridge: Harvard University Press, 1996), 253–63.
88 Allen Colquhoun was one of the few who noted the regressive dimension of the implied "return." See Colquhoun, "Regionalism and Technology," in *Modernity and the Classical Tradition: Architectural Essays 1980–1987* (Cambridge: MIT Press, 1989), 207–11. For major writings on regionalism, see Vincent Canizaro (ed.), *Architectural Regionalism* (New York: Princeton Architectural Press, 2007).
89 Jameson, *The Seeds of Time*, 193.
90 Kenneth Frampton, "Critical Regionalism Revisited: Reflections on the Mediatory Potential of Built-Form," in *Vernacular Modernism: Heimat, Globalization, and the Built Environment*, ed. M. Umbach and H. Huppauf (California: Stanford University Press, 2005), 193.
91 Kenneth Frampton, https://www.sah.org/publications-and-research/sah-newsletter/sah-newsletter-ind/2018/05/21/2018-plenary-talk-by-kenneth-frampton# (accessed May 26, 2018).
92 Jameson, *The Seeds of Time*.
93 See Tom Avermaete, V. Patteeuw, Lea-Catherine Szacka and H. Teerds, "Critical Regionalism Revisited," *OASE*, no. 103 (May 2019): 1–10, and the *Architectural Review*, issue 1466 (Spring 2019).
94 Fredric Jameson, *Allegory and Ideology* (London: Verso, 2019), 37.

POSTSCRIPT

Inflation: World Architecture

> National *literature* is now a rather unmeaning term; the epoch of *world literature* is at hand, and everyone must strive to hasten its approach.
> —J. W. Goethe (1827; original emphases)

> National one-sidedness and narrow-mindedness become more and more impossible, and from the numerous national and local literatures there arises a world literature.
> —K. Marx, *The Communist Manifesto* (1848)

As I sat to write the following pages, I received an email from Kenneth Frampton saying that he had completed the fifth edition of *A Critical History*, published late in 2020.[1] In an earlier personal conversation, when asked how a fifth edition would relate to the *critical concept* as formulated in the introduction to the first edition of the book, his response was something like "It's gone!" Would he have given the same answer if the question had been raised when the book's fourth edition was published? In any event, our interest here centers on the content of these editions and the fact that a departure from the book's first edition was already anticipated in the third, with the last chapter of Part III titled "World Architecture and Reflective Practice." Before taking up the notion of "world architecture," it should be emphasized that the leading title of Part III has not changed since the publication of the first edition of the book (1980). It reads "Critical Assessment and Extension into the Present," followed by different cycles of periodization depending on which edition of the book you pick: from 1925–78 (first edition) to 1925–84 (second edition) to 1925–91 (third and fourth editions). Noteworthy is the double connotations of the phrase "extension into the present": it could mean either that there will be future sequels to the book or/and that modern architecture has been an "incomplete" project since 1978, the decade roughly comprising the rise of the postmodern condition. Accordingly, only Parts I and II of the book have remained focused on "modern architecture." In contrast, the subjects discussed in Part III explicitly announced the end of the canon of the International Style architecture. Still, while the lead title of Part III has remained the same, a new chapter has been added to the end of each subsequent edition of the book.

Now, regardless of what other reasons the author and the publisher might have had for these editions, what remains consistent is Frampton's insistence on critical engagement with the temporality of architecture at each turn of the *present*. Thus, while the "critical" has remained the book's main project for 40 years, Frampton has become increasingly inclined to marry pragmatism with a phenomenological take on Marxism. If critical had to be articulated in the light of challenges launched against "national identity," at another point, he launched Critical Regionalism as a stand against the overwhelming presence and experience of the commodity form in the realm of culture. In this permutation, "reflective practice" was introduced in the third edition of the book as a way to reconsider critical practice at a time (roughly around 1990) when "the spontaneous urbanization of the world" and "the loss of the *finite* city as a significant cultural object" had left "building with no choice but to exist in its historical moment."[2] Accordingly, it is essential to reflect on the preface to the third edition, particularly the idea of "reflective practice" advanced by the sociologist Donald Shon (1983), and then attend to the notion of "world architecture." In what follows, the importance of *historicity* for Frampton's critical historiography of architecture in late capitalism is highlighted.

In the preface to the book's third edition, Frampton underlines the importance of reflective practice.[3] The preface is dedicated to four countries (see below), from where selected work is discussed in the last chapter of Part III. Aside from a long quotation of the epigraph to the last chapter of the third edition of *A Critical History*, Frampton draws on Schon's idea of reflective practice to underline various attempts to demystify technical rationality, the guiding principle pursued by most professionals who played a significant role in organizing postwar Western society at large. Schon's argument also considers the radical criticism of the late 1960s, launched against most institutions of the emerging system known today as late capitalism. On one end of Schon's critical spectrum are Ivan Illich and his distrust of the instrumental logic informing the professional world. At the other end, he mentions Christopher Alexander, whose design theories were taught in most American architecture schools during the 1970s. In addition to *Notes on the Synthesis of Form* (1964), what appealed to Schon was Alexander's associative theory and the correspondence he makes between "pattern languages" in architecture, which he "saw as 'part of nature'—and 'patterns of events,' leading to 'the quality without a name' in which 'timeless way of building' achieves fulfillment."[4] Interestingly enough, Frampton mentions Alexander for the first time in the postscript to the third edition of *A Critical History*, and about his and Serge Chermayeff's criticism of row-rise, high-density housing, a typology that, according to Frampton, has frequently been demonstrated since the end of the 1950s to be "both practical and eminently liveable."[5] What Frampton saw as useful in Schon's criticism of professionals' technically informed and problem-solving attitude was the author's advocacy for "knowing-in-action." In this line of consideration, Frampton highlights the necessity for architects to engage with the client and the actuality of the circumstances, both technical and cultural, which, in one form or another, are accountable for the work's purpose and its final form and aesthetics. Thus, the dialogue between architect and client is presented as essential for realizing architecture that neither follows the mainstream aesthetic nor is obsessed with the technologically driven spectacle informing the present culture. This is important because each of the four countries, Finland, France, Spain and Japan, are part of a "well-developed" universe. The selected work presented in the book's final pages shows a "remarkably high level of general practice."[6]

Accordingly, by the third edition of the book, Frampton was still making a distinction between architecture associable with Critical Regionalism and that which was "conditioned by a mode of beholding" that, in return, would oblige the historian to avoid writing "an absolute history." To this end, and following Fredric Jameson's observation that Critical Regionalism does have the potential to invent a different relationship with technology beyond the modernist celebratory or nostalgic positions, Frampton wrote in 2005 that "the prospect of transfiguring the modern transcends all those critical categories oscillating between the modern, the postmodern, and the anti-modern to leave us disarmed, as it were, before the relentless technoscientific modernization of our age."[7] Seemingly, the works chosen from the mentioned four countries do engage with technology differently and validate the other two tropes important for Frampton's discourse on the critical: we are reminded of the ever-anachronistic character of the process of building due to constant technological inventions, and the present situation that is marked by the disappearance of the line separating the rural from the cosmopolitan. This being the case, "world architecture" is also concerned with the creative recoding of the historically accumulated culture of the building that is not yet intimidated by the two tenets of the modernist approach to technology: the romantic yearning for the lost traditional craft, and the futuristic embracement of technology. Neither *recodings* is validated by Frampton's "six points of resistance." Instead, he highlights the ethics involved in the dialectics between the *what*—the character of the building—and the *how*—a host of Semperian themes relevant to tectonics, that is, earth-work, frame-work and cladding, to mention the three most important ones.

In the same preface, we are also reminded of "the exceptional capacity of the best high-tech offices but also the equally impressive levels of tectonic sophistication to be found among more humanist lines of practice, as is evident say in the work of the Portuguese master Alvaro Siza." Thus, between Siza and Renzo Piano, a juxtaposition that might be considered a replacement for Aalto and Mies is discussed in Chapter 6 of this volume. However, this juxtaposition should not be taken as a happy ending but as a potential response to the ongoing crisis of architecture. Despite and because of "world architecture," Frampton tried to expand and include diverse work produced globally and beyond those strictly sitting in the orbit of Critical Regionalism. Thus, considering the diversity and scope of architecture produced in the four corners of the world, it is convincing that *inflation* in architecture should be included in any critical architecture assessment.

To better understand the proposed notion of inflation and recoding of Critical Regionalism, some ideas from Jameson's text "Third-World Literature in the Era of Multinational Capitalism,"[8] introduced in the previous chapter, are reiterated here. The intention here is to associate Critical Regionalism with the loss of the canon, architecture formulated in the context of the ongoing Western theorization of architecture since Vitruvius's *The Ten Books on Architecture*. Although it is not clear if Frampton has read Jameson's text, we should revisit the inclusion of "world architecture" in the title of the last chapter of the third edition of *A Critical History* in the light of Jameson's notion of "world literature," which Goethe had theorized long ago. According to John Pizer, J. W. Goethe also wrote about *Weltmarkt*, evidently wanting to establish a rapport among the "monetary, material, and communicative underlying cultural transnationalism" of the time.[9] As part of the commodity form market, apropos, architecture today is circulating the world beyond national boundaries. Digital media offers architects access to various architectural production techniques (programs), which also contribute to the formation of the subjectivity central to the capitalistic ideological drive for homogenizing technological progress as an end in itself. This unfolding has put both critics and historians in a guarded position. It might be a historical coincidence that the digital surge coincided with the end of the era of Theory, the theorization of architecture in the light of philosophical ideas. However, the concept of inflation also recalls the Marxian concepts of world history and the world market as allegories for a particular totality. Having said this, and as far as it concerns architecture, Jameson's text is helpful in two different ways. First, literature has, in many ways, a closer rapport with culture than with the prevailing technical apparatus. Conversely, architecture in modernity has closer ties with the given political economy, which most often determines the state of technology as such, but more importantly with technologies of construction, labor skills and materials, the total of which informs the production and consumption of the final work.[10] Second, because architecture is comprehended and appropriated mostly in the sphere of everyday life, to overcome *inflation*, criticism of world architecture should focus on the double-edged function of culture technique. This observation is not explicitly addressed in Jameson's text, though it is tacitly implied when he writes that literature in the Third World is in many ways political. This proclamation is inevitable in the age of capitalism when the "local being" is already positioned against the "universal being."[11] Thus, the political is central to the culture-technique dichotomy, a strategy paramount in Frampton's writing, though stated differently. For example, it is suggested in Critical Regionalism that in most countries, especially those located outside of the orbit of the First World, an ongoing conflict exists between local traditions and the abstract and formal implications of technology. A de facto acceptance of world architecture, on the other hand, safeguards against fragmentation and the demise of national identity in the age of capitalist globalization. This observation is important at a time when the old separation between technique and culture, essential for the formation of modern architecture (*Bauen*) during the early decades of the past century, has now vanished, at least in the First World. This development is also crucial because, in the context of the contemporary transformation from mechanical to digital reproducibility, the technical and the cultural are interwoven to the point where the digitally reproduced surface is considered a definitive but reductive definition of architecture's contemporaneity.[12] Therefore, the state of such a fusion underlines the *common* in the contemporary inflation of architecture.

We return now to the old center/periphery dichotomy, which in the light of the above considerations is transfigured into differential indexes that should be mapped regarding two unfoldings: first, almost all nations today embrace the production and consumption system of capitalism, marketed under the rubric of global modernization. Second, national culture in various countries is most often informed by the conflict between the remnants of local culture and the consumerism championed by late capitalism, the regime of which remains anonymous given the scope of corporate networks. Whereas the dominant architecture produced in the centers has already internalized the spectacle of the commodity form, architecture produced in peripheries is by nature political in one way or another. Still, because of the technique-culture centrality, architecture produced at the periphery demonstrates traces of resistance against both the process of homogenization (cultural) and digitalization (technical). The implied rift speaks for the "unequal development" as part of the subsequent processes of modernization despite the claim that fruits of progress are evenly distributed across the globe, a phenomenon absent even in everyday life of the First World. Here, Critical Regionalism is recalled once again regarding the negative dialectics implied in the desire for simultaneous attendance in "the place of production" and "the production of place,"[13] a temporal missed encounter essential to vernacular still breathing in peripheries.

Notwithstanding the overwhelming presence of spectacle today, historiography should draw from the Thompsonian "experience of the mole of History burrowing through a long past and creating its specific traditions in the process."[14] At the present situation of capitalistic modernization, the idea of world architecture is a helpful category to grasp allegorically the totality with which capitalism has woven into the Real as experienced in both peripheries and centers. Frampton's historiography of Modern Architecture offers the starting point and "prism" for expanding the scope of criticism beyond the canon established by the International Style architecture (the 1930s) and into contemporary architecture that tends to welcome the technical at the expense of the cultural. In an attempt to address the crisis of historicism either in the national identity form or the zeitgeist,[15] this book's retrospective reading of Frampton's oeuvre offers an historico-theoretical awareness of the predicament of architecture's contemporaneity, broadening the scope of knowledge in architecture beyond the 1980s.

Notes

1   The correspondence took place on July 14, 2019.
2   Kenneth Frampton, "Postscript" to the third edition of *Critical History* (1992), 342–43; original emphasis.
3   Donald A. Aschon, *The Reflective Practitioner: How Professionals Think in Action* (New York: Basic Books, 1983).
4   See Hanno-Walter Kruft, *A History of Architectural Theory from Vitruvius to the Present* (New York: Princeton Architectural Press, 1994), 443.
5   Kenneth Frampton, *Modern Architecture: A Critical History* (London: Thames & Hudson, 1992), 342.
6   Kenneth Frampton, "Preface to the Third Edition," in *A Critical History* (1992), 7.
7   Kenneth Frampton, "Critical Regionalism Revisited: Reflections on the Mediatory Potential of Built-Form," in *Vernacular Modernism: Heimat, Globalization, and the Built Environment*, ed. M. Umbach and H. Huppauf (California: Stanford University Press, 2005), 193.
8   Fredric Jameson, "Third-World Literature in the Era of Multinational Capitalism," *Social Text* 15 (Autumn 1986): 65–88.
9   John Pizer, "Goethe's 'World Literature' Paradigm and Contemporary Cultural Globalization," *Comparative Literature* 52.3 (Autumn 2000): 213–27. He continues that J. W. Goethe's resignation was regarding "the impossibility of creating a 'classical' (national) German literature may have made the formulation of a 'world literature' the only possible alternative to cultural fragmentation" (216).

10 On this subject, see Arantes Pedro Fiori, *The Rent of Form: Architecture and Labor in the Digital Age* (Minneapolis: University of Minnesota Press, 2019).
11 Harry Harootunian, *Uneven Development: Reflections on Japan's Modern History* (New York: Columbia University Press, 2019), 260.
12 This phenomenon has been discussed in "Surface: The A-tectonic of Roofing and Wrapping," in *Architecture and Spectacle: A Critique*, ed. Gevork Hartoonian (London: Routledge, 2016), 233–54.
13 Here we benefit from Harry Harootunian's reflections on the situation of Japanese intellectuals during the 1920s. See Harootunian, *Uneven Development*, Chapter 6, 198–213.
14 Jameson, "Third-World Literature," 81.
15 On historicism, see Allen Colquhoun, "Three Kinds of Historicism," in *Modernity and the Classical Tradition: Architectural Essays, 1980–1987* (Cambridge: MIT Press, 1989). The essay was originally published in *Architectural Design* 53, 9/10 (1983).

INDEX

Aalto, Alvar 66–68, 92–93, 99–100, 101–2, 111. *See* Chapters 6 and 7; tectonics
Adorno, Theodor 6–7, 38, 81–82, 108–9, 178–79
Alberti, L. Battista 37–38, 61–62, 158–59
Alexander, Christopher 200
Althusser, Louis 148–49
Anderson, Stanford 185–86
Ando, Tadao 163, 172–73, 191–92
Archigram 131–32
Argan, Giulio 64–65, 109–11
Arendt, Hannah 2–4, 7–9, 19–20, 22–23, 25–26, 63, 67–68, 70–71, 72–73, 74–77, 81–82, 107–8, 119, 130, 132–34, 149–50, 155–56, 158, 163, 177–78, 180–81, 183–85
Asplund, Gunnar 65–66
Aureli, Vittorio 73–74
Avant-garde 63–64, 74–76, 84, 85, 95, 101–2, 146, 178, 180–81, 185–86, 190–91
  critique of 180
  and Kitsch 86
  neo- 146–47
  strategic 182–83
  See Greenberg, C.
autonomy 34, 35–36, 38, 42, 45, 49, 81, 90–91, 180
  formal 42–43, 171–72
  semi- 49

Baird, George 19–20
Banham, Reyner 20–22, 34–35, 49, 52–53, 92
  new brutalism 93–95

Bauhaus school 68–70, 77–78, 116–18, 132, 145–46
Bauen 203
Baukunst 43–45
Behrens, Peter 74–75, 95–97
Benjamin, Walter 2–4, 5–6, 7–8, 13, 14, 16, 17–27, 28, 59–60, 61, 63–64, 73–74, 86–87, 88–89, 109–11, 130–32, 146, 156–57, 166, 178–79, 186–87, 190–91
  Angelus Novus 16–17
  constellation 6
  and Heidegger 133–34
  loss of aura 26–27, 187–88
  periodization 28
  philosophy of history 7–9, 14–17, 27–28, 33, 130, 133–34, 146–47, 163, 191
Bergdoll, Barry 38–39
Berlage, Hendrik Petrus 98–99
Bloch, Ernst 37–38, 166, 184
Botta, Mario 153–54, 170–71, 172–73, 174–75, 186
Botticher, Carl 50–52
Boullée, E. 42–43
Brunelleschi, Filippo 37–38, 39–40, 62, 64–65
Brutalism 52–53, 113. *See* Banham, new brutalism
Burger, Peter 74–75, 180, 190–91

Carpo, Mario 37–38
Casabella 132–33
Caygill, Howard 190–91
Cedra, Ildefons 47–48
Chermayeff, Serge 200–1
Choay, Françoise 46–47, 86

Choisy, Auguste 43, 45
Classicism 65, 66–67, 95, 108–9, 117–18
  neo 41–45, 141–42
  Romantic 98–99, 141–42
Colquhoun, Alan 33–34
Commodity 191–92
  aesthetic of 24, 121
  fetishism 23–24, 28, 48–49
  form 19, 177–78, 180–81, 182–83, 184–85, 186–87
constellation 13–14, 16
  montage and 14. *See also* Benjamin, W.
Constructivism 65, 73–74, 125–26, 131–32, 180, 193
  Russian 68–70, 101, 153–57, 168–69, 185
Contemporaneity 5, 114–15, 202–3
  of architecture 6, 34, 158
Costa, Lucio 116–17
Cox, Anthony 116–17
Cret, Philippe 89–90
Crystal Palace 41–42, 50. *See* Paxton
Cunningham, David 35–36

Dal Co, Francesco 146, 173–74
Danesi, Sylvia 67–68
De Stijl 77–78
  Manifesto 101
de Carlo, Giancarlo 112–13
Digital 202–3
  reproducibility 9
Drew, Philip 141
Duiker, Johannes 149

Eiffel tower 52–53
Eisenman, Peter 35–36, 38, 65–66, 70–71, 120
Eisenstein, Sergei 154–55
enlightenment 15–16, 17–18, 20–21, 23–24, 28–29, 33, 34, 40–45, 49, 66–67, 68–70, 77, 90, 98, 191, 193
  concept of autonomy 42

fabrication 14
Ferriss, Hugh 84–85
Flyjvberg, Bent 190–91
Foster, Hal 34, 175

Foster, Norman
  Center Pompidou 110
  Willis-Faber & Dumas 105–6, 109–11
Foucault, Michel 45, 147–48
Fourier, Charles 43–45, 46–47, 49, 50–52
Frankfurt School 81–82, 109, 178–79
Freud, Sigmund 35–36
Friedman, Yona 73–74
Fuller, Buckminster 82–83, 131–32

Gannon, Todd 21–22
Garnier, Tony 19–20
  Garden City 42, 47
Giedion, Sigfried 20–22, 37–38, 52, 63–64, 70–72, 77, 140–41, 145–47. *See* monumentality
Gilly, Friedrich 45–46
Globalization 181–82
  capitalist 203
Goethe, J. W. 41–42, 199, 202
  Weltmarkt 203
Gramsci, Antonio 190–91
Graves, Michael 176–77
Greenberg, Clement 86, 178–79
Gregotti, Vittorio 70–72, 89
Gropius, Walter 105–6, 145–46

Habermas, Jürgen 22, 59, 70–71, 75–76, 85, 175
Habraken, N. J. 132
Hamilton, Richard 125–26
Haring, Hugo 146
  Organicism 146
Harootunian, Harry 18–19
Harris, Harwell Hamilton 172–73, 181–82
Haussmann, Baron George 15–16, 46–48, 50–52
Hegel, G. W. F. 41–42
Heidegger, Martin 2–5, 13–14, 16–17, 19–21, 22–24, 25–27, 45–46, 75–76, 86–87, 131–32, 133–34, 141, 174–75, 185
  Bridge 27–28
  dwelling 19, 109–12, 130–31, 183–84
  placemaking 8–9, 26–27
  raum 26–27, 111, 184
  technology 22, 34–35, 163, 187–88
Herron, Ron 131–32
Heterotopic 140–41

INDEX

Hilberseimer, Ludwig 49
historicism 18–19, 25–26. *See also*
    Benjamin, W.
historiography 33–34, 35–36, 37–38, 45–46
    critical 34–35, 38–39, 54
Hitchcock, Henry-Russell 83–84, 91,
    113–15, 163
    new tradition 84
Hobsbawm, Eric 43–45, 68–70
Horkheimer, Max 6–7, 34–35.
    See also Adorno, T.
Howard, Ebenzer 47–48
Howard, John Galen 172–73
Humanism 19–20, 95–97, 98–99, 101,
    123–24, 139–40, 147–48, 156–57,
    190–91
    Aalto 145–46, 152
    Palladian 123–24
    See 148
humanization 158–59, 174–75
    of architecture 149
    Aalto 152

ideology 53–54, 72
    architectural 38, 42, 70
    modernity 33
    operative 148–49
    state 67–68, 77–78
Illich, Ivan 200
Independent Group 125–26

Jameson, Fredric 18–19, 33, 164–65, 174–75,
    182, 187–88, 191–92, 193, 203
Jencks, Charles 21–22
Johnson, Philip 82–83, 98–99, 113–15, 163

Kahn, Louis 43, 47–48, 82–83, 88–90,
    125–26, 170–71, 174–75
    served-service 73–74, 189–90
Klee, Paul 16–17. *See Angelus Novus*,
    Benjamin
Koolhaas, Rem 67–68, 155–56
Koselleck, Reinhart 77–78, 176–77
Kraus, Rosalind 34

Labrouste, Henri 42–43, 45
Lacan, Jacques 1
Lane, Barbara Miller 68–70

Laugier, Marc-Antoine 36–37
Le Corbusier 65, 67–68, 72–73, 75–76,
    77–78, 81–82, 93–95, 112–16,
    117–18, 124, 125–28, 130–31,
    144–46, 155–56
    dom-ino 52–53, 83–84, 88–89
    five points 106–7, 108–9
    humanism 148
    monumentalization. *See* Chapter 4
    League of Nations Palace 97. *See*
    monumentalization of vernacular
Ledoux, Claude Nicolas 14–15, 42–45,
    131–32
Lefaivre, Liane 170–71, 181–83
Lefebvre, Henri 123–24
Lequeu, J. 42–43
Levin, Neil 61–62, 63
Lissitzky, El 68–70
Loos, Adolf 4–5, 67–68, 107, 108–9,
    114–15, 140, 141–42, 148–49,
    171–72, 177–78, 180–81, 188
    Raumplan 75–76, 108–9
Lubetkin, Berthold 116–17, 155–56
Lyotard, Jean-François 132–33

Maki, Fumihiko 131–32
Malevich, Kazimir 95
    Suprematism 98–99
Marcuse, Hebert 84–85, 170–71
Marx, Karl 36–37, 48–49
Mathesius, Hermann 74–75, 77–78
May, Ernst 184–85
Maybeck, Bernard 172–73
mega-form 49, 54, 75–76
megalopolis 19–20, 113, 176–77, 184–85
Melnikov, Konstantin 155–56
Mendelsohn, Eric 67–68, 91
Meyer, Hannes 68–70, 72–73, 145–46
Mies van der Rohe, Ludwig
    Aalto and 8–9
    Beinahe nichts 4–5
    new national gallery 95
    See Chapter 6
Modernization 113–14, 117–19, 122–23,
    170–72, 175, 176, 178
    cultural 178, 191–92
    global 168–69, 203
    technoscientific 201

INDEX

Moholy-Nagy, Laszalo 68–70, 72–74, 75–76
Monumentality 59–60, 61–62, 63–64, 83
  and authenticity 88–89
  classical 97
  new- 85
  neo- 84
  See Giedion
monumentalization
  Le Corbusier, Chapter 4
  Mies, Chapter 4
  of technique 98–99, 139, 146–47
  of vernacular 83, 139–40
  Japanese 166–68
Moravanszky, Akos 152
Morris, William 107–8, 109, 118–19, 123–24
  Red-House 108–9
Mumford, Lewis 91–92
  regionalism 172–74
  See Chapter 7
Munch, Edvard 16–17
Murphy, Douglas 46–47

Nervi, Luigi 52–53
Neue Sachlichkeit 24–25, 68–70, 72–73, 82–83, 132, 171–72. See also new-objectivity
Neumeyer, Fritz 95–97, 116–18
Neutra, Richard 114–17
new brutalism 93–95, 112–13, 118–23, 125–26. *See* Banham
New Deal 82–83, 86, 88–89
new empiricism 91, 123
New Objectivity 101
new tradition 86. *See* Hitchcock, H. R.
Niemeyer, Oscar 116
Nietzsche, Fredrick 74–75
new-objectivity. *See* neue schlichkeit
Norberg-Schultz, Christian 19–20, 120–23, 126–27, 129–31

oppositions 19, 155–56, 184
Osborne, Peter 20–21
Otero-Pailos, Jorge 86–87, 123

Payne, Alina 62
Paxton, John 50. *See* crystal palace
Pearson, Paul David 142–43
Pelkonen, Eeva-Liisa 143–45

Perrault, Claude 42–43
Perret, Auguste 45, 52–53, 95–97
periodization 6–7, 8–9, 22, 25–27, 28, 90, 92–102. *See* Benjamin, W.
Perspecta 180–81
Pevsner, Nikolaus 120–22
Phantasmagoria 48–49, 50, 107
phenomenology 25–26, 34–35, 86–87, 100–101, 120–23, 187–88
Photomontage 61–62, 63–64
Piano, Renzo 158–59, 203
Piranesi, G. Battista 41–43, 45, 156–57
Pizer, John 203
place-form 113, 183
place-making 4–5, 8–9, 158–59, 189–90
Poggioli, Renato 179
Porphyrios, Demetri 147–48, 149, 157–58
Portman, John 111
Portoghesi, Paolo 72
Postmodernism 19–20, 21–22, 86, 87–89, 101–2, 124, 157–58, 181–83, 191–92
  theorization of 18–19
product-form 105–6, 109–11
Productivism 156–58
Pugin, Augustus 70

Raumplan. *See* Loos, A.
Raymond, Antonin 116–18
Realism 181–82
Reinhardt, Ad 95
Renaissance 33–34, 95–98
  humanism 37–38
  perspectival regime 28
reproducibility
  digital 37–38
  mechanical 36–37
resistance 16–17, 26–27, 183
Richards, James M. 86
Richardson, H. H. 143–44
Ricoeur, Paul 86, 164–65, 166–68, 169, 175–76, 177–78, 180–81
Riegl, Alois 74–75, 122–23
Rimpl, Herbert 70
Rivera, Diago 84–85
Roberts, Henry 46–47
Roberts, John 168–69, 180
Rockefeller center 84–85

Rodchenko, Aleksandr 155–56
Rossi, Aldo 67–68, 70–71, 129–30, 132–33, 185
Roth, Alfred 114–15
Rowe, Colin 174–75
Rudofsky, B. 19–20
Ruskin, John 67–68

Sakakura, Junzo 117–18
Scarpa, Carlo 174–75
Schapiro, Meyer 92–93
Schindler, Rudolf 114–15, 116–17
Schinkel, Friedrich 42–43, 45–46
   Altes Museum 43, 65–66
Schivelbusch, Wolfgang 25–26
Scholem, Gerhard 16–17. *See* Benjamin, W.
Scott Brown, Denise 132–33
Schnaidt, Claude 132
Semiautonomous 36–37, 42
Semper, Gottfried 74–75, 151–52, 189–90
   Stoffwechsel 152
Sert, Jose Luis 85
Shon, Donald 200
Simmel, George 36–37
Siza, Alvaro 171–72, 175, 188, 202
Smithsons 52–53, 111, 120–26, 128–29, 187–88
Soufflot, Jacques-Germain 38–39, 44
   Ste-Genevieve 8, 38, 39
Spectacle 26–27, 28, 87–88, 93–95
Stam, Mart 73–74
Stern, Rober 72
Stierli, Martino 59–60
Stirling, James 119–20, 124, 125–28, 170–71. *See* Chapter 5
Sullivan, Henry 67–68, 129–30
Summerson, John 126–27
Szacka, Lea-Catherine 72

Tafuri, Manfredo 2, 5, 16–17, 22, 24–25, 33–35, 45, 70–71, 87–88, 109–11, 113, 119, 120–22, 129–31, 146–48, 156–57
Tange, Kenzo 73–74, 117–18, 166–68
Tatlin, Vladimir 52–53, 157–58

Technology 19, 21–22, 23–24, 26–27, 50–52, 61–62, 63–65, 72–73, 86–87, 92, 95–97, 130–32, 184–85, 188, 191
   and materiality 7–8
   instrumental logic 133–34
   nihilism of 26–27, 95
   See Benjamin, W.; Heidegger, M.
technification
   of architecture 75–76
   of culture 62–63
tectonics 82–83, 86–87, 89–90, 98–100, 101, 152, 153–54, 185–87, 189–90, 191–92
   Aalto 140–41, 150–51
   Miesian 92–97, 100–1, 140–41, 157–59
   Utzon 141
Teige, Karel 83, 97
Terragni, Giuseppe 8–9, 59–60
   Casa del Fascio. *See* Terragni, Chapter 3
Tessenow, Heinrich 70
theatricalization 116–17
totality 83, 123, 164–65
Tschumi, Bernard 155–56
Tzonis, Alexander 170–71, 181–83

Utzon, Jorn 141, 174–75, 182–83, 188–90, 191–92. *See* tectonics

van de Velde, Henry 74–75, 77–78, 152
van Doesburg, Theo 72–73
van Eck, Caroline 42
van Eesteren, Cornelis 72–73
van Eyck, Aldo 113
Vertov, Dziga 155–56
Vattimo, Giani 174–75
Venturi, Robert 87–88, 132–33, 144–45, 157–58, 185
Vesnin, Alexandrovich 149
Vidler, Anthony 122–23, 155–56
Visconti, Luchino 188

Wagner, Martin 184–85
Wagner, Otto 93–95
Wagner, Richard 74–75
Webb, Michael 130–31
Webber, Melvin 86
Werkbund 74–75, 107–8

Westernization 166–68
Winckelmann, J. J. 41–42
Wittkower, Rudolf 19–20, 122–23
Wittwer, Hans 72–73
Wölfflin, Heinrich 118–19
Woods, Shadrach 113

Wern Christopher 42
Wright, F. L. 47–48, 52–53, 82–84, 88–90, 92–95, 98–100, 114–15, 116–17, 125–26, 139–40

Zevi, Bruno 22, 139–40

www.ingramcontent.com/pod-product-compliance
Lightning Source LLC
Chambersburg PA
CBHW021141230426
43667CB00005B/209